Running Microsoft Workloads on AWS

Active Directory, Databases, Development, and More

Ryan Pothecary

Apress®

Running Microsoft Workloads on AWS: Active Directory, Databases,
Development, and More

Ryan Pothecary
Tonyrefail, UK

ISBN-13 (pbk): 978-1-4842-6627-4   ISBN-13 (electronic): 978-1-4842-6628-1
https://doi.org/10.1007/978-1-4842-6628-1

Managing Director, Apress Media LLC: Welmoed Spahr
Acquisitions Editor: Susan McDermott
Development Editor: Laura Berendson
Coordinating Editor: Rita Fernando

Cover designed by eStudioCalamar

Cover image designed by Pixabay

Distributed to the book trade worldwide by Springer Science+Business Media New York, 1 New York Plaza, New York, NY 10004. Phone 1-800-SPRINGER, fax (201) 348-4505, e-mail orders-ny@springer-sbm.com, or visit www.springeronline.com. Apress Media, LLC is a California LLC and the sole member (owner) is Springer Science + Business Media Finance Inc (SSBM Finance Inc). SSBM Finance Inc is a **Delaware** corporation.

For information on translations, please e-mail booktranslations@springernature.com; for reprint, paperback, or audio rights, please e-mail bookpermissions@springernature.com.

Apress titles may be purchased in bulk for academic, corporate, or promotional use. eBook versions and licenses are also available for most titles. For more information, reference our Print and eBook Bulk Sales web page at http://www.apress.com/bulk-sales.

Any source code or other supplementary material referenced by the author in this book is available to readers on GitHub via the book's product page, located at www.apress.com/9781484266274. For more detailed information, please visit http://www.apress.com/source-code.

Printed on acid-free paper

For my wife Tracy and our family, William,
Alex, George, and Daisy

Table of Contents

About the Author

Ryan Pothecary is Senior Specialist Solution Architect for a cloud-based services company, which he joined 4 years ago. He has worked on the AWS platform for the last 8 years as part of a near 30-year career in IT. Over the last 4 years, he's worked directly with customers and partners who are moving to the AWS Cloud. He specializes in helping customers move Microsoft Workloads to AWS and works with customers throughout their entire cloud journey. He is also a member of a community of engineers, architects, and consultants who help customers run Microsoft Workloads on AWS in every part of the world. Outside of work, he is determined to learn how to play the guitar his wife bought him, even though he has small stubby fingers.

About the Technical Reviewers

Sanjay Dandeker is a Senior Professional Services Consultant at a public cloud providor. He works closely with financial services customers to deliver technical and business outcomes to support and accelerate the adoption of cloud services within a highly regulated environment.

His role involves helping customers to define and deliver their cloud strategy as well as architecting, building, and testing global infrastructure solutions to support cloud native and migration of applications to AWS.

Mark J. Easton works as a cloud solutions architect, helping gaming companies take advantage of cloud computing. He lives in a small, riverside town in England, with his wife, his three sons, and a crazy poodle. When not working, he can often be found writing or developing indie games.

Acknowledgments

I could not have written this book without the support of my wonderful wife, Tracy, who graduated university to become a mental health nurse and since starting this book has single-handedly homeschooled our children while looking after her father who suffers from dementia and who I love very very much. I'm also very proud of our children William, Alex, George, and Daisy. You are amazing, most of the time.

I'd also like to thank my friends and tech reviewers Sanjay Dandeker and Mark Easton for their support in taking on this project while juggling work, family, and pandemics. This book is better because of you. I'd also like to thank the supportive people at Apress, in particular Rita and Susan. Also Kevin Higgins and Lee Petford for additional support and all-round awesomeness.

Finally, there are a whole host of very clever people who have helped me write this by sharing their knowledge and wisdom.

> The ProServe 2017 team of Abrar, Waqar, Aamer, Darius, Steve E, Ben B, Neil, Pete, Tony, Paul F, Roughty, Rob C, Matt, Russell, Mario, Ritesh (#1 fan), Adam, Steve M, Tom, Gregson, Oli, Andy, Eamonn, and Pedro.

> The GSP dream team – Kevin, Stefan, Mark, and Ron.

> Partner trainers – Luca, Rob, Tom, George, Oli, Max, Vernon, Emil, Mark, Rotem, Gaby, Mahmoud, and all the team.

> SSA gurus – George, Rogier, Dudu, Andy, Baris, Andreas, Dan, Ralph, Sai, Borja, Chris, and Alexis.

> TFC heros – Frank, Greg, Jesse, Thorr, Kirk, Sepehr, Chris, Rodney, Alex, Boris, Andy, Anil, Hans, Brian B, Brian L, Garry, Javy, Lance, Luis, Matthew, Pete P, Ron, Shijaz, Zlatan, and many many more.

> Tom Hayes, Dave Bowring, and finally Bob Harris for starting me on this adventure.

Introduction

In 2020, the world changed.

As COVID-19 swept through the globe, all of us were affected. Some of us lost loved ones or had to recover from illness ourselves. Others have had to adapt their lives to manage homeschooling while being isolated from family and friends. Most of us had to find a different way to work when travel was not possible or we were asked to lock down.

You may have heard of *the Cloud* and wondered if the claims of saving money and the promise of agility and innovation are actually true. Your business may have been making plans for its first steps into this area before 2020 and like many other companies, may have decided to accelerate those plans.

You may have no experience of Amazon Web Services directly, but you would have certainly used some of its services during the last year. From watching Netflix, Prime Video, BBC, Hulu, or talking with friends over Zoom, Twitter, Facebook, or Slack to shopping online with Tesco, Whole Foods, Sainsbury's, or a small online bookstore called Amazon.

And there are millions of other businesses using AWS all over the world.

AWS celebrated its 15th birthday in March 2021; it was the first of the so-called Hyperscale Public Cloud providers. During those 15 years, it listened to its customers and developed services that solved some of the challenges facing businesses running IT systems over the years. While doing that, slowly but surely, its impact has changed the world.

It's true that over the last 15 years, things have changed. The way we watch television, the way we listen to music, how we shop, and even how we communicate with each other.

But when I think of the impact of AWS, I think of a quote from global healthcare business Novartis that stated "39 years of Computational Chemistry was condensed into 9 hours" during a project where they screened 10 million compounds against a common cancer target. The amazing thing about that story is that the case study is from 2013. Can you imagine how much better it is today? Companies like Pfizer, AstraZeneca, and Moderna have been using AWS to develop and test COVID-19 vaccines too.

But it's not just healthcare companies using AWS, every single industry is embracing the potential of Public Cloud services on this planet (and even on Mars thanks to NASA's Perseverance rover).

The goal of this book is to help you use AWS for your Microsoft workloads. Microsoft has its own public cloud platform, Azure, and they make it very easy for users of its software to sign up for an Azure account. The thinking must be that if customers start using Azure, it'll become sticky and they'll continue using it.

This book will show you that *you have other options* when it comes to Cloud Platforms. We look at a large range of AWS services, a lot of them built specifically for AWS customers who have Microsoft workloads.

If writing a technology book is like trying to hit a moving target, then writing an AWS book would be like hitting the same target, but this time blindfolded and riding a bike.

AWS changes every single day. It is a technology platform that is in constant motion, but the things you'll learn from this book will be invaluable in helping you move your business and its Microsoft Workloads to AWS and return some real value.

We not only discuss the AWS Services that you'll find in the AWS Management Console but also highlight services that are not so visible and you may not have heard of before.

I hope you find this book useful, I hope you find it accessible and enjoyable, and I hope some parts make you smile. Overall, I hope you learn that Microsoft Workloads are not only supported on AWS but encouraged to grow and transform.

Enjoy and stay safe.

Ryan (April 2021)

CHAPTER 1

Wait, I Can Run Windows on AWS?

I was speaking to a customer. We were talking about a plan to migrate thousands of Microsoft servers currently running in the company's data centers to AWS. At one point, the customer said, "I've been working on AWS projects for the last 18 months and only found out last week that you can run Microsoft servers on AWS."

I put my headset on mute, screamed, took a moment, clicked the headset back off mute again.

Sadly, I've done that more than once. In fact, if you are ever on a call with me and I go on mute, I'm either on a train or screaming.

The scream isn't directed at the customer, of course; you either know these things or you don't. There are plenty of things I have no clue about such as Cricket, Opera, or how to be financially stable.

The scream is in frustration at perception. The perception that the only place to run Microsoft workloads in a public cloud is with Microsoft and their Azure platform.

These moments of frustration are happening less and less these days. People are better informed and have taken the time to explore all of the information across all of the cloud platforms that are available. They've run proof of concept (PoC) workloads and reached their own conclusions.

Today, I find that most customers are surprised by the actual number of Microsoft workloads that run on AWS. Published figures from the IDC, a marketing intelligence company, reported the percentage at almost double that running on Microsoft Azure. So, if you are planning to run your Microsoft workloads on AWS, you'd be in good company.

This is a very brief chapter on how we got to *here*.

© Ryan Pothecary 2021
R. Pothecary, *Running Microsoft Workloads on AWS*, https://doi.org/10.1007/978-1-4842-6628-1_1

We now live in a world where many of the everyday services you use, such as listening to music on Spotify, chilling with Netflix, managing your money with Capital One, grocery shopping online with Sainsbury's, getting a driving license in the United Kingdom with the DVLA, and almost everything in between, are connected. Cloud computing platforms have changed how IT services are consumed by the public and, more importantly, how IT services are delivered and run across a massive number of businesses.

And the surprising thing is that even with almost every single business using or planning to use cloud platforms, it currently only accounts for 4% of overall IT Services spend by businesses. What is mind-blowing to me is that with every company big or small that I know moving or having moved to the cloud, just how many *other* IT systems are out there.

If the general consensus states that the *Digital Revolution* started in 1975, then we have to marvel at how far we've come in just 45 short years. I've heard comparisons that the cloud computing platforms of today mirror the huge mainframe solutions of the 1970s and 1980s. There is some logic to that comparison. With both, you pay for processing time, but after that the similarities become somewhat hazy. Even in my advancing years, I have no recollection of these huge monsters other than what I saw in films and TV shows. Personal computing during the 1980s put this new technology in the reach of families, and even though those machines were quickly replaced at the end of the decade by the IBM PC and the hundreds of far more affordable clones from HP, Dell, Compaq, and so on, they started the world *using computers* in their everyday lives more and more.

And it was here that Microsoft gave us Windows 3.0, which started a domination of the IT industry that has lasted more than 30 years. It seems impossible to get realistic data on the number of machines that have run or are running the numerous versions of Microsoft Windows made since version 3.0 came out in 1990. TechCrunch reported 450 *million* copies of Windows 7 sold since its launch in 2009 through to 2011. Research by Gartner told us that the two-billionth computer was shipped in 2008, and a conservative guess would be that 90% of those ran a version of Microsoft Windows. From all the stats I've seen on the subject, it's fair to say that the number of licenses for Windows systems sold since 1990 would cover everyone on Earth.

In 2008, a year before Microsoft released Windows 7, a small subsidiary of an online book retailer launched a service that let you create virtual servers and pay for them by the hour. They called the servers *instances*, and you connected to them over the Internet.

This wasn't the first of what they called *services*; they had already launched a service called the Simple Storage Service or S3, which lets you store significant amounts of data and address that data via web requests. Then there was the Simple Queue Service, or SQS, which is a messaging service for distributed systems. All of these services had been in beta for a couple of years beforehand.

When you signed up for an Amazon *Web Services* account, the Management Console let you start one of these virtual server *EC2 Instances* and gave you some options of what operating system you wanted to use when it started. One of these options was Microsoft Windows Server 2003. As new Microsoft operating systems are launched, they are typically available to be used on AWS within a week of release. This has happened so far with Windows Server versions 2008, 2012, 2016, and currently 2019 as well as all of the *R2* significant updates. Since Windows Server 2012, they have used the Datacenter Edition version of the operating system, primarily for licensing purposes. We discuss the topic of Licensing in Chapter 3.

You'll note here that only the Server Editions of Microsoft Windows are available; there are no *Home* or *Personal* versions available from AWS.

If ever you find yourself attending one of the many official AWS events they host all across the globe, you might well have heard during one of these presentations the staggering number of new services or significant updates to functionality that they release each and every year.

As a customer of AWS, I've always found this amazing. When I first logged on to the AWS Console, not that long ago in 2014, I'm pretty sure that there were around 30 services available. I remember thinking I'm never going to be able to learn how to use all those services. Today, there are in the region of 200 AWS Services available in the AWS Management Console, and I *know* I'm never going to be able to learn how to use them all.

Everything from Compute and Storage through to Machine Learning, Robotics, and Satellite Control Services. It's often been said during these AWS presentations that upward of 90% of services and functional enhancements that are developed come from customer requests. If this is the case, then what new services can we expect next? Perhaps industry-focused services for retail, financial services, or healthcare? Perhaps more experimental services like the recently launched Quantum Compute service, Amazon Braket.

As with other AWS services that have been launched over the past 10 years or more, these services are made available to everyone with an AWS account, which effectively democratizes their usage for all. It's going to be an interesting time as incredibly powerful technology is available to everyone on a per-usage basis and is no longer just available to huge enterprises with the deep pockets to be able to run such systems. We must all remember, however, that with great power comes great responsibility. The ethics of this technological democratization will continue to be an ongoing debate. We want customers to benefit from having access to all the services that AWS offer, but what if some of those customers don't share our same politics and values?

And what has happened to Microsoft during this time? A fall from grace followed by a resurrection into being a global cloud provider that can compete with AWS for being the biggest.

It's well documented that Microsoft's stewardship during the Steve Ballmer era was difficult. A company that could do no wrong for such a long period of time was caught napping more than once and has played catch-up ever since.

The importance of the Internet in how we access information, how we consume services, and now in how we live our everyday lives initially passed Microsoft by without them really noticing. They were far too focused on the huge launch of Windows 95 to even include an Internet browser in the release. It's rumored that it came to an agreement with Spyglass Software to repackage its browser as Internet Explorer and would pay them for every copy sold. But Microsoft didn't sell a single Internet Explorer because they packaged it into an update to Windows 95, and the whole matter between Spyglass and Microsoft had to be dealt with in the law courts.

When they included Internet Explorer as part of the Windows 95+ and 98 operating systems, it was argued that they were creating a competitive advantage over the likes of companies like Netscape, and they were subsequently embroiled in legal battles for the next 5 years. It was one of Microsoft's darkest hours.

You could then forgive Microsoft for letting the future importance of the growing smartphone industry pass it by when the Apple iPhone was released in 2007. It was the year that the infamous Windows Vista was released, the first major release of an operating system by the company that was universally criticized. It took 2 years to recover and release Windows 7, which until the recent launch of Windows 10 was the most popular operating system available.

Microsoft entered the smartphone market in 2011 by licensing its Windows Mobile OS, and then in 2014 it went ahead with a full acquisition of Nokia, which also found itself struggling under the enormous dominance of not only the iPhone but now Google's Android phones.

Microsoft Azure became commercially available in 2010, just 2 years behind AWS going public, so why is it that when asked to compare platforms, a common answer is that the AWS Cloud is far more mature and production ready? My guess is that it's due to the circumstances involved in the creation of the platforms. AWS came into being following the lessons learned in redeveloping the Amazon.com retail platform. Its chief goals at the time would be security, availability, reliability, and the ease to make updates to the code, whereas the goals around the creation of Azure were solely not to be left behind in yet another technological race like they were with the Internet and smartphones.

And it's here that I'll stop with the comparisons. My thoughts are if you are moving from your on-premises traditional, IT infrastructure to using the cloud, then you are doing *the right thing* regardless of which provider you choose. The key is to make sure you are getting the most out of those cloud platforms, which we will cover in more detail later on in this book.

Why Cloud?

Why are businesses throughout the world adopting cloud technology? What makes it so special and how is it different from traditional IT? As someone who has held roles in IT infrastructure services for many years, my goals can be summarized as follows:

1. Keep all IT systems running.

2. Allow users to access those systems.

3. Make new IT systems available when needed.

4. Repeat.

I spent years creating *Gold Build* server images to deploy to physical servers in data center racks. Setting up monitoring systems and working on capacity management so that I would have enough servers in place when my business needed them. Developing processes around all of this to make sure no mistakes were made and that our customers received the platforms they believed they needed when they needed them. A move to virtualization allowed for an increase in speed in getting platforms to our customers, but our processes soon put a halt to that when customers didn't get the kind of performance from the servers that they had before.

By the time we got to grips with running a virtualization platform that provided the performance our customers expected and added some automation to make the management easier and deliver services at the velocity they wanted, we thought we were doing well. Before cloud, I would argue that the only innovation to come out of the last years of server infrastructure was virtualization, and the benefit of that was purely in getting more bang for your buck in terms of cost savings. Today's data center infrastructure is predominantly virtualized and runs on products from two different vendors: VMware and Microsoft. Microsoft's Hyper-V solution has only 10% of the market, so with VMware having such a huge install base, it made sense for AWS to partner with VMware in 2017 to launch VMware Cloud on AWS.

My own personal journey with AWS began in 2014. On my first day in a brand-new company, my new CTO talked to me about the benefits of cloud and in particular AWS, and I had an epiphany. I swore to myself that I would only ever use cloud technology and never step foot in another data center again.

That year, however, I saw my new company moving out of its data center, and I spent far too much of my time in one. But that was the last year I stepped foot in a data center. A record I intend to keep.

The general tenets of public cloud that we discussed on that day remain the same today:

- Self-Service

- Elastic

- API-Driven

- Global

- Utility Pricing

Let me briefly explain each of them while you work out the impact on your business.

Self-Service is an easy one and had already been available with some service providers via a web service provisioning system for quite some time. The thought of allowing users, or departments, to provision their own systems puts you in one of two states. You are either relieved that you don't have to spend time doing fairly low-value work, or it terrifies you at the idea that the control of new IT systems is now in the hands of users and not the IT department. Historically, everything IT related was in the control of an IT department that made sure everything was secure and manageable. When we get to Chapter 8, which concerns itself with operations, you will understand that the biggest challenge with cloud adoption is one of culture and not technology.

When my CTO explained *Elastic* to me, my eyes lit up. Capacity management in an IT infrastructure is a continual and often cumbersome task. Typically, the customers I've seen have a predictable rate of consumption of their IT services. Dynamic changes in my IT systems were to be avoided, because that normally meant things were going wrong, so I always provisioned for the potential peaks in usage that were expected and very rarely reduced below that.

But now here was a cloud platform where I could set up something called *autoscaling*, which added Amazon EC2 Instances automatically and then removed them automatically when they weren't needed.

Of course, this led into a discussion about mutable and immutable infrastructure, which is a subject we will explore in Chapter 3.

Next, we have *API-Driven,* which again is something that has been around for a while in limited ways but has added immense benefits to the AWS Cloud ecosystem. All AWS Services expose their functionality via APIs, which are commands used to directly access this functionality. The AWS Management Console does this behind the scenes itself. After you've configured an EC2 instance the way you want it and finally click *Launch*, the console issues an API call to the EC2 service to do the actual work.

Taking this a step further, with the help of the Software Development Kits (SDKs) that are available, we can actually write code that can query AWS Services, grab data, and perform actions. We will discuss how important this tenet is during our chapter on development.

Global is quite self-explanatory but also vitally important because of the way it changes the way we think about resilience and availability. AWS was built with availability and resilience ingrained into its design across every service. It is built on what we call Regions and Availability Zones. Regions are geographic areas that contain *two or more* availability zones. It's easy to think of an availability zone as a data center, although the reality is that an availability zone can be more than one physical data center, but it is, at the very least, a single physical data center building.

Businesses are very sensitive over the placement of their data centers, preferring them to be separated by a geographic distance, and each availability zone is a *meaningful distance* away from the other in the region. Your curiosity might be piqued by the term *meaningful distance* – why doesn't AWS just publish the exact minimum distance? I guess for the exact same reason that AWS does not publish the exact location of each of its availability zones or the data centers that operate in each of these zones. When you think about it, the exact postal address is not really important. What is critical is that there is a distance between them that separates them from an incident that might impact an entire data center.

We will discuss this further in the next chapter.

The last public cloud tenet is Utility, or allowing the user to pay for the AWS services that they consume when they are using them and then stop paying for them the second they stop using them. It's the same way we pay for electricity or gas or any other utility. The impact of this should form a part of your whole cloud strategy. Whereas historically we've left servers to run 24/7 because we've already paid the capital expenditure for the physical asset (even though there's always an ongoing cost, such as electricity, etc.), this new payment model enables us to save money if we only run our servers when they are needed. A common example is that of a development environment where all your devs are in a single time zone. By running your servers for just 8 hours a day for 5 days a week, it allows you to reduce your costs by 75% by shutting them down out of working hours and weekends.

It's a significant shift in our operations and management of servers, but then there are also significant costs to be saved by stopping services that are not being used. The power of consuming public cloud services with this pay-as-you-go model shifts the focus for business from a CapEx to OpEx model, and this tenet alone is often a driver to move to the cloud.

What Are Your Goals in Moving to the Cloud?

It's a question I often ask my classes when teaching. The answers I get back usually revolve around cost savings. I sometimes get a response of "because it's popular!"

I love that response. It's a very honest statement as IT departments are sometimes caught up in technological trends. It's part of the job to make sure that you are aware of the latest developments within the industry, and this can sometimes influence your strategy.

If being on-trend is your sole reason for moving to AWS or any other cloud provider, please stop. Your move to the cloud is going to be unsuccessful, frustrating, and may well cost you 2 years of your life that you are not going to get back.

Is *cost* your motivation? This is a little trickier. You can certainly save money moving to the cloud. If you take your IT estate **exactly** as it is now and move it to the cloud, you will save some money, but not much. Maybe by performing right-sizing during the migration, you are going to save some more money. If you create some automation using tags to stop Amazon EC2 Instances that are not needed from running overnight and on weekends, you'll save even more money. You can also purchase Reserved Instances and use Spot Instances and save stacks of money.

All of these things are very achievable, but they all require some effort to make them happen. And more importantly, they require ongoing discipline and management to make sure your bills are not creeping up. The problem comes in keeping that initial number of servers you've migrated constant. It's the easiest way to prove you are getting a ROI. But in all reality, the number of virtual servers you migrated will slowly start to increase as your developers and business units explore the other AWS Services available to them.

Is *speed to market* your reason for undertaking this move to the cloud? Now we're talking! Agility and speed are absolutely achievable if you also commit to revising your operational processes to work in a more agile manner. Years of performing a consultative role in cloud migrations have taught me a few things. One of which is that technology is never the challenge. If we have technical issues, these are things we can think about and fix. Cultural challenges are often the real issue which is more difficult to address.

Businesses have used technology in a certain way for the last 40 years, and how the new way cloud platforms operate has to be reflected in the operational processes that are going to be used. It may take 90 seconds to create and launch an Amazon EC2 instance. But, if you surround this agility with 4 weeks of Change Control process followed by interventions from the Network, Build, and Application teams, then you lose a huge benefit of moving to the cloud.

Governance, not control.

Our final answer to "why move to the cloud" is innovation. If this is your reason, then BINGO! You are a winner; take a prize from the top shelf.

Giving your teams the ability to learn, explore, and use those AWS Services such as analytics, machine learning, and IoT to create services that can help your customers or create new revenue streams for your businesses will add more value to your move to the cloud than any of the other reasons we've heard.

Build on!

Let's continue in the next chapter.

CHAPTER 2

AWS 101

If you've been using AWS for a while, then please feel free to skip or skim this chapter. Still here? Great! Welcome to the Amazon Web Services Cloud Platform.

I think you're going to like it.

If this is all new to you, you are free to read through this chapter a number of times. I'll also include links to some great videos that explain some concepts in more detail. Before we go any further, I'll set some clear expectations about this chapter.

I'll cover a small number of topics here – just the big important stuff that you'll need to know before we get to the next chapter. We'll cover accounts, global infrastructure, and some networking fundamentals. You'll understand quickly that there is a lot more to learn, and we discuss other AWS services in ensuing chapters as we use them. The purpose of this book is not to provide a comprehensive deep dive into AWS, but instead to focus specifically on the foundational components required in running Microsoft workloads on the platform.

AWS Accounts

Let's start at the beginning. You've just signed up for an AWS account via `http://aws.amazon.com`, and you've chosen the Basic (free) support tier and are ready to rock.

You made a note of the account number, didn't you? You are certainly going to need that. In this AWS Account, you have the ability to create Virtual Private Clouds (VPCs), which can be thought of as customer-isolated data centers. Each VPC has a range of IP addresses that it can use based on a Classless Inter-Domain Routing (CIDR) block that you specify and configure when you create the VPC, just like your own data center.

Similarly, you'll be able to configure isolated network subnets within your CIDR block, and this is where you will run your Amazon EC2 Instances (virtual servers).

In this single AWS Account, you'll have a number of service limits, such as only being able to create a maximum of five VPCs per Region and limits about the number of virtual machines you can launch at any one time.

It's really easy to increase these service limits – you just log a service ticket in the AWS Management Console, which is then passed to AWS engineers and account staff to action on your behalf. Many of these limits are in place for new accounts to avoid inadvertently running up a large bill while you're learning!

Perhaps at this point, you might be thinking that this single AWS Account will be all you'll ever need to host your entire enterprise. A few years ago, I did see AWS customers who only had one or two accounts. But now, it is common to see customers running over 50 accounts to manage their growing environments. You may ask, why is that?

The ability to open multiple AWS Accounts leads to challenges that require a more mature cloud approach to solve.

An employee can open an account and, within a small amount of time, with just a credit card and some personal details, start AWS Services that are costly or that centralized IT departments feel that they shouldn't be running.

For example, if that employee is a developer charged with creating a production-ready application, you may find that once the project is complete, the application "needs to" stay in that account. So now centralized IT has inherited an AWS account they had no involvement in creating and may be outside of something they wish to support.

You're thinking, "OK, this isn't a huge problem, we can fix this." But think of this scenario times a hundred. What happens when you've got a hundred rogue accounts? This was once a very common scenario with large enterprises that hadn't yet formalized their cloud strategy. However, these days, many organizations have processes in place to deal with the situation or better still have the means to prevent it happening altogether.

What about shared services like Identity (Active Directory), Logging, Security, Monitoring, Deployment tools, and so on? Where do these tools live and how are they able to serve all these different accounts?

This is why AWS developed services to help enterprises that need multi-account strategies. Two AWS services that you'll need to investigate closer if you need help here are AWS Organizations and AWS Control Tower.

Regions and Availability Zones

Now that you have an understanding of AWS Accounts, the next question should be: *where* are you going to run your services?

As mentioned in the previous chapter, AWS segments its global infrastructure into Regions and Availability Zones. A Region is an independently isolated geographic area containing two or more Availability Zones, which in turn are the data centers from where your services will run. At the time of writing this book, AWS has 25 regions covering EMEA, APAC, and the Americas. Some of these regions have two Availability Zones, but most have three and some have significantly more such as the Virginia (US-EAST-1) region which has six.

There are also some regions that you have to request to use before they become available to you such as the regions AWS has in China plus the two GovCloud regions in the US. New Regions and Availability Zones are launched by AWS each year and expand the availability of services across the globe by making them available to where customers want to use them.

We should also cover Edge Locations and Points of Presence (PoPs), while we are here. PoPs are far more numerous than Regions and Availability Zones and allow content to be made available closer to the users who need to access it. They are typically used for specific AWS services such as S3 and CloudFront, where you want to get the content as close as possible to the end users to improve performance.

I'm going to reward all your hard work at this time with a little break. Take the next hour and 34 minutes to watch a keynote address from James Hamilton, Distinguished Engineer at AWS, who explains how AWS built the backbone infrastructure that it uses for all of its cloud services. It's an incredible presentation and required viewing for every AWS user. Go to https://youtu.be/AyOAjFNPAbA or search James Hamilton re:Invent 2016.

Designing for Availability

There's an often-quoted saying from the CTO of Amazon.com, Dr. Werner Vogels, "Everything will eventually fail over time."

I've often heard it paraphrased as "Everything fails, all the time," which takes the logic away from the original statement and sounds like something Eeyore would say to Winnie the Pooh.

The original statement is logical and obvious, but the true understanding of this statement is often ignored by businesses moving to the cloud where I often see single points of failure within a design. Yet moving to AWS Cloud is the perfect opportunity to ensure that your infrastructure is designed for availability as AWS provide you with the foundations and tools to enable you to do this.

The exact level of availability is dependent on your business requirements and the costs you are willing to bear. Typically, companies span their servers over a number of Availability Zones (AZs) within a single region. There are super low latency connections between these AZs, which is great for fast failover should an EC2 instance or an AZ fail.

Perhaps you work for a business that has to comply with industry regulations where building your application across AZs is not good enough. In these cases, you can look to designing your services to cover more than a single region. Multi-region designs are very common for larger enterprises and with some thought can work very well. Ensuring that any AWS service you depend upon is available in the regions you plan to use is a good first step!

Back in the data center heyday of the early 2000s, if your company needed *High Availability*, they would run a production copy of critical applications in a single data center and *also* a standby copy in a separate data center. When I reflect on how much time, effort, and huge sums of *money* that went into providing disaster recovery systems, I shudder.

With the ability to template an entire data center infrastructure using "Infrastructure as Code" tools such as AWS CloudFormation or HashiCorp's Terraform, you have the ability to run that template in any AWS Region to create a brand-new environment within a very short time. I still find it amazing when I build a data center in AWS in minutes and think back to when the same thing would have taken the best part of 12–18 months.

When you have the capability to create an entire data center at your fingertips, does it affect your businesses' DR strategy? Do you still need your servers or EC2 instances running 24/7 in a remote location? The reality is that you just need an up-to-date copy of your data available, a working template of your infrastructure, and a DNS or load balancing service. I admit it's a simplification. There are other considerations, like how to ensure that the exact EC2 Instance type will be available for your sole use at any given time, and this requires some thought and an investigation into EC2 *Reserved Instances*. AWS published a whitepaper on the subject.[1]

---

[1]https://d1.awsstatic.com/whitepapers/Storage/Backup_and_Recovery_Approaches_Using_AWS.pdf

Another consideration in choosing which of the 25 regions to use is *Where are your users?*

Cloud gives you the perfect opportunity to create your entire infrastructure very quickly, in an ever-increasing number of locations, throughout the world. So even if you are based in the East Coast of the United States, you can create the application platform exactly where your users run it, even in China.

How do you deliver content to your users if they are spread around the globe? Do you have to create AWS environments in each region? Of course not, you can use the Edge locations and Points of Presence (PoPs) I mentioned earlier in this chapter alongside a service like AWS CloudFront to deliver your content as close to your users as possible while maintaining the "core" of your application in one of the AWS regions.

Virtual Private Cloud (VPC)

Let's dive a little deeper into what a Virtual Private Cloud (VPC) is and what you can do with it. A VPC allows you to build your own virtual networking within an AWS Region. When you create a VPC, you have to assign it a *Classless Inter-Domain Routing (CIDR) block*, which is a fancy name for a range of IP addresses that can be used inside your VPC. In fact, you can create multiple VPCs within a region and even use the same or overlapping CIDR blocks if your heart desires. The AWS internal networking infrastructure ensures they are completely isolated and cannot communicate with each other. It's generally not good practice to have overlapping CIDR blocks within your account, but I'm simply making the point that how you design your network is completely within your power and not defined by AWS. Although each VPC is completely isolated from the other, we will discuss how you can enable communication between VPCs shortly.

Just as you have in your own data centers, your network is segmented further into smaller blocks of IP addresses from the assigned CIDR range with "subnets." It's within these subnets that your EC2 Instances will reside. By default, there is no communication in or out of your VPC until you add one of the available *Gateways*. Internet Gateways (IGW) connect subnets directly to the Internet and require a change to the subnet routing table to allow nonlocal traffic to be sent to the IGW. We also have Virtual Private Gateways (VGW) which enable connectivity to your own data centers via VPN or AWS Direct Connects.

IP addresses are supplied to your EC2 Instances when they launch by means of the built-in DHCP service. This service, called the DHCP Option Set, allows you to set a number of values for the instances you run inside your VPC. The values are for settings like Domain Name Servers (DNS) or NTP Servers if you need to change the preconfigured defaults. We will be changing some of these settings during Chapter 10 when we discuss Identity.

Before we move on from VPCs, I want to highlight two important features: VPC Flow Logs and VPC Peering. VPC Flow Logs capture information about the IP traffic inside your VPC. All this data is then stored in another AWS Service called CloudWatch in 1-minute intervals. VPC Flow Logs need to be enabled at the VPC, subnet, or network interface level. Incredibly important from a security perspective that you have available logs should anything untoward happen. VPC Flow Logs provide valuable information regarding traffic that has been accepted or rejected by hosts inside your VPC. It should be noted that this shows the message header including ports and IPs but not the actual data itself.

Finally, at the top of this section, I explained that VPCs are customer-isolated networks, which is correct, but there are ways to provide connectivity between VPCs. You could use Internet Gateways to communicate over the Internet of course, but a far more efficient and private way is to set up VPC Peering.

VPC Peering creates a network link between VPCs using the AWS backbone infrastructure. One side of the VPC Peering connection makes a request to peer, and once the other side accepts the peering request to connect, they must both add routes to their respective routing tables. One thing to note here is that VPC Peering is nontransitive, which basically means that peering to a particular VPC does not give you the access to any VPCs that it is in turn peered to. Figure 2-1 demonstrates this.

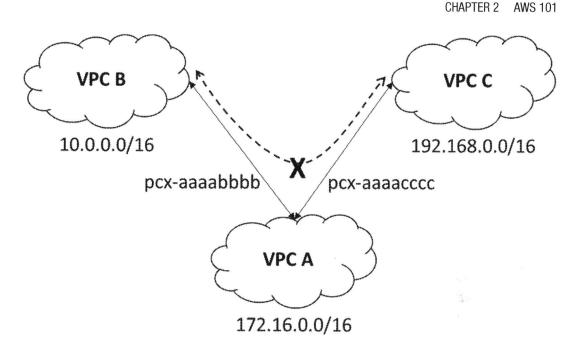

Figure 2-1. *VPC Peering is nontransitive*

In this figure, VPC-A is connected via peering to both VPC-B and VPC-C. However, that does not mean that VPC-B and VPC-C are allowed any form of direct network communication betweeen each other. To enable those VPCs to communicate will require another VPC Peering request directly between B and C.

Security Groups and NACLs

Traditionally, we had our network configured with a small number of subnets – each subnet serving a group of servers which have similar roles. For instance, my web servers lived in their own isolated subnet, and I could open up firewall-controlled access to just HTTP and HTTPS traffic to reach those servers. The firewall rules I put in place on each subnet provided access to every server inside. Simples. If I had a web server farm of 50 servers, I didn't need to add 50 separate firewall rules; I simply added a single rule, and every server residing inside that subnet was subject to the rule applied.

Network Access Control Lists (NACLs) are available on AWS and provide a very similar function. You assign the NACL to a VPC subnet and then add the network ports to be allowed in and what traffic you want to allow out. This kind of access control affects all EC2 instances that reside in that subnet. NACLs are stateless, which means you have to explicitly *allow* either side of a connection (inbound and outbound). The important thing to remember is that NACLs operate at the subnet level and are stateless.

Let's take the previous example and expand it to propose that one of my EC2 instances also needs access to a database server residing in a different subnet. The change to the NACL means that *every* EC2 Instance in that subnet now has that access. This could be something I don't want to happen. The use of NACLs requires some thought and planning.

Security groups are instance-bound stateful firewalls.

Let's look into that statement in more detail. Security Groups (SGs) are required to be attached to an EC2 Instance before it is launched – they provide network port–based firewall functionality in a stateful way. This means that if I specify what inbound network ports to enable, the security group will allow outbound traffic required for that connection. SGs can be attached to multiple EC2 instances and will allow inbound and outbound access to all of the individual instances based on the rules you've specified. Putting multiple EC2 Instances in an SG will not automatically allow them to communicate with each other. With a security group, you only need to specify what ports to allow; all other traffic is implicitly denied.

Since Security Groups are bound to an EC2 Instance network interface, they ensure tighter security and more flexibility. However, anything that is more flexible inevitably ends up having an administrative burden, and typically you can end up with a lot of security groups, so some good housekeeping skills are often needed. Personally, I feel that this housekeeping overhead is outweighed by the knowledge that a security group is attached to each and every Instance before it is launched.

Identity and Access Management

Now that we've covered the AWS global infrastructure, let's move back to our AWS Account and log in to the AWS Management Console. When you first create an account, you'll only have the administrator (root) account available. At this stage, we need to discuss the AWS Identity and Access Management (IAM) service.

There are two different types of identity you need to concern yourself with when using AWS – identities that provide access to the AWS Cloud and then the more traditional operating system identities that access the server Instances that you can create.

You'll need an identity that will let you manage your AWS Cloud account. This identity is part of a service called AWS Identity and Access Management or IAM for short. IAM lets you create user accounts and assign security policies to let you perform any action within the AWS Management Console, the AWS Command Line, or programmatically with a Software Development Kit (SDK). These accounts are what you will use to create VPCs and EC2 instances and other related AWS services.

When you launch an EC2 Instance running a Windows Server Machine Image, a local administrator user account that is part of the local server administrators group will be automatically created for you. The very last question you are asked during the EC2 Instance creation wizard is to specify what key pair to use. Key pairs are created in each account and are used to decrypt the administrator password for this administrator account.

You can also join your EC2 Instance to an Active Directory domain during the launch process, which will still supply a local administrator account that you may use but also allows you to log in with an Active Directory Domain account.

Identity is a big subject, and we will cover it in depth during Chapter 10.

Responsibility Model

Let's discuss boundaries, shall we?

In this new cloudy way of running IT systems, who does what and what are the things that you need to focus on? From day one, AWS has operated what they call the Shared Responsibility Model. The concept behind this model is to define clear lines of responsibility between AWS and their customers. The demarcation is very clear. Security *of* the cloud is the responsibility of AWS, and Security *in* the cloud rests with the customer.

The AWS Cloud is made up of physical hardware, data centers, physical security, network connections, power, and so on (wait, did you think it was an actual cloud?)

While the data, solutions, platforms, and environments using AWS Services like S3 or EC2 are the responsibility of the customer, AWS gives you the building blocks, and you are responsible for what you build (see Figure 2-2).

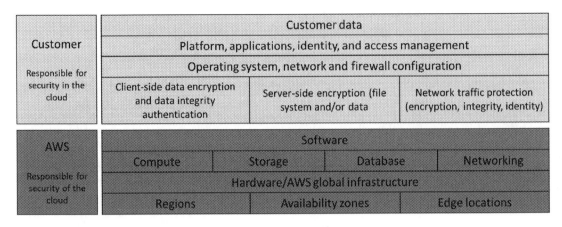

Customer	Customer data		
Responsible for security in the cloud	Platform, applications, identity, and access management		
	Operating system, network and firewall configuration		
	Client-side data encryption and data integrity authentication	Server-side encryption (file system and/or data	Network traffic protection (encryption, integrity, identity)
AWS	Software		
Responsible for security of the cloud	Compute	Storage	Database	Networking
	Hardware/AWS global infrastructure		
	Regions	Availability zones	Edge locations

Figure 2-2. *AWS's Shared Responsibility Model*

Security

AWS take security seriously. Very, very seriously. Their mantra has always been "security is job zero," and it has built a large number of services specifically focused on customer security. It's quite a change of approach compared to legacy data center hosting where forms of security were bolted onto a platform either before it went into production or, Lord forbid, afterward.

Inside AWS, there are teams focused on security detection and prevention and a large number of security consultants who will work with you to ensure that you are following best practices. For example, one of the most popular AWS services is its cloud storage service S3. When you create an S3 bucket, it's not accessible to anyone, and to allow people to access it, you have to explicitly configure the S3 bucket yourself. There are services, like AWS Trusted Advisor, which monitor your account to benchmark it against best practices and provide security warnings for configurations that don't meet these best practices as well as provide recommendations on ways to reduce costs, improve performance, and add fault tolerance.

Amazon Macie uses machine learning to classify the data you have inside AWS, categorize it by sensitivity, and protect it so that you are aware where your important data is and safeguard it for you. AWS Shield provides protection from Distributed Denial of Service (DDoS) attacks, which are a particularly difficult form of attack to protect a business against since it involves what looks like normal Internet web traffic; the issue comes when so much of this traffic arrives at the server that it prevents legitimate requests getting through and denies your users of a service. There are lots of these services – you won't need to understand them all in depth for the purposes of this book, but I think it's useful to have an understanding of what is available and how they'll fit into your AWS environment.

How about security on the operating systems we manage ourselves? AWS Inspector provides an automated security assessment service that helps you test the security state of your running instances.

A great place to start this is right here: `https://aws.amazon.com/products/security/`.

Monitoring

Now that we understand that we are responsible for what we run on AWS, let's quickly take a look at what monitoring is available and how we can detect issues within our AWS Cloud environment.

Monitoring is split into two elements with AWS. You've got traditional system-based monitoring such as availability, capacity, application, operating system logs, and so on. Then there's monitoring of the cloud itself – and understanding what network traffic goes in and out of your cloud environment, alerts from AWS Services, and so on.

Traditional monitoring suites have not been very *cloud-aware*. They were designed for physical or virtual servers in data centers whose sole purpose was to keep running for as long a time as possible. In Chapter 3, we discuss the idea that if a server fails, we aren't particularly concerned what is wrong with it, but more about whether a replacement server will be up and running with all the same application and content in just a few minutes.

But AWS comes with a whole host of monitoring services ready to use. We cover these in more depth during Chapter 8 and in particular how they apply and can be used for our Microsoft Workloads. They include services such as AWS CloudWatch, AWS CloudTrail, and Flow Logs. They allow us to set up events that can trigger remedial actions and automate the whole process of ensuring that services are available.

Further Learning

Working on AWS involves constant learning – not only due to the large number of AWS services they have in the Management Console these days, but more importantly the incredible number of significant updates and improvements that existing services receive.

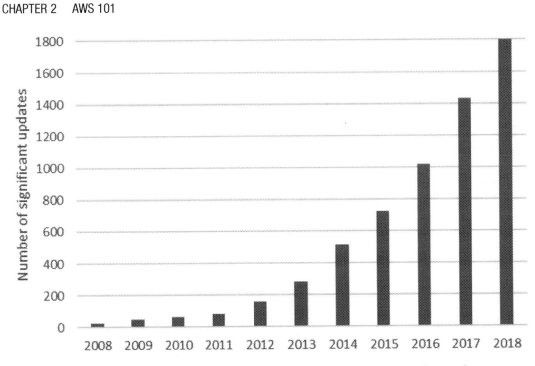

Figure 2-3. *Significant changes to the AWS platform from 2008 through 2018*

Let's take a minute to appreciate the graph in Figure 2-3. It shows the amount of significant changes and new services from 2008 through to 2018. I find it amazing that so many improvements can occur on some services that are now more than 10 years old. And it's heartwarming to know that over 90% of these improvements come directly from customers. Customer interactions either directly with AWS Support or via the large amount of Solution Architects and Professional Services Consultants can result in the opening of a Product Feature Request (PFR) which informs the service team road map and can lead to a new feature released for everyone to use.

How do you learn more about AWS?

There are plenty of good third-party tools and sites to learn about AWS – places like A Cloud Guru, Linux Academy, Cloud Academy, Udemy, and YouTube. Most of these companies also offer training on other cloud platforms.

AWS has its own training that provides classroom and digital training, a lot of it for free. AWS has its own certifications also. At the current time, it consists of 12 qualifications that you can achieve ranging at the very start of your AWS knowledge with the *Cloud Practitioner* exam right through to professional-level *Development and Architecture* exams and now specialty exams in areas such as *Security, Networking,* and *Machine Learning.* You can learn more about AWS training here: `https://aws.amazon.com/training/`.

My advice on the next steps for learning about AWS is to take things slowly. The AWS Cloud platform is now too broad for you to become an expert in all of it. Nor will you ever need to. Just understand the services that you are going to use and go from there. Plus, make sure you revisit services often. If a brand-new AWS service does not give you the functionality you need in comparison with what you have been running in your data center today, don't write off using it in the future because as we've learned, things change quickly!

Summary

In this chapter, we've covered the big building blocks of the AWS Cloud – the elements that are prerequisite knowledge before we dive deeper in the chapters to come.

We discussed AWS Accounts and touched upon multi-account strategies, the AWS global infrastructure of Regions, AZs, and PoPs. We had a very brief discussion on the AWS mantra of designing for Availability and then discussed the networking side of AWS with virtual private clouds, security groups, and NACLS.

We talked about identity, security, and the AWS Responsibility Model as well as Monitoring. All of these are big subjects, and justice cannot be done with a few paragraphs. We will discuss all of these from the perspective of Microsoft Workloads throughout the course of this book.

Lastly, we discussed further learning. I've used AWS every working day for the last 8 years, and I learn multiple new things every day. This new cloudy way of running our IT services has changed the game; it has brought untold benefits in the democratization of technology, and it is not stopping any time soon.

CHAPTER 3

Server

If you are considering Amazon Web Services as the cloud provider for your Microsoft workloads, then this chapter on all things Windows Server is going to be an important one for you. In later chapters of this book, we discuss containers and serverless, and we also cover AWS services such as Amazon RDS or AWS Directory Services which can replace the need to run and maintain servers. However, especially at the start of your cloud journey, you'll predominantly be using Amazon Elastic Compute Cloud (EC2) virtual machines to act as the servers for your Microsoft workloads.

In fact, it's so popular to run Microsoft Windows Server on Amazon EC2 that AWS saw an increase of 400% during 2014–2017, as customers who traditionally saw AWS as Linux-only found that their Microsoft Workloads ran just as fast and reliably as they did in their own data centers (I would argue even more so).

There's a quote attributed to Andy Warhol, "Perception precedes reality."

Even with this massive growth of running Windows on Amazon EC2, I've still seen companies who start their cloud journey with AWS and then look at Microsoft Azure when it comes to finding a home for their Microsoft workloads.

Why? I guess the logic is that since you're running Microsoft software, it must be better to run it on a Microsoft cloud platform.

It should make sense. But my own conversations with companies and the large number of stories shared at AWS events suggest that businesses have not found that particular logic to be true.

This is why companies large and small overwhelmingly choose AWS to run their Microsoft workloads. There's an often-quoted statistic you may have seen at AWS events or in one of their many presentations.

AWS runs 58% of all Microsoft Windows Server running in the cloud.

So, it's reassuring to know that you'll be in good company as we continue through this chapter on Windows Server.

© Ryan Pothecary 2021
R. Pothecary, *Running Microsoft Workloads on AWS*, https://doi.org/10.1007/978-1-4842-6628-1_3

Amazon EC2

Later in this book, we dip our toe into the capabilities of containers for Microsoft Workloads on AWS, and we also look at the fascinating world of Serverless technology and how it can revolutionize how you create solutions. But when starting their cloud journey and migrating from their on-premises data center, a large number of AWS customers start using Amazon EC2 and never feel the need to change.

Amazon EC2 is AWS's virtual server service (AWS calls them Instances). They form a powerful reason why customers are making the move to the cloud. No other AWS service typifies the pay-as-you-go nature of public cloud platforms than virtual servers.

Available when you need them, and the moment you don't, simply click stop or terminate and you'll not pay a single penny more. Imagine a data center full of servers which you need to service those Black Friday or holiday periods, when you have hundreds of thousands of users shopping on your retail website. Picture that same data center in January or February once the rush has subsided, and you are left with all that equipment which you no longer need until the next big sale. Now imagine being able to click a single switch and return all those servers to their vendors and not pay anything until you need them once more. Powerful stuff.

Amazon EC2 came out of a beta period that it had been running in since 2006 and was officially launched in October 2008, and it started supporting Microsoft Windows Server on day one.

Amazon EC2 comprises a few separate components which we will look at during this section:

- Instance type
- Amazon Machine Image
- EC2 configuration
- Tags
- Storage
- Security groups
- Virtual instance

Amazon Machine Image (AMI)

The first option you have when creating an Amazon EC2 Instance is what operating system you want to run. AWS have their own Linux distribution called Amazon Linux as well as various other Linux distros from Red Hat, SUSE, and Ubuntu. They also have various editions of Microsoft Windows Server starting at 2012 and including 2016 and 2019. It's also possible for you to bring your own server image into AWS and run those out of support editions such as 2008 and 2003.

These operating systems are packaged in a software configuration called an Amazon Machine Image (AMI). AWS provides us with a number of AMIs to choose from (Figure 3-1), and they update these AMIs every month with the latest security updates. Apart from the AWS-provided AMIs and AMIs you can create yourself, there are also community AMIs and AMIs that can be shared between AWS accounts. Finally, there is the AWS Marketplace where ISV partners and hardware vendors like F5, Cisco, Sophos, Barracuda, and so on provide ready-to-run AMIs with their software already preconfigured. There is an additional charge for these images which is clearly shown before you agree to use the image.

Figure 3-1. *AMI list*

Every AMI has a unique AMI-ID such as `ami-019b399cca02b2cd3` which is the current AMI-ID for Microsoft Windows Server 2019 in London. If I search for the same image in a different region, it will have a different AMI-ID, and every month when AWS updates the image, it'll have another unique AMI-ID.

Amazon EC2 Instance Type

In the same way as you have different server configurations in your data center, AWS offers nearly 400 different instance types (Figure 3-2) for you to choose from. These instance types are categorized in families, and each family fits around different use cases.

- General purpose
- Compute optimized
- Memory optimized
- Storage optimized
- Accelerated computing

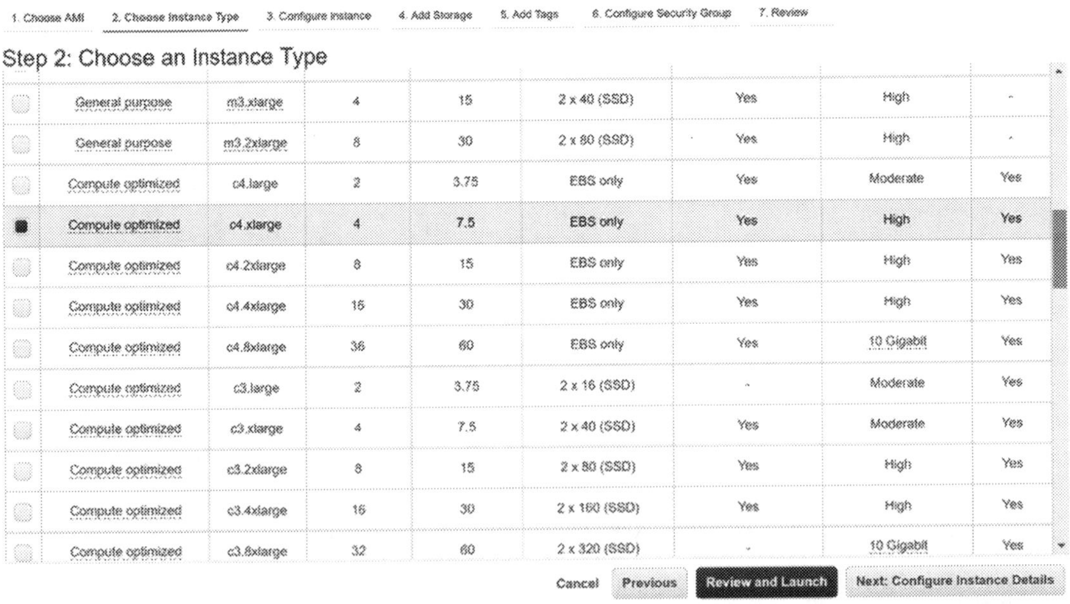

| | 1. Choose AMI | 2. Choose Instance Type | 3. Configure Instance | 4. Add Storage | 5. Add Tags | 6. Configure Security Group | 7. Review | |

Step 2: Choose an Instance Type

○	General purpose	m3.xlarge	4	15	2 x 40 (SSD)	Yes	High	-
○	General purpose	m3.2xlarge	8	30	2 x 80 (SSD)	Yes	High	-
○	Compute optimized	c4.large	2	3.75	EBS only	Yes	Moderate	Yes
●	Compute optimized	c4.xlarge	4	7.5	EBS only	Yes	High	Yes
○	Compute optimized	c4.2xlarge	8	15	EBS only	Yes	High	Yes
○	Compute optimized	c4.4xlarge	16	30	EBS only	Yes	High	Yes
○	Compute optimized	c4.8xlarge	36	60	EBS only	Yes	10 Gigabit	Yes
○	Compute optimized	c3.large	2	3.75	2 x 16 (SSD)	-	Moderate	Yes
○	Compute optimized	c3.xlarge	4	7.5	2 x 40 (SSD)	Yes	Moderate	Yes
○	Compute optimized	c3.2xlarge	8	15	2 x 80 (SSD)	Yes	High	Yes
○	Compute optimized	c3.4xlarge	16	30	2 x 160 (SSD)	Yes	High	Yes
○	Compute optimized	c3.8xlarge	32	60	2 x 320 (SSD)	-	10 Gigabit	Yes

Cancel   Previous   Review and Launch   Next: Configure Instance Details

Figure 3-2. *Amazon EC2 Instance types*

AWS also offer different CPUs from different manufacturers including Intel, AMD, and its own ARM-based Graviton and Graviton2 processor. They also offer instances with AMD Radeon and NVIDIA GPUs and instances which come with AWS's own Inferentia processor, specially built to aid Machine Learning workloads. If you have a use case for it, there's also an instance type that comes with a field-programmable gate array (FPGA) which allows customizable hardware acceleration.

Naming conventions for instance types include *family*, *generation*, and *size*, for example, C5.Large. Here, the family is C (for compute optimized), 5 for generation, and Large for the size, which in this case is a 2 vCPU, 4GB RAM EC2 instance.

Configuring Your Instance

You've chosen what spec of server you want and what operating system it will run; the next stage is to provide the configuration of network, IAM role, domain, and so on. This screen (Figure 3-3) has a lot of configuration options. Don't be put off by this; you can accept the defaults and click network, but it's worth spending a minute here and checking that you've selected the correct VPC and network subnets and whether you wish to have this instance automatically join an AWS Directory Service Domain (or an on-premises domain that you're advertising with AWS AD Connector).

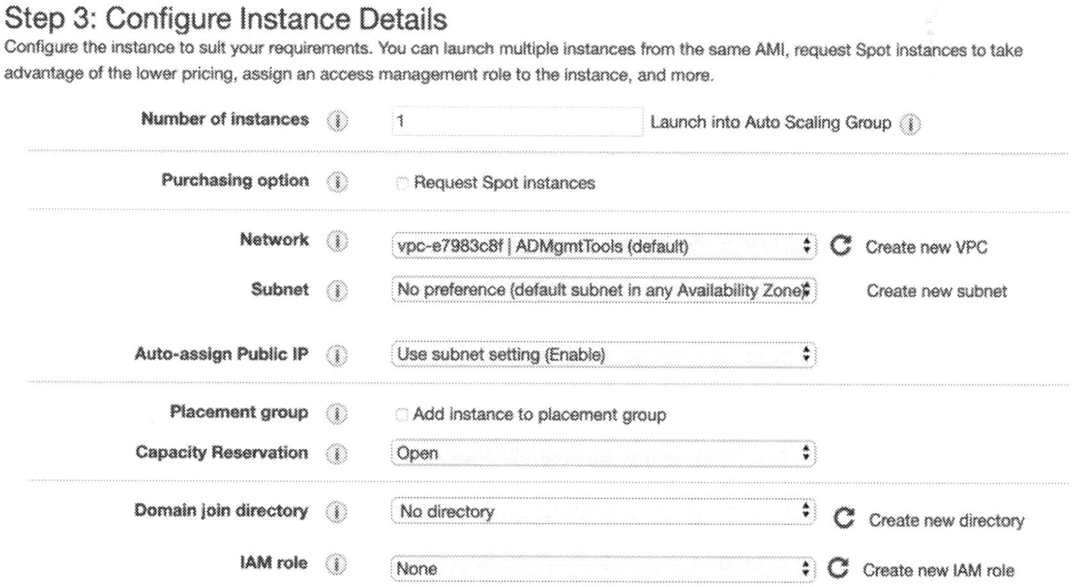

Step 3: Configure Instance Details

Configure the instance to suit your requirements. You can launch multiple instances from the same AMI, request Spot instances to take advantage of the lower pricing, assign an access management role to the instance, and more.

Number of instances ⓘ	1 Launch into Auto Scaling Group ⓘ
Purchasing option ⓘ	☐ Request Spot instances
Network ⓘ	vpc-e7983c8f | ADMgmtTools (default) ⟳ Create new VPC
Subnet ⓘ	No preference (default subnet in any Availability Zone) Create new subnet
Auto-assign Public IP ⓘ	Use subnet setting (Enable)
Placement group ⓘ	☐ Add instance to placement group
Capacity Reservation ⓘ	Open
Domain join directory ⓘ	No directory ⟳ Create new directory
IAM role ⓘ	None ⟳ Create new IAM role

Figure 3-3. *Configure instance details*

If you click the Advanced Details arrow, you'll get the option of adding a Bash or PowerShell script into the User Data section. This script will be run during the first boot of the machine and may be used to add Windows roles or features or configure the instance in some way that will make it useful when the server starts up (`https://docs.aws.amazon.com/AWSEC2/latest/WindowsGuide/ec2-windows-user-data.html`).

You can also use this configuration screen to choose to launch the instance as a Dedicated Instance or Host. Very useful if you want to Bring Your Own License (BYOL).

Storage

You now have the option of adding storage (Figure 3-4) for the root volume (the C:\ drive) and any additional drives you may need up to a maximum of 23 further drivers covering up to a Z:\drive. You can use the built-in Disk Management tool inside Windows Server to change the drive letter and apply software RAID if you need it.

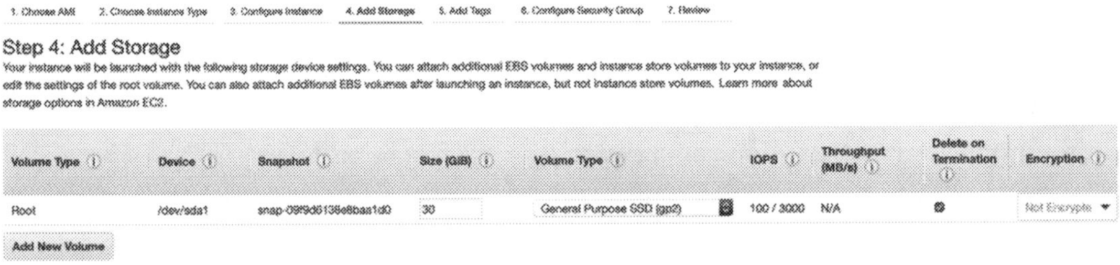

Figure 3-4. *Storage*

There are many different volumes available to you. You can change the size of each volume; however, the root volume cannot be more than 2048GB since that is all that is allowed by the operating system. There is also a maximum size of 16TiB for a nonroot volume. With some volume types, you can change the amount of IOPS you require the volume to have.

You also have the ability to encrypt each volume using the default AWS KMS key that is created in your account, or you can bring your own key and use that.

The EBS volume types available to you include

- General Purpose SSD (gp2)

- General Purpose SSD (gp3)

- Provisioned IOPS SSD (io1)

- Provisioned IOPS SSD (io2)

- Cold HDD (sc1)

- Throughput Optimized HDD (ST1)

- Magnetic

There are also directly-attached-to-the-hardware *instance store* volumes available on certain Amazon EC2 instance types, and of course there are other storage services such as Amazon S3 or AWS FSx for Windows Server. We discuss all of these different storage services later in this chapter.

One thing to finally mention is the Delete on Termination checkbox. This deletes the EBS volume if the attached Amazon EC2 Instance is terminated and avoids having orphaned EBS volumes costing you money in your account.

Tags

Don't skip over this section!

Tagging is something that AWS talks about a lot, and for good reason. These small bits of metadata can help you automate and manage your AWS infrastructure and help you find resources which are really useful when you have a lot of resources in your AWS Account.

Tags may not be the most exciting thing in your life (if they are, then you should talk to someone), but they *will* make your life easier.

Tags are labels that you give to an AWS resource. They have two elements, a key and a value. You can see in Figure 3-5 that when creating an Amazon EC2 instance, you have the ability of not only providing any number of tags to the EC2 instance but you are also tagging the storage and network components at the same time.

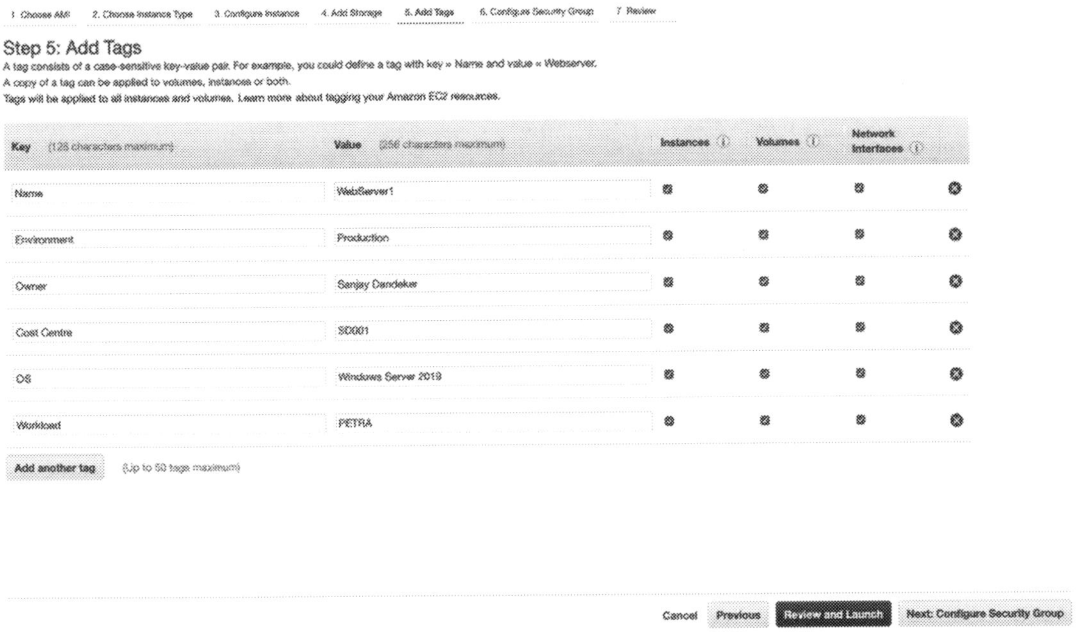

Figure 3-5. Tags

However, regardless of how useful they are, a lot of AWS customers still dont use them or don't have a strategy when it comes to tags. This is why AWS provides the ability to enforce tagging by the implementation of AWS Config rules. AWS Config continuously monitors your AWS account and has the ability to stop or terminate AWS resources if tagging is missing.

Security Groups

AWS Security Groups (Figure 3-6) are instance-bound stateful software firewalls.

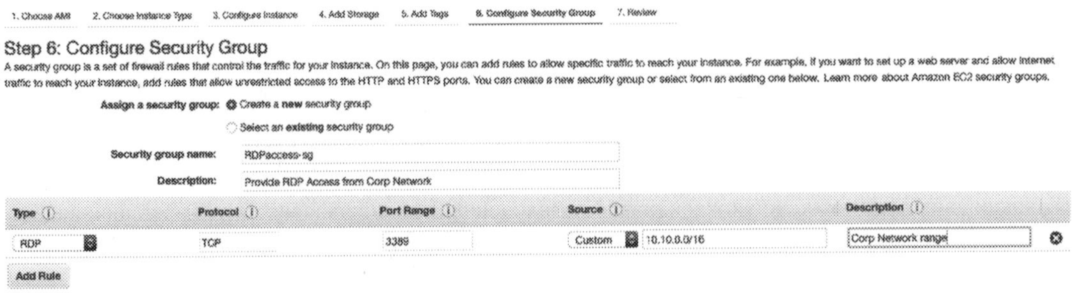

Figure 3-6. Security Groups

Let's think back to our data center–based architectures. You would have had networks that were public and private – maybe a traditional web, application, and database solution using three separate subnets for each layer. These subnets were isolated from each other to protect the servers running inside them. Between each subnet, we allowed certain network ports to communicate.

Firewall rules were typically configured at a subnet level. It was easier to manage, and less firewall rules meant we had better performance. The issue comes when every server sitting in a subnet has an open firewall port that they may not need.

AWS Security Groups provide a port-based firewall attached to every single Amazon EC2 instance. You must have a security group assigned to your instance; otherwise, it won't launch.

Security groups are stateful, which means that I just need to configure what network ports are allowed 'In' to the server; all ports are allowed out. For each security group, you have to configure what network ports are allowed and from which destination.

A neat drop-down box will give you an idea of common ports to select, or you can simply add your own custom port and either TCP or UDP Protocol.

The source can be Custom, Anywhere, or My IP. If you choose My IP, the wizard will look up your current Internet IP address and use that. Obviously, be careful since that address can change without you knowing if you don't have a static IP from your service provider.

You will get a warning message if you are allowing open access from Anywhere, which is the whole Internet (0.0.0.0/0), and it's always good practice to allow access from known IP addresses only.

Review, Key Pairs, and Launch!

After security groups, you'll see the final review screen where you must launch your instance. This screen will highlight your configuration choices and also tell you if this EC2 Instance is included in the free-tier options. It will also highlight once again if you have any security group rules that leave your instance exposed.

After clicking launch, you'll then see a pop-up screen (Figure 3-7) asking you to select or create a key pair.

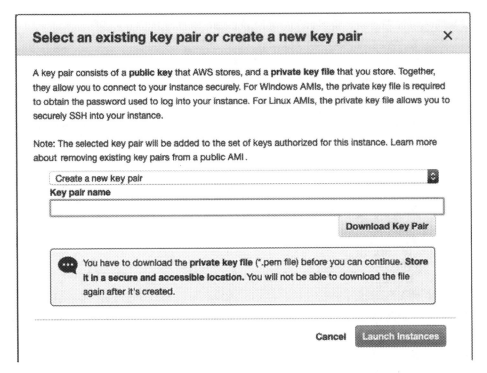

Figure 3-7. *Final review screen and key pair creation*

An Amazon EC2 key pair is a 2048-bit SSH2 RSA key, consisting of a public and private side, that is a crucial part of your security credentials. AWS stores the public key, and you download and store the private key which will be used rather than a password when connecting to your Amazon EC2 instances.

When creating an Amazon EC2 instance, you must choose which key pair to use before you launch the instance if you want to connect to it.

On Linux Instances, you'll use your private key as part of the SSH command, whereas with Microsoft Windows instances, you'll need the private key to decrypt the local administrator password that will allow you to interactively log in.

Key pairs are not needed if you automatically join an Active Directory domain during the initial launch of the Instance, and you don't need or have no use for the local administrator account. You can also launch an Instance without using a key pair, but you will not be able to connect to it.

Perfect for server roles which don't need anyone loggin on to them (which should really be the majority of all servers).

EC2Launch

Now that you've finally launched your Amazon EC2 Instance, what exactly happens?

Each Microsoft Windows instance has an agent called EC2Launch.

Previously called EC2Config in all pre-Windows 2016 editions, AWS decided to create an updated helper service for Windows Server 2016 and 2019.

EC2Launch is a set of PowerShell scripts that help configure and initialize your Microsoft Windows Server instance during the first boot. After the first launch, the script is automatically disabled and must be rescheduled using Windows Task Scheduler to run again.

The `InitializeInstance.ps1` script can be found in the `%Programfiles%\Amazon\EC2-Windows\Launch\Scripts` folder and performs a number of functions such as

- Add network routes to the KMS license server

- Set the computer name

- Add DNS suffixes

- Set the administrator password

- Set up a new wallpaper with instance information

- Execute any scripts in the user data section

There are also some other PowerShell scripts which come under the EC2Launch umbrella such as

- InitializeDisks.ps1 – Initializes EBS and instance store volumes.

- SendEventLogs.ps1 – Sends certain EventLogs to the console based on filters.

- SendWindowsIsReady.ps1 – Sends a simple Windows is ready message to the console.

- SysprepInstance.ps1 – SysPreps the instance using a default Unattend.xml. There are also batch files called BeforeSysprep.cmd, SysprepSpecialize.cmd, and Randomize-LocalAdminPassword.ps1 all to be used for the SysPrep process.

If you've not used SysPrep before, then an explanation of the process is at the start of the next section.

If you'd like to change any of these settings, AWS has created an application called EC2LaunchSettingsUI.exe which can be found here:

```
%ProgramFiles%\Amazon\EC2Launch\Settings\EC2LaunchSettingsUI.exe
```

Amazon EC2 Startup

It currently takes approximately 90 seconds to start an Amazon EC2 instance running Windows Server 2019. AWS has put a lot of effort in reducing this time significantly over the years. Startup time is crucial if we want our cloud environments to be dynamic, responsive, and agile. If we are using AWS's own Auto Scaling service to dynamically grow (and shrink) our server infrastructure in response to real-life usage, then we need new servers to be available, and useful, to us immediately.

So how do AWS do this?

If you've ever tried building a fleet of Microsoft Windows Servers, you'll be aware of Microsoft's SysPrep process. It's something you run on a Golden image, which is a server image that contains all the software and configuration you need preinstalled.

SysPrep strips the image of all unique system identifiers and hostname to mitigate the issue of having two identical machines running on your network at the same time. When you start up an image that has been SysPrep'd, you'll need to add a unique hostname, and the SysPrep will make that server unique on the network.

This takes time – even if you are using unattend files that help to automate the process.

I mentioned earlier that Amazon EC2 uses pre-created images called AMIs; these AMI Image files are stored on Amazon S3 and must be copied down from S3 to Amazon EBS block storage to form your root volume.

Next comes the SysPrep part; each server must be unique, remember? AWS have developed workflow, caching, and image management to complete that entire process in under 90 seconds for the latest release of its Amazon-provided AMIs, the ones you see and choose from during the first step of the Launch Instance process.

If you are using older versions or your own AMIs, then the startup process will be longer since the image will need to run a full SysPrep before it's available.

Once the server has started, it will execute the commands that you may have added to the user data section of the Amazon EC2 Launch wizard. The user data section contains either command-line scripts, preceded by `<script>` and ending in `</script>`, or Microsoft PowerShell beginning with `<powershell>` and ending in `</powershell>`. More info here: `https://docs.aws.amazon.com/AWSEC2/latest/WindowsGuide/ec2-windows-user-data.html`.

Amazon Machine Image

An Amazon Machine Image is a software configuration that comprises a choice of operating system provided via an Amazon EBS snapshot, security permissions that determine which AWS accounts can use the AMI, and finally a mapping to determine what EBS volumes to attach when it's launched. Basically, it saves you from standing in a cold data center feeding CDs to a server until it becomes useful.

As mentioned previously, AWS provides you with a *lot* of AMIs to choose from. There are the regularly updated Quick Start, or Amazon-provided, AMIs, then there are community AMIs, marketplace AMIs, and AMIs shared to your AWS account from other AWS accounts.

You have the ability to create or import your own AMIs. Creating an AMI is very easy. Find a running Amazon EC2 instance you want to use, select it, and choose Create Image (Figure 3-8) from the Action Image and Templates menu.

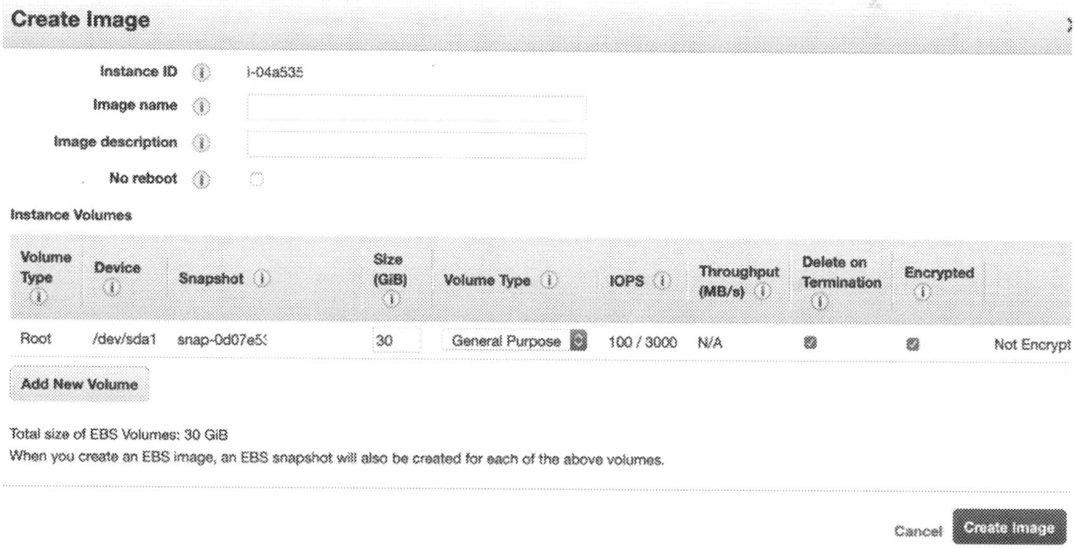

Create Image

Instance ID		i-04a535
Image name		
Image description		
No reboot		☐

Instance Volumes

Volume Type	Device	Snapshot	Size (GiB)	Volume Type	IOPS	Throughput (MB/s)	Delete on Termination	Encrypted	
Root	/dev/sda1	snap-0d07e5	30	General Purpose	100 / 3000	N/A	☒	☒	Not Encrypt

Add New Volume

Total size of EBS Volumes: 30 GiB
When you create an EBS image, an EBS snapshot will also be created for each of the above volumes.

Cancel   **Create Image**

Figure 3-8. *Create Image screen*

The newly created image will show in your EC2 console under Images. It will have been assigned a unique AMI-ID. From this screen, you can make the AMI public – it's private by default – or allow specific AWS accounts to use it.

If you make the AMI public, then it will be added to the community AMI's section. AWS has a "use at your own discretion" policy when it comes to community AMIs.

My own personal preference is not to use community AMIs unless I know who the source/owner is. Even then I'd weigh up the effort of just quickly reproducing the image myself.

You can also import an image from VMware using the command-line VM Import/Export tool, or you can use the brilliant AWS Server Migration Service which you can run on VMware, Hyper-V, and Azure.

Whatever tool you use, you'll end up with an AMI that you can select when launching your Amazon EC2 instance.

One tip to keep in mind is to make sure you also create a local user account with administrator permissions before you start the process. You may be using the image on a different Active Directory domain, or you may be unable to decrypt the local administrator's password.

There are a host of prerequisites to check off if you are importing a server from VMware or Hyper-V, such as ensuring that no antivirus is running. A full list of things to look out for can be found here: `https://docs.aws.amazon.com/vm-import/latest/userguide/vmie_prereqs.html`.

The Quick Start/Amazon-provided images are updated every month, just a few days after the Microsoft "Patch-Tuesday" release of updates, with the latest security hotfixes. After this process, they will have a brand-new AMI-ID.

It's important to remember this if you plan to create an immutable infrastructure where you've automated a rebuild of your application stack with the latest updates rather than making changes on the fly. An immutable infrastructure can be a difficult concept for those of us used to running and managing Windows estates ourselves. However, it is entirely possible to achieve on AWS and has benefits in uptime and manageability compared to an infrastructure where changes are being made directly on individual servers.

AWS Image Builder

Although start times of the latest Microsoft Windows Server AMIs on Amazon EC2 are an amazing 90 seconds, that leaves you with just a plain server. What you really need is a super-fast start time *with* all the tools and apps you need, ready to run.

There are many ways to accomplish this; we've been using configuration management tools like Chef and Puppet for years, joined by Ansible, among many others. Microsoft has its own System Center Configuration Manager or even PowerShell DSC to add to this list.

Companies have been using all of these tools very happily on AWS for years, and for completeness we should also mention some AWS Services such as AWS OpsWorks or the sublime AWS Systems Manager (more on that later).

But all these tools have one thing in common, their actions happen *after* the server is first built and comes to a ready state. You really need to investigate the time it takes from launch to useful – a state where all required roles or applications are installed and the server can be used.

Add this stage onto your server launch time, and you can quickly go from 90 seconds to 5 minutes or more (sometimes much more). So, what is the effect of this delay? You most keenly feel this if the server is part of an Amazon Auto Scaling Group where you have to wait 5 minutes or more every time you scale up. If the startup time is significant, the current peak (and reason for scaling) may have subsided by the time a working server is available to share the load.

The answer is to prebake AMI images based on the server role or application. Here, you take a current base AMI and add whatever applications and tools you need, then you save it as an AMI that you'll be ready to use. Sound good?

Ah-ha! You've fallen into my carefully laid trap.

Yes, prebaking AMIs *does* make the startup process faster, and of course that can only be seen as a good thing, *but* you've now taken on the responsibility of managing a herd of AMIs that have to be updated *every-single-month-until-you-die*.

Dry your eyes.

AWS has another solution that can really help here.

AWS Image Builder was launched at AWS re:Invent in 2019 with the sole purpose of making the creation and maintenance of AMIs a whole lot easier.

AWS Image Builder creates an image pipeline (Figure 3-9) that, once configured, can be scheduled to run independently of any action from yourself.

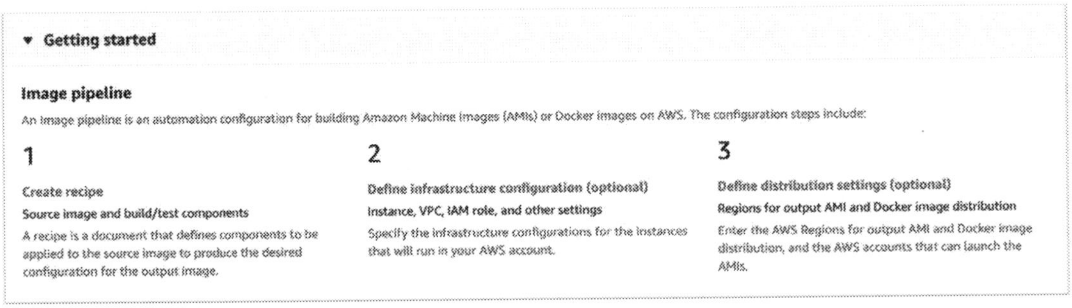

Getting started
Image pipeline
An image pipeline is an automation configuration for building Amazon Machine Images (AMIs) or Docker images on AWS. The configuration steps include:
1
Create recipe
Source image and build/test components
A recipe is a document that defines components to be applied to the source image to produce the desired configuration for the output image.
2
Define infrastructure configuration (optional)
Instance, VPC, IAM role, and other settings
Specify the infrastructure configurations for the instances that will run in your AWS account.
3
Define distribution settings (optional)
Regions for output AMI and Docker image distribution
Enter the AWS Regions for output AMI and Docker image distribution, and the AWS accounts that can launch the AMIs.

Figure 3-9. *The AWS Image Builder pipeline process*

Once you click the Create Pipeline button, you'll be taken through a wizard which firstly asks you for a pipeline name and a schedule. You can choose to run it manually when you need it or on a regular schedule that you define.

During the wizard, you will create an image recipe, similar to Chef. The next screen allows you to update an existing image recipe or create a new one; you can also select the base or source image to build upon. In Figure 3-10, I've selected the Quick Start (Amazon-provided) Windows Server 2019 AMI.

Source image Info
Select image
Select managed images
Enter custom AMI ID
Image Operating System (OS)
Amazon Linux
Windows
Ubuntu
ubuntu
CentOS
CentOS
Red Hat Enterprise Linux (RHEL)
Red Hat
SUSE Linux Enterprise Server (SLES)
SuSE
Image origin
Quick start (Amazon-managed)
Images owned by me
Images shared with me
Image name
Windows Server 2019 English Core Base x86

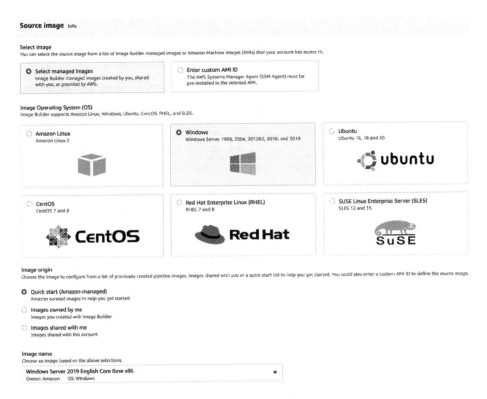

Figure 3-10. *AWS Image Builder configuration first step*

The next section of this step involves creating build and test components. Build components are configuration items that detail how to download, install, and configure a software package on your Amazon EC2 instance. AWS provide you with a host of build components covering common scenarios. You can also create your own or share build components between AWS accounts.

Once you've selected or created what you need, you can change the installation order, in case of dependencies.

Creating a build component is easy with an example build document available to follow. AWS have provided some good documentation here: `https://docs.aws.amazon.com/imagebuilder/latest/userguide/image-builder-application-documents.html`.

There is even a standalone executable that will allow you to run your build components locally. You simply save your build configurations as `.yml` YAML files and then use `AWSTOE.EXE` to run them (`https://docs.aws.amazon.com/imagebuilder/latest/userguide/image-builder-component-manager-local.html`).

Next, you'll want to test this image before you start using it, and AWS Image Builder has some standard test components already created for you to use, or of course you can create your own tests.

The final step in this section is to choose which EBS volume to use as the root C:\ drive volume, the size, the type of EBS volume, and whether you need it encrypted or not.

Creating the pipeline and defining a recipe using build and test components is really the bulk of the AWS Image Builder tasks you'll need to complete. But there are also two optional tasks should you wish to change the defaults here.

First up is the infrastructure configuration. Now that we've got all the elements of our AMI selected, AWS Image Builder will launch an Amazon EC2 instance to build this image for us. Then it creates the image from a snapshot and terminates the build Instance, leaving a working AMI for us to use.

The infrastructure configuration step tells Image Builder where to create this build instance. You can leave it at the defaults, use an existing configuration, or create a new configuration. With this option, you can provide IAM roles, EC2 instance types, VPCs, and subnet settings as well as SNS notifications and any tags you want to use.

The last step is to configure the distribution of this AMI once it's built. Once again, you can use the defaults or create and use new Distribution Settings. It's here that you can specify additional accounts to share the AMI with alongside any license configurations you've created with AWS License Manager. So, if you've installed Microsoft SQL Server using Bring Your Own License on this AMI, then you'll be able to track them and enforce usage based on the licenses you own.

The process is now complete; you'll see an Amazon EC2 instance start and terminate while the AMI is building, and you'll have a freshly baked AMI ready for consumption.

You can tie the AWS Image Builder process into a larger full-scale immutable infrastructure process using AWS Code Pipeline.

AWS have created a blog post to show you how to do just that using CloudFormation to set up all the resources needed to run the pipeline:

```
https://aws.amazon.com/blogs/mt/create-immutable-servers-using-
ec2-image-builder-aws-codepipeline/
```

Amazon Elastic Block Storage

Amazon EBS is a great example of how AWS take something and iterate on it constantly to transform what should be a standard cloud service into a service that is itself transformational. It's common to think of Amazon EBS as several large SAN devices all connected together, but the actual scale of Amazon EBS is something difficult to comprehend. EBS volumes can be as large as 16TB, and AWS customers run millions of these volumes every single day.

It offers 99.999% service availability and has an annual failure rate of between 0.1 and 0.2%, which is 10x more superior than normal SAN devices using industry standard disks.

The Amazon EBS service (Figure 3-11) is a standalone block-level storage service that runs independently of services like Amazon EC2. It's important to point this out since we associate EC2 and EBS closely with each other. Every single AWS Availability Zone has its own Amazon EBS hardware which automatically replicates Amazon EBS volumes within an Availability Zone.

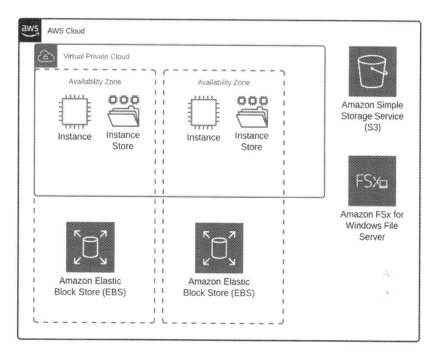

Figure 3-11. *AWS storage services in relation to Amazon EC2*

Take a minute to appreciate that statement.

Since Amazon EBS automatically replicates a volume, then should a volume suffer an outage, we don't suffer any data loss. Keep this in mind when thinking about using OS-level RAID, which we've been using on-premises for the last 30 years for reliability, but which now can be focused purely on the performance benefit.

As with every AWS storage service, there are multiple different tiers to choose from, and the service itself has a host of functionality that we need to be aware of.

You can create an Amazon EBS volume at the same time you create an Amazon EC2 instance or create it separately in the EBS section of the Amazon EC2 console and then attach it to a running Amazon EC2 instance. Amazon EBS also provides point-in-time snapshot capabilities which are stored in an Amazon S3 bucket in your AWS account. You can use these snapshots to create an Amazon EBS volume if required.

If you work with infrastructure or databases, then you'll know that storage performance is critical to the smooth running of a service. And Amazon EBS provides an increasing number of different types of EBS volumes, all of which have their own performance profile, use case, and price points.

At a high level, we have either Solid-State Disks (SSD) or Magnetic Hard Disk Drives (HDD), but these are broken down further into separate Amazon EBS volume types.

SSD GP2 volumes are the default storage you see when you launch an Amazon EC2 Instance. It provides burstable performance up to 3000 IOPS (input/output operations per second) on baseline IOPS of between 100 and 16,000 (for volumes larger than 5334GB). As is the case with most storage, performance is linked to volume size. The larger the volume, the more disks are needed and the higher the IOPS. A rule of thumb for GP2 volumes is 3 IOPS per GB of storage.

The burstable nature of GP2 volumes is similar in concept to the burstable T-Family of Amazon EC2 instances. You have a baseline level of performance, and while you are running at that level, you are earning virtual I/O credits which are used if you need more performance from a volume for short durations. The higher the amount of storage, the faster you earn credits. If your baseline I/O performance is higher than the burstable IOPS, then you'll not be able to use it.

SSD GP3 volumes don't have the burstable nature of GP2. They have a consistent baseline of 3000 IOPS, and you can increase that by up to 500 IOPS per GB without the need to increase the actual amount of storage. GP3 was announced at AWS re:Invent 2020 and is the next generation of Amazon EBS volume with 4x faster throughput than GP2 and at a lower price point.

SSD Io1 volumes are the first generation of provisioned IOPS storage used for scenarios where you need very fast storage performance. Io1 volumes have a provisioned IOPS ratio of 50:1, meaning a 100GB Io1 volume has 5000 IOPS.

SSD Io2 volumes are the latest generation of provisioned IOPS storage for customers who need single-digit millisecond latency, with a durability of 99.999% and 10x higher IOPS with a provisioned IOPS ratio of 500:1, giving a 100GB volume 50,000 IOPS.

Also at AWS re:Invent 2020, a new tier of EBS storage was announced, called Io2 Block Express. This provides submillisecond latency and 4000MB/s throughput.

Further information on general-purpose and provisioned IOPS volumes can be found here: `https://docs.aws.amazon.com/AWSEC2/latest/UserGuide/ebs-volume-types.html`.

But we not only need very fast and powerful SSD storage, we sometimes need slower and less expensive storage. If I was running Microsoft SQL Server on Amazon EC2, then a GP2 or Io2 volume would be the wrong thing to use for my backup drive. It would just be a waste of money. That's why AWS also cover us with Magnetic HDD–based EBS volumes.

Here, there are two options.

ST1 Throughput Optimized HDD has a maximum throughput per volume of 500MiB/s. Like GP2, it uses burstable performance to increase a baseline performance. If you have workloads that have large sequential data such as Hadoop/Amazon EMR or Data Warehouses and so on, then ST1 volumes can be a great balance between providing you the performance you need at a great price.

There are also SC1 Cold HDD volumes; if you require infrequent access to data, then SC1 could be the right fit for you.

Finally, there's a volume that you only really get to see if you are creating a volume from scratch, and that is *magnetic volumes*. These are a previous generation of storage that still have a use case, and AWS keeps them running. These have some constraints such as a limit of only 1TB and an average of just 100 IOPS. If you have data you simply cannot move to Amazon S3, then a magnetic volume might be the right answer for you.

It's worth noting that none of the HDD volumes can be used as a root (boot) volume.

Amazon EBS also has a feature called Data Lifecycle Manager. Its sole purpose is to make your life easier and save you money. Sounds good huh?

With Amazon Data Lifecycle Manager (Amazon DLM), you can define how long you need the snapshots associated with an Amazon EC2 and EBS volume. You can set policies, and Amazon DLM automates the snapshot lifecycle based on your policies. For example, I take a snapshot on Monday evening as part of my regular backup process of my Amazon EC2 instance. This snapshot is stored on Amazon S3 forever until I decide to move it or delete it. There are snapshots that are quickly stale and of no use to me, and there are snapshots I have to keep for compliance reasons.

One neat feature of Amazon DLM is that it automates the copying of snapshots across regions. This is perfect for your low-cost "pilot-light" disaster recovery process. Amazon S3 has a similar feature called Amazon S3 lifecycle policy which is used to manage data deletion policy and on which tier of Amazon S3 the data should reside.

If you are running workloads that demand even more performance of your Amazon EBS volume, then AWS announced a brand-new Instance type called an Amazon EC2 R5b. These virtual rocket ships can deliver 3x better EBS performance than a standard Amazon EC2 R5 instance type, delivering 7500 MB/s bandwidth and 260,000 IOPS.

One final thing to consider from a Microsoft Workloads viewpoint is the traditional role that RAID arrays provide for reliability and performance.

Firstly, AWS recommends that RAID 5 and 6 are not used since the parity disk required for these configurations takes away from performance, not add to it.

AWS do however support RAID 0 and 1 configurations at the operating system level. With RAID 0, we would create multiple volumes and then use OS configuration to make them one big volume. This can provide you with a huge increase in performance over the per-volume performance you'd get from Amazon EBS.

Although single disk failures are covered under EBS's replication technology, entire EBS failures are rare but possible and if that were to occur then you would lose data. It's often quoted that Amazon EBS is 10x more reliable than the standard commodity disks you'd use in your data center.

There's a discussion to be had with your business regarding risk vs. performance. Using Amazon DLM, you can at least maintain very regular snapshots should you need them!

AWS FSx for Windows File Server

A shared file system is something we've had on-premises for years; they are used for our home directories and shared folders, and a lot of our applications use them. But they only existed in AWS via their Amazon EFS service which is NFS compatible and used for Linux operating systems only. After the release of Amazon EFS in 2015, it took AWS a further 3 years to launch its SMB counterpart for Microsoft Windows. But when it did finally arrive, it did so with a bang.

Firstly, Amazon FSx comes in two completely separate editions. There's Amazon FSx for Windows File Server, and then there's Amazon FSx for Lustre. Lustre is a high-performance file system used by the high-performance compute (HPC) crowd.

Secondly, Amazon FSx was the only service, at that time, that launched with full PCI-DSS, SOC, and ISO compliance from day one.

Thirdly, it's fast – submillisecond latency and hundreds of thousand IOPS per file system. It can also store up to 64TB per file system and allows you to specify what throughput capacity you need. There is also a built-in caching system used to increase performance.

When you create an Amazon FSx file system, you have the option to set up a maintenance window where it allows the service to be patched and also provides backups of the file system for you. Resilience is in the form of the option of single or multi-AZ implementations, and Amazon FSx handles all the file over for you should something go wrong.

Amazon FSx for Windows File Server (Figure 3-12) is a fully managed service that runs on top of a dedicated Amazon EC2 instance (or two if using multi-AZ configuration). As with the similar fully managed service, AWS Directory Service for Microsoft Active Directory, you don't actually see the Amazon EC2 instances in your account. These are isolated in the AWS Management layer and are presented to your AWS Account as an AWS Elastic Network Interface (ENI).

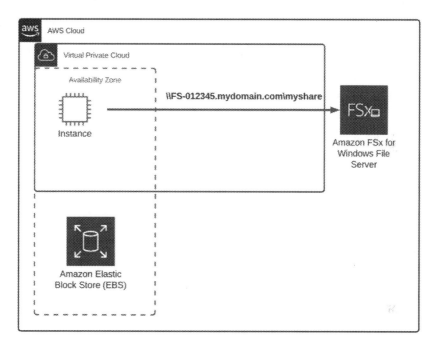

Figure 3-12. *Amazon FSx for Windows File Server*

As with all AWS storage services, you can encrypt the storage with no performance overhead using your AWS KMS key or a custom key.

Of course, AWS can't really provide an NTFS Microsoft Windows file system without some integration with Active Directory. At launch, Amazon FSx was integrated with AWS's own AWS Directory Service for Microsoft Active Directory. Since then, they quickly added support for customers' own managed Active Directory domains which can be running on Amazon EC2 or even still on-premises in your data center.

Apart from acting as a Windows File Server, one of the most common scenarios for using Amazon FSx is running high availability for Microsoft SQL Server. Here, Amazon FSx can be used as the shared storage witness for either SQL Server failover cluster instance deployments or availability groups.

Take a look at the AWS whitepaper "Best Practises for deploying SQL Server on AWS," which can be found here:

`https://d1.awsstatic.com/whitepapers/best-practices-for-deploying-microsoft-sql-server-on-aws.pdf`

An excellent AWS blog on this topic can be found here: `https://aws.amazon.com/blogs/storage/simplify-your-microsoft-sql-server-high-availability-deployments-using-amazon-fsx-for-windows-file-server/`.

Saving Money with Amazon EC2 Reserved Instances

AWS offers their services on pay-as-you-go pricing which is a revelation compared to the cost of running services on-premises. If you don't need a server, simply click stop or terminate, and that bill will go away. However, speaking with other IT companies and AWS partners, the preceding concept is one of the most difficult to implement for many new AWS customers.

We are just not used to switching things off. Sometimes, it's for good reason; the application we are running is used 24/7. Other times, it's more a mindset change. Maybe we don't trust that they'll come back on again, maybe we think we will lose data, or maybe if there's a chance of any kind of issue, then it's just not worth the effort to switch our servers off.

Even though AWS shows us how truly magical a potential DevOps future can be with our infrastructure fully automated and self-healing while we relax on a beach, they also understand that this potential may not be your reality. There will be customers who want or need to leave all of their Amazon EC2 instances running 24/7/365.

AWS pride themselves on what they call Customer Obsession. It's one of the leadership principles inherited from their Amazon parents. Since AWS knows there are customers who simply have to keep some services running 24/7, then it doesn't seem very Customer Obsessed to charge the same flat fee that's charged to those customers who can stop and start a service as and when they need it. It seems as if the customers who have to run all the time are somehow disadvantaged.

That's why AWS over the years have announced a lot of different ways of paying for the same thing.

Six months after launching Amazon EC2, AWS gave us Reserved Instances (RIs). This is a payment mechanism only. You find the Amazon EC2 instance you want and then choose the term (1 year or 3 years) and whether to pay all of the cost up front for the largest discount or perhaps Partial Upfront or No Upfront payment for less discount.

In the Amazon EC2 console, there's a section for Reserved Instances. Here, you can search for AWS RIs that meet your criteria and then add them to your basket. If you've already purchased an RI that you no longer need, then you can sell it on the Reserved Instance Marketplace (Figure 3-13) which is managed by AWS.

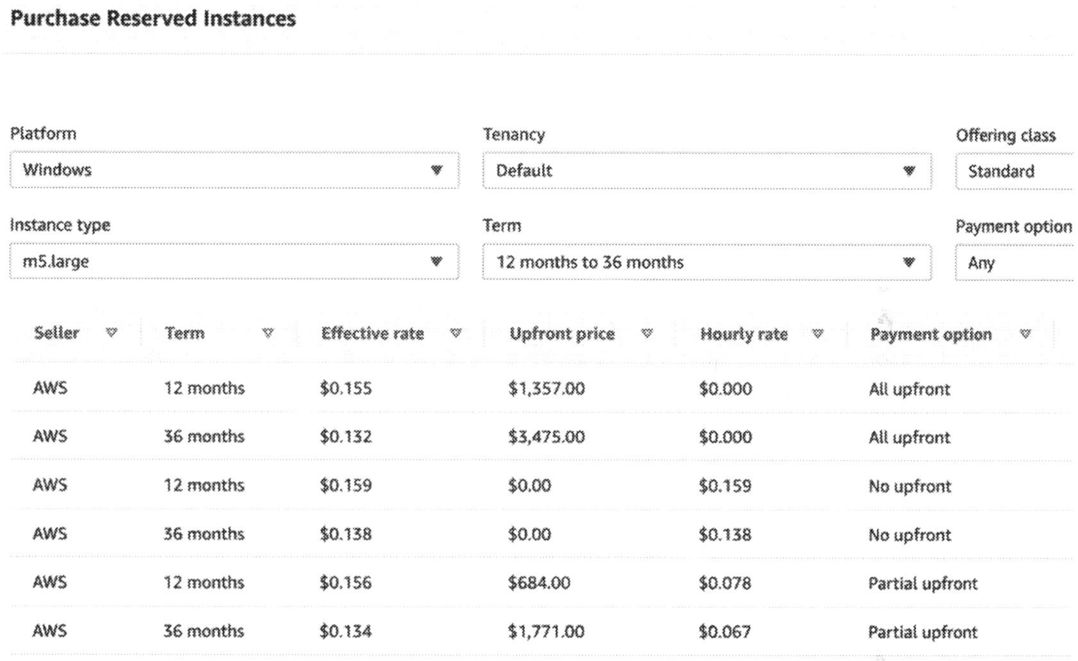

Purchase Reserved Instances

Platform		Tenancy		Offering class
Windows ▽		Default ▽		Standard
Instance type		**Term**		**Payment option**
m5.large ▽		12 months to 36 months ▽		Any

Seller ▽	Term ▽	Effective rate ▽	Upfront price ▽	Hourly rate ▽	Payment option ▽
AWS	12 months	$0.155	$1,357.00	$0.000	All upfront
AWS	36 months	$0.132	$3,475.00	$0.000	All upfront
AWS	12 months	$0.159	$0.00	$0.159	No upfront
AWS	36 months	$0.138	$0.00	$0.138	No upfront
AWS	12 months	$0.156	$684.00	$0.078	Partial upfront
AWS	36 months	$0.134	$1,771.00	$0.067	Partial upfront

Figure 3-13. *AWS Reserved Instances*

If you are running an on-demand EC2 instance of the same type and in the same availability zone as the RI you've just purchased, then it'll be converted to the cheaper price of the Reserved Instance immediately.

Reserved Instance pricing is typically 60% lower than an on-demand EC2 Instance of the same type, so why don't we just use Reserved Instances rather than On-Demand Instances and save ourselves a few bucks? Remember that Reserved Instances are a commitment for 1 year or 3 years, and so use them wisely. With On-Demand Instances, you can stop the instance, and you stop paying for it. Not the same for Reserved Instances, if you stop a Reserved Instance, you continue to pay for the reservation you made.

The use case mentioned in AWS's launch announcement focused more on being able to reserve EC2 capacity should you need it for your disaster recovery environment. There's a neater way of ensuring you have the Amazon EC2 capacity you need that doesn't have the commitment of Reserved Instances and is a lot more flexible.

On-Demand Capacity Reservations (ODCR) was launched in October 2018 to allow AWS's customers to ensure that specific Amazon EC2 Instance types are available when they need them. As soon as you create an ODCR, you are charged for the instance whether you have one running or not. ODCR can be used in conjunction with AWS Reserved Instance and Savings Plans pricing. If you have already created an ODCR, then you can ensure that any Amazon EC2 instance that is launched will use that ODCR by selecting the Capacity Reservation setting in step 3 of the Amazon EC2 Launch wizard (Figure 3-14).

Figure 3-14. *On-Demand Capacity Reservations*

Reserved Instances are a great way to save money, but they have some constraints. You have to be careful when purchasing because the EC2 instance type you choose will stay with the Reserved Instance for the duration of the commitment (up to 3 years). This is an issue because we want to ensure that our cloud environments are agile and flexible. AWS don't want customers having Reserved Instances for instance types they no longer use or would get value out of.

AWS have the concept of Convertible Reserved Instances where you *can* make changes. There's a slightly lower discount for these Convertible RIs. Table 3-1 has a comparison between standard and Convertible Reserved Instances.

Table 3-1. *Comparison between RIs and Convertible RIs*

Standard Reserved Instance	Convertible Reserved Instance
Enables you to modify Availability Zone, scope, networking type, and instance size (within the same instance type)	*Enables you to exchange one or more Convertible Reserved Instances for another Convertible Reserved Instance with a different configuration, including instance family, operating system, and tenancy*
	There are no limits to how many times you can perform and exchange, as long as the target Convertible Reserved Instance is of an equal or higher value than the one you are exchanging
Can be sold on the Reserved Instance Marketplace	*Cannot be sold on the Reserved Instance Marketplace*

Reserving Amazon EC2 makes sense for those workloads that you can't afford to switch off. But IT is quickly evolving, and running applications on virtual servers isn't the only game in town anymore. How can I get the same Reserved Instance benefit on the other AWS compute services?

Savings Plans

Once again, Savings Plans is purely a pricing mechanism where you pay less (up to 72% less) than standard On-Demand costs in exchange of a commitment over 1 or 3 years.

Didn't we just cover that with Reserved Instances? What's the difference?

Reserved Instances only work with Amazon EC2. Savings Plans works across EC2, AWS Lambda, and AWS Fargate. So, if you are going down the route of rearchitecting or refactoring your IT estate, then Savings Plans offers you more flexibility here. It also offers more flexibility in that you only have to commit to a specific amount of compute power. If you exceed the Savings Plan agreement, then your costs will revert to On-Demand pricing. It also allows you to move EC2 instances between regions, and you can move to different instance types.

Spot Instances

You can see that AWS provides you with lots of different pricing mechanisms and, using features like Reserved Instances or Savings Plans, can help you if you have workloads that run continuously or for long periods.

What about if I only need an Amazon EC2 instance for a short period, maybe to help with a batch process, payroll run, or graphics rendering, and when that job is complete, I then hand back my instances?

Surely, On-Demand Instances cover this use case.

You can certainly use On-Demand Instances for this use case, but there is an alternative and one that can offer up to 90% discount compared to using On-Demand Instances.

Amazon EC2 Spot Instances take advantage of the unused compute capacity available inside the AWS Cloud to provide you with an Amazon EC2 instance that works and performs in exactly the same way as an On-Demand Instance but at an average of 70–90% discount in cost.

The original use case when it was launched in 2009 was those times where there is flexibility in when your application can run or if you need large amounts of compute capacity urgently. I would also add to that, if you have a workload that can be distributed and run over multiple individual EC2 instances and there is no hard deadline to complete the process, then Amazon EC2 Spot Instances are perfect.

Since that 2009 announcement, the AWS service teams have added a host of new features (Figure 3-15), and also the AWS global infrastructure has expanded exponentially.

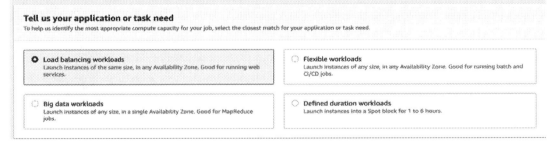

Figure 3-15. *Amazon EC2 Spot Instances*

Originally, when setting up Spot instances, you would be asked for the price you are willing to pay, per Instance, for the increased Spot instance capacity you will need.

Now we know that the Amazon EC2 On-Demand cost per hour is pretty steady. There are some variations in different Regions, but basically it's much the same.

That's not the case with Spot. The prices of EC2 Spot Instance go up and down dynamically based on how much spare capacity is being used in that Region and Availability Zone. On Monday morning, if all of AWS's customers decided to spin up a C5.Large EC2 instance, then the Spot price for that instance type will go up as general AWS capacity increases.

If the Spot price I set for the instance is higher than the current Spot price, then great; I get an EC2 instance at a great price. But if the price I set is lower than the current Spot price, then the EC2 instance will be terminated with a short 2-minute warning.

That's the big difference between Spot and On-Demand. If I run On-Demand Instances, I've got that instance until I decide to terminate it, whereas with Spot, the instance might be taken away from me if the per-AZ Spot price increases.

Depending on the workload I'm running, I could choose a safe, slightly higher Spot price to ensure that I keep my Spot instances until the workload is complete. Or I could decide to set a very low, aggressive Spot price, gain from bigger savings, but risk that the Spot instance is taken away.

I'm sure you like the idea of saving between 70 and 90% off your AWS bill each month. You probably don't like the concept of having running servers interrupted when the Spot price increases.

I mentioned elsewhere in this book the quote from Amazon CTO Dr. Werner Vogels, "Everything fails eventually," and AWS have been relentless in championing this different approach to running IT services where we expect and plan for failure. I can use those same concepts here with Amazon EC2 Spot Instances (Figure 3-16).

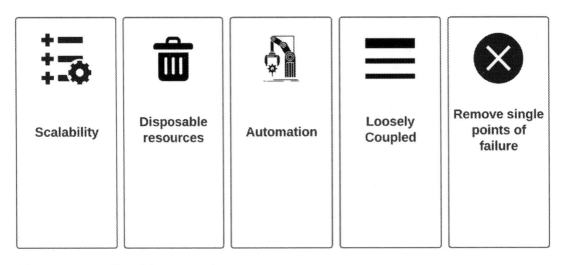

| Scalability | Disposable resources | Automation | Loosely Coupled | Remove single points of failure |

Figure 3-16. Cloud best practices

Netflix has long been an industry leader in the way it created a distributed, loosely coupled, and vastly scalable infrastructure on top of AWS. They are a heavy user of Amazon EC2 Spot Instances to help them transfer media into different formats. They also quite literally wrote the book on testing their ability to survive failure using their Chaos Monkey application which randomly shuts down EC2 Instances in their production environment to ensure they never have any single points of failure. You can read more about that here: https://netflix.github.io/chaosmonkey/.

But we don't all have the cloud maturity of Netflix, and AWS have given us some additional features around Spot Instances that can really help.

Amazon EC2 Spot Fleet allows you to build a fleet of instances consisting of both Spot and On-Demand. Here, AWS will ensure that you have enough compute capacity you need and will replace EC2 Spot Instances if they are terminated. All that's needed from you is the number of instances you'd like, and AWS do the rest.

Amazon EC2 Spot Fleet takes away all of the management need to maintain a large number of Spot instances (Figure 3-17).

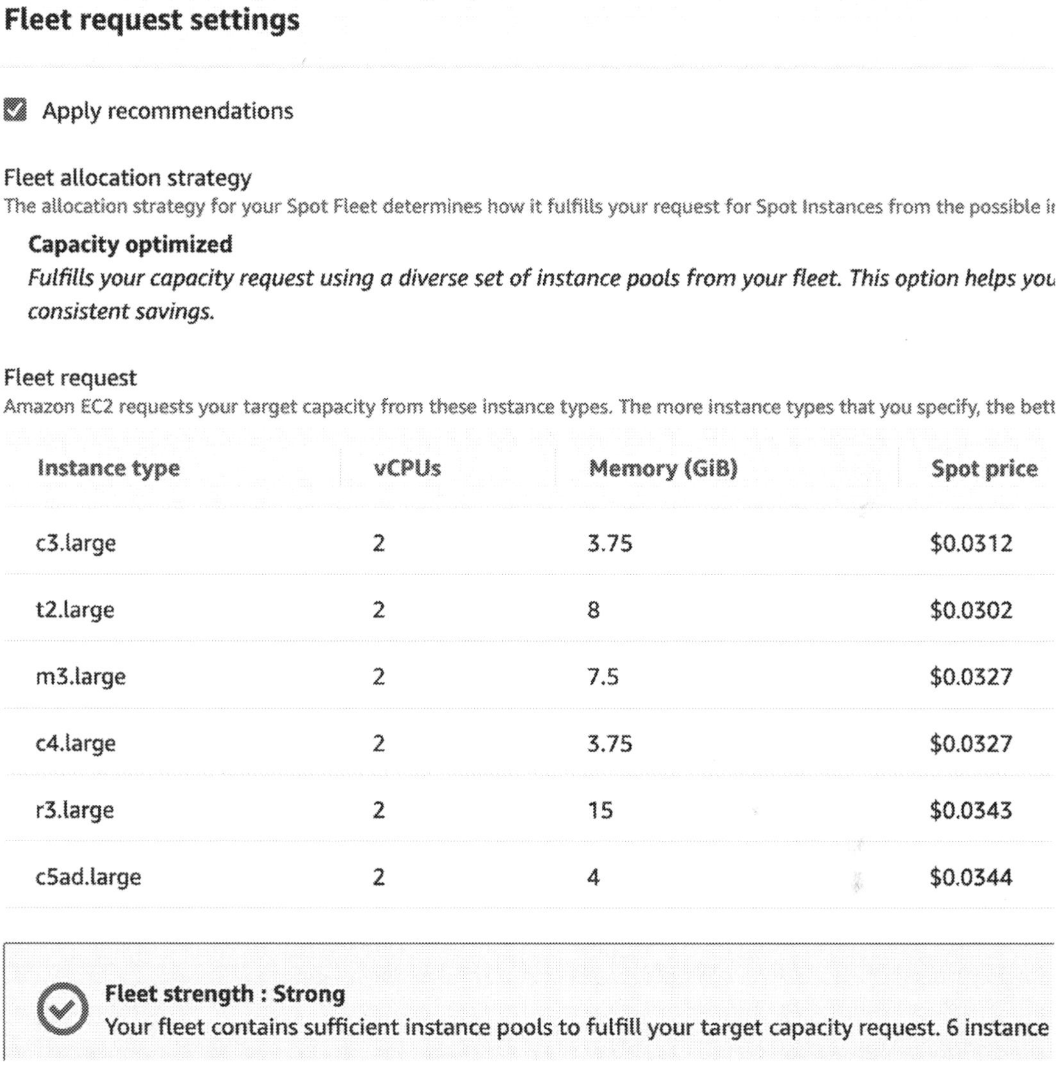

Fleet request settings

☑ Apply recommendations

Fleet allocation strategy

The allocation strategy for your Spot Fleet determines how it fulfills your request for Spot Instances from the possible in

Capacity optimized
Fulfills your capacity request using a diverse set of instance pools from your fleet. This option helps you consistent savings.

Fleet request

Amazon EC2 requests your target capacity from these instance types. The more instance types that you specify, the bett

Instance type	vCPUs	Memory (GiB)	Spot price
c3.large	2	3.75	$0.0312
t2.large	2	8	$0.0302
m3.large	2	7.5	$0.0327
c4.large	2	3.75	$0.0327
r3.large	2	15	$0.0343
c5ad.large	2	4	$0.0344

⊘ **Fleet strength : Strong**
Your fleet contains sufficient instance pools to fulfill your target capacity request. 6 instance

Figure 3-17. *Amazon EC2 Spot Fleet*

Finally, we cover the last use case of using Amazon EC2 Spot Instances, and that's the company that needs additional compute power for a short time and does not want it taken away. Say hello to Amazon EC2 Spot block.

You can create an Amazon EC2 Spot block and define a time of up to 6 hours where you will absolutely keep the Spot instances you've created. This can be done at the command line using the following command:

```
aws ec2 request-spot-instances \
```

```
--instance-count 5 \
--block-duration-minutes 120 \
--type "one-time" \
--launch-specification file://specification.json
```

Using the Amazon EC2 console, you'll see a section dedicated to Spot instances, and it's here that you can see pricing history over the last 3 months. You'll be forgiving in assuming that the graph will be very dynamic, showing the price fluctuations of the Spot instances. However, you'll see that mostly the price of Spot instances are very stable, thanks in part to the huge amount of capacity inside AWS these days. Figure 3-18 shows Spot pricing over the last 3 months with savings between 52 and 63% compared to on-demand pricing.

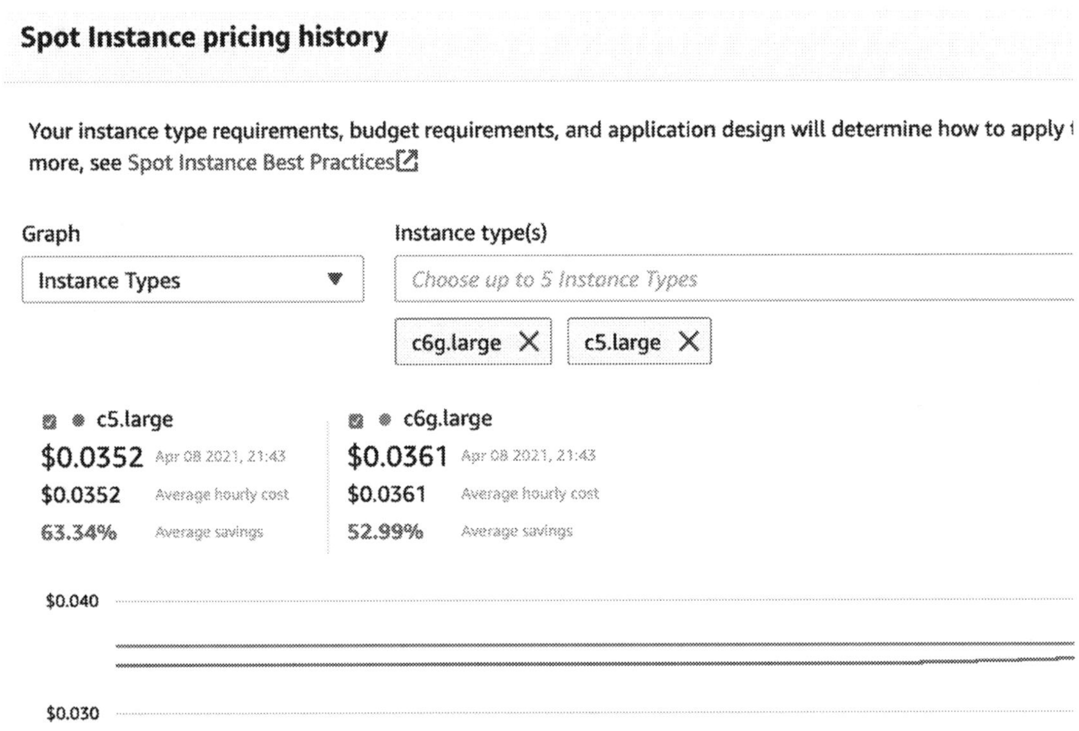

Spot Instance pricing history

Your instance type requirements, budget requirements, and application design will determine how to apply 1 more, see Spot Instance Best Practices⤴

Graph	Instance type(s)
Instance Types ▼	Choose up to 5 Instance Types
	c6g.large ✕ c5.large ✕

☑ ● c5.large

$0.0352 Apr 08 2021, 21:43

$0.0352 Average hourly cost

63.34% Average savings

☑ ● c6g.large

$0.0361 Apr 08 2021, 21:43

$0.0361 Average hourly cost

52.99% Average savings

$0.040

$0.030

Figure 3-18. *Amazon EC2 Spot pricing over the last 3 months*

Historically, only about 5% of Spot instances are terminated by AWS.

When considering saving money in AWS using Spot instances, Reserved Instances, or Savings Plans, it's really worth remembering that all of these features are just pricing mechanisms. However you pay for it, you'll get the same Amazon EC2 Instance using all these different methods.

That's not the case for the next type of EC2 Instance we will discuss.

Amazon EC2 Dedicated Hosts and Instances

Over the last few sections, we've discussed a lot of ways to save money by using different payment mechanisms for running the same Amazon EC2 instances. In the final section on this topic, we discuss possibly the most important part of Amazon EC2 from a Microsoft workloads' perspective, and that's Dedicated Hosts and Instances.

Simply, Amazon EC2 Dedicated Instances run on hardware that is dedicated to a single customer. The Dedicated instances are isolated at the physical host level from any instances running in any *other* AWS accounts. Dedicated instances, however, can run Amazon EC2 instances that share the same physical host as other EC2 instances that belong to the same AWS account. With Dedicated instances, AWS determine which host your instances run on.

Why is this important?

Some software licensing requires that it must be used on infrastructure that is dedicated for your sole use. Dedicated instances can work in this scenario.

Dedicated Hosts take this concept further and provide you with a physical server for your sole use that allows you visibility to the physical sockets and cores of the server and as such is perfect for Bring Your Own License uses.

Table 3-2 provides a comparison between Dedicated Hosts and Dedicated Instances.

Table 3-2. Differences between Dedicated Hosts and Instances

	Dedicated Host	Dedicated Instance
Billing	Per-host billing	Per-instance billing
Visibility of sockets and cores	Yes	No visibility
Host and instance affinity	Allows you to constantly deploy to the same physical server	Not supported
Targeted instance placement	Provides visibility and control over how instances are placed	Not supported
Automatic instance recovery	Supported	Supported
BYOL	Supported	Not supported

If you wish to run Microsoft SQL Server on Dedicated Hosts, then you'll need to bring your own Amazon Machine Image, since the Amazon-provided AMIs or marketplace AMIs are not compatible with Dedicated Hosts. Dedicated Hosts can work with On-Demand, Reserved Instances, and also Savings Plans to save you money. Keep in mind that you pay per host, per hour.

It may seem like we are going backward by talking about dedicated physical servers running in the cloud. The reality is that AWS created them to fill a very important use case for those customers who have invested huge sums in Microsoft licensing and wish to get the most out of it.

Licensing

This is what happens when I talk to customers about licensing:

> "Would you like to talk about Microsoft Licensing on AWS?"

> <everyone has an urgent conference call to join>

> "OK, instead, would you like to learn how to save a huge amount of money?"

> <everyone sits back down again>

Yes, discussing Microsoft licensing isn't everyone's idea of fun, but learning about this subject can save you a huge amount of money on your AWS billing every month.

It may surprise you to learn that AWS is Microsoft's largest customer when it comes to SPLA licenses. SPLA is Microsoft's Service Provider License Agreement (SPLA) and allows IT companies to purchase software licenses and then sell them to their customers as part of a service. SPLA became popular back in the early 2000s with companies delivering web hosting or server management services.

When you use the Amazon EC2 console to launch a Windows Server EC2 instance, you are using what AWS calls a license-included EC2 instance. AWS provides the Microsoft server and Microsoft SQL Server licenses here via their SPLA agreement with Microsoft. If you want to know how much that license is costing you, then a quick comparison between Amazon Linux and Microsoft server AMIs running on the same instance type will tell you. The cost will be dependent on the number of vCPUs your instance type has, and on the larger instance type, the difference can be around 40%. Making sure your business understands the impact of BYOL on their AWS bills can have a significant impact on TCO (total cost of operations – there's no ownership when you're using AWS).

License-included may look like you are paying vast sums for Microsoft licenses, but there are significant benefits to using it. Firstly, and most obviously, you may not actually own Microsoft licenses in your business, and using AWS's On-Demand Instances with license-included is a quick and easy way to acquire what you need when you need them.

Secondly, your licenses may be tied to a certain edition of a Microsoft product, whereas license-included allows you to use current, future, and legacy versions of Microsoft software. There are no software upgrade fees.

Next, you don't have to *manage licenses*. Just imagine! AWS handles all of that for you. No more visits to the procurement team. No more spreadsheets – hooray!

Also, it provides you with the freedom to run EC2 instances in the way you wish as and when you want to. I've heard tales of businesses running EC2 instances 24/7 simply because they've already invested in the server license they brought into AWS.

Finally, it will free you from the traditional "enterprise agreements" that cost you an arm and a leg and locked you into a contract for the next 3 years. For years, businesses have been trapped in enterprise agreements with no way out due to the huge cost increase they'd face without them. Enterprise agreements therefore have largely dictated what technology a business would use. They even dictate what cloud provider to use, and I would bet that a significant number of Azure customers found themselves using that platform based on "free credits" via their enterprise agreement.

This can all change.

AWS license-included covers Windows Server editions with two administrative remote desktop connections and also Microsoft SQL Server using standard, web, or enterprise editions.

Please don't discount license-included just because it's not the cheapest game in town. It's certainly the most flexible.

We see in Figure 3-19 the options you have when it comes to Microsoft licenses on AWS. Microsoft licensing can seem very complex if it's not something you deal with every day, and applying this to AWS can seem daunting. Figure 3-19 shows this isn't the case.

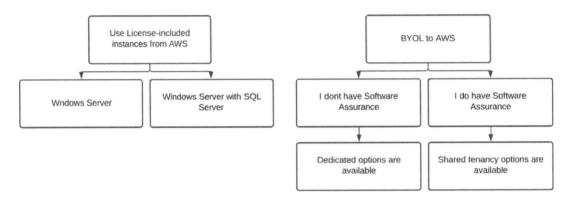

Figure 3-19. *Microsoft licensing options*

When businesses agree to purchase an enterprise agreement with Microsoft, they are provided something called "Software Assurance" (SA) free for the first 3 years, and thereafter they have to renew separately. Software assurance gives the customer the benefit of 24/7 support, upgrades, training, and something called "License Mobility." License mobility is a simple agreement that allows the purchaser to run certain Microsoft licenses in multi-tenanted environments – like the cloud.

Sounds nice huh? Most enterprise-sized businesses would use an enterprise agreement, but for some other businesses, it's just way too expensive.

Don't worry if you have software assurance or not; AWS has different options to allow you to get the most benefit out of your license investment.

Bringing Licenses to Shared or Default Tenancy

If you have license mobility via software assurance, you'll be able to bring a number of Microsoft server licenses to AWS and use the default or shared tenancy option. Shared tenancy is what you use if you just go and launch a quick on-demand EC2 instance. With shared tenancy, you are running Amazon EC2 instances on hardware that you share with other customers, but of course you are totally isolated and protected from them.

There are Microsoft products that have License Mobility benefits, such as

- Microsoft SQL Server

- Microsoft Exchange

- SharePoint

- Dynamics

- System Center

- Remote Desktop Services

And there are products that do not, such as

- Windows Server

- Windows desktop

- Microsoft Office

- MSDN software

If you have any of these licenses, hang tight; there are options for you on the next page.

The most popular software to license this way is Microsoft SQL Server which is licensed via virtual CPU or vCPU. Microsoft has determined that there is a 4 vCPU minimum usage, so even EC2 instance types with 2 vCPUs get hit with a 4 vCPU license requirement. AWS hold a list of all its EC2 Instance types and the number of vCPUs you'll need to license here: `https://aws.amazon.com/windows/resources/licensemobility/sql/`.

If you are running high-availability solutions, then it's worth noting that SQL's passive failover benefits are allowed for all versions of SQL Server from 2014 to current. This means that the primary server should be licensed per vCPU, but any secondary server does not need a license.

To allow the use of your licenses on AWS shared tenancy, you'll need to complete a form and submit it to Microsoft. More information can be found here:

`https://aws.amazon.com/windows/resources/licensemobility/`

AWS have really gone above and beyond to ensure that businesses using Microsoft SQL Server are taken care of – from the R-family of Memory-optimized Amazon EC2 instances which have a ratio of less vCPU (and therefore less licenses) to RAM to the ability to optimize vCPUs by disabling hyperthreading which will reduce license count by more than 50%.

Options for BYOL Without License Mobility

Licenses that are not eligible for license mobility, such as Windows Server or SQL Server without software assurance, can be installed on AWS Dedicated Hosts with a rather large caveat. The license must have been purchased before October 2019. Considering we are halfway through 2021 already, then, the number of businesses that still fall into this category is getting smaller and smaller.

So why this constraint? In the summer of 2019, Microsoft decided to rewrite your license agreement to make it harder for its customers to use cloud platforms like AWS or Google Cloud Platform and to give its Azure service an advantage.

Whether that works out for them in the long run will be interesting to see.

Personally, I think IT leaders are firmly over being forced to choose one technology over another because they would be penalized over license costs. I'm sure you'd agree that it's not very customer focused.

Around the same time, Microsoft announced their Azure Hybrid Use Benefit (AHUB) which provided Linux-type pricing for your Windows Servers if you had active software assurance.

Comparing the two, AWS's Dedicated Host option is considerably cheaper due to the fact that Microsoft expects you to pay for Software Assurance to get the benefit.

If you need help understanding the best way to get the most benefit from the licenses you own, then AWS can help you. Just reach out to them via their dedicated Microsoft on AWS email address `microsoft@amazon.com`.

The other way that AWS can help you is via their own Optimization and Licensing Assessment (OLA) where they actively work with you to look at your current licensing situation and show you ways to reduce costs, right-size your compute, and reuse your licenses.

The AWS Optimization and Licensing Assessment can be found here: `https://aws.amazon.com/windows/optimization-and-licensing-assessment/`.

AWS License Manager

Imagine, You have a large IT landscape – Amazon EC2 instances in multiple VPCs and also in multiple AWS accounts. You also have several on-premises data centers which host several thousand servers that are yet to migrate to the cloud. From a licensing perspective, you have multiple editions of Windows Server, SQL Server, and even some Oracle licenses. You have a centralized asset management application and the various licensing contracts with multiple vendors you store on a spreadsheet. Imagine the effort required to keep track of it all as EC2 instances are dynamically started, stopped, or terminated.

That scenario, or at least a version of it, may be familiar to you. There is someone in your organization responsible for ensuring that you are compliant from a licensing standpoint. Maybe tomorrow when you arrive at work, you should buy them a coffee; it is the very least they deserve. Because managing licenses is difficult and requires superhuman effort.

This is why at re:Invent 2018, AWS launched a brand-new totally free service called AWS License Manager. This service can keep track of AWS and also on-premises license usage and also ensure that you are never out of compliance by enforcing that usage so that your teams can't launch Amazon EC2 instances if there are no licenses to cover them.

AWS License Manager manages Windows Server, SQL Server, and Oracle licenses. You can check licenses based on vCPUS, cores, sockets, or instances. All it requires is for you to enter the number of licenses you own for that product, and AWS License Manager will do the rest.

In Figure 3-20, you can see that I've switched on the Enforce license limit option. This is what will stop Amazon EC2 instances from launching if your licenses run out. You can also configure rules that will determine where those licenses will be used.

License type

The counting model used for the license. This may not track the terms of your agreement with your licensor. Amazon RDS is only supported for vCPUs.

> vCPUs   ▼

Number of vCPUs - *optional*

SNS notifications are sent when the license type reaches its limits. To configure the SNS topic, go to Settings.

> 100   ⬍   vCPUs

Only numeric values allowed. Max: 100000

☑ **Enforce license limit**

> Helps prevent usage after available license types are exhausted, e.g. an instance launch requiring new license types will be blocked to prevent overuse. Not supported for RDS.

▼ **Rules** - *optional*

Rules does not support Amazon RDS.

Rule type   **Rule value**

Specify the rules to be applied for license usage   Enter value for selected rule

> Tenancy   ▲ | You can select one or more tenancy types ▼ | Remove |

> **Minimum vCPUs**
> Resource must have minimum vCPU count in order   Dedicated Host ✕
> to use the license. Default: 1

> **Maximum vCPUs**
> Resource must have maximum vCPU count in order   Enter value for selected rule   Remove
> to use the license. Default: unbounded, limit: 10000

> **Tenancy**
> Defines where the license can be used. If set,   *l*
> restrict license usage to selected tenancies.

> **vCPU Optimization**   iscover and track your products. License Manager tracks instances with the selected
> Honor CPU options optimization if it is configured   included in the instance cost.
> on resource launch.

Figure 3-20. *Configuring license enforcement and rules with AWS License Manager*

You can also use SQL License Manager to create a host resource group which is a collection of the Amazon EC2 Dedicated Hosts we discussed earlier. AWS License Manager will track license usage on these Dedicated Hosts. AWS License Manager also gives you a dashboard to show exactly what license configurations you have for different products and how many servers or instances are using them. No more spreadsheets.

AWS License Manager can also do automated discovery of new software when EC2s are running as well as rules that will exclude AWS accounts or instances from coming under its control based on AWS tags.

AWS Systems Manager

AWS Systems Manager is my favorite service.

I mention that fact to everyone – people who attend classes I teach, customers who I meet, colleagues I work with, postal workers who deliver mail, complete strangers in the street. What is it about AWS Systems Manager that puts it above approximately 200 other services?

Thank you for asking. You may want to take a seat for this one.

I think it is the perfect example of what an AWS Service should be. By that I mean that it was created by customers asking AWS for specific functionality; AWS then went off and created that new feature and added other new features as well, all the while looking at how they work as a whole as well as in isolation until you end up with a service that is the IT equivalent of a Swiss army knife, and then you keep going, adding new functionality and updating existing features, and you never ever stop.

AWS Systems Manager had humble beginnings. It began life as a simple feature that allowed you to run a command on your EC2 instances, and it was buried at the bottom of the Amazon EC2 console behind far more flashier services like Spot instances and EBS. I would argue that the vast majority of AWS customers didn't even know it was there (Figure 3-21).

At this time, its features came under the banner of EC2 SSM (Amazon Simple Systems Manager), but it grew. Launching "Run Command" at AWS re:Invent 2015, it received polite applause, but by the time AWS re:Invent 2016 came along, it had been joined by an army of capabilities such as "State Manager," "Automations," "Patch Manager," "Maintenance Windows," "Inventory Manager," and "Parameter Store," among others.

It's the little service that could.

At re:Invent 2016, they brought these capabilities together under a single banner called EC2 Systems Manager, but that couldn't contain it for long because with even more features being added, eventually AWS gave us a full-blown service called AWS Systems Manager.

This is the service that has grown the most during my time working with AWS, and it integrates with services like Amazon CloudWatch, AWS Directory Services, and of course Amazon EC2. Brand-new standalone services like AWS Image Builder and AWS License Manager, which we discussed earlier in this chapter, are effectively built out of the features of AWS Systems Manager. That's why it's my favorite service.

SYSTEMS MANAGER
SERVICES

   Run Command

   State Manager

   Automations

   Patch Compliance

   Patch Baselines

SYSTEMS MANAGER
SHARED RESOURCES

   Managed Instances

   Activations

   Documents

   Maintenance Windows

Figure 3-21. *The original EC2 Systems Manager*

Fresh-faced after a graphical revamp in early 2021 (Figure 3-22), AWS Systems
Manager's functionality covers a huge amount of what an administrator would need to
do to ensure the health of their server estate. We will cover the main capabilities over the
next few pages, but AWS Systems Manager is divided into logical categories.

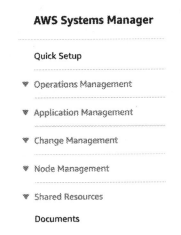

AWS Systems Manager

   Quick Setup

▼ Operations Management

▼ Application Management

▼ Change Management

▼ Node Management

▼ Shared Resources

   Documents

Figure 3-22. *The current AWS Systems Manager*

Operations Management covers capabilities like Explorer, OpsCenter, and Personal
Health Dashboard.

Application Management covers Application Manager, AppConfig, and Parameter
Store.

Change Management has Automation, Maintenance Windows, and Change Manager.

Node Management covers the largest group of features, all focused on Amazon EC2 such as Run Command, State Manager, Session Manager, and Distributor.

Before we discuss some of the key capabilities, you'll need to understand how AWS Systems Manager works.

AWS Systems Manager works with what it calls "managed instances." Managed instances are Amazon EC2 instances which have the AWS SSM Agent installed and running, an IAM role giving permissions to AWS Systems Manager and network access to the service.

The AWS SSM Agent is installed already if you use one of the Amazon-provided AMIs for Amazon Linux, Ubuntu, MacOS, and Windows Server. If your AMI is not covered here, then you can find and install the AWS SSM Agent from here: `https://docs.aws.amazon.com/systems-manager/latest/userguide/sysman-install-win.html`.

Then you'll need network access. AWS Systems Manager requires HTTPS port 443 open to outbound traffic from the potential "managed instance," and you can do this in one of two ways. One way is by allowing port 443 *out* of your instance to the AWS Systems Manager endpoints which are

```
ec2messages.regionidentifier.amazonaws.com
ssmmessages.regionidentifier.amazonaws.com
ssm.regionidentifier.amazonaws.com
```

For example, in the eu-west-2 region, you would use

```
ec2messages.eu-west-2.amazonaws.com
ssmmessages.eu-west-2.amazonaws.com
ssm.eu-west-2.amazonaws.com
```

The other way, useful if your Amazon EC2 Instance does not have Internet access, is to create an AWS endpoint.

This great blog and video will show you how to quickly create an endpoint for use with AWS Systems Manager:

```
https://aws.amazon.com/premiumsupport/knowledge-center/ec2-systems-manager-
vpc-endpoints/
```

The next thing you'll need is to create an AWS IAM instance profile and an IAM service role that you'll attach to your Amazon EC2 instances when they launch and will give that instance the permissions to use the Systems Manager service. By default, a service doesn't have permissions to use another service, so we have to give it a policy to allow it.

AWS Systems Manager has a quick setup feature that will configure all of the IAM elements you'll need as well as provide some default settings for the capabilities that AWS Systems Manager has. AWS Quick Setup (Figure 3-23) is very useful and automates a lot of the setup tasks that otherwise take time and effort.

AWS Quick Setup
Automated and simplified setups
based on best practices

AWS Quick Setup helps you configure frequently used AWS services and features across your organization with fewer clicks.

How it works

 1. Choose a home Region

Quick Setup creates the AWS resources used to deploy all of your configurations in the AWS Region you specify. The home Region can't be changed once chosen.

 2. Choose a configuration type

Quick Setup provides a library of configuration types that automate common setup tasks and deploy configurations for services based on best practices.

 3. Specify configuration options

Specify your preferred values for the options of the configuration type you chose, and which resources to target with your configuration. With Quick Setup, you can deploy configurations to a single AWS Region for your current account. Quick Setup also integrates with AWS Organizations so you can target multiple organization units (OUs) and Regions.

 4. Deploy and review

Deploy your configuration, and review the summarized results. You can use the summary page to troubleshoot failed deployments, and to view more details about your configuration. The summary page also notifies you when new versions of relevant software become available, as well as newly supported features and Regions.

Figure 3-23. *AWS Systems Manager quick setup*

It all started with "Run Command" which, as the name suggests, lets you run a command on an EC2 Instance. I sense you are a little disappointed after such a huge buildup. Not only can it run a command on a single machine, but it can run on your entire fleet or just selective machines based on tags. Still need convincing? It has a host of AWS-created "documents" that it runs, anything from "ApplyChefRecipes" through to "CreateVSSSnapshot." It'll let you install software, configure software, and run a batch file or a PowerShell script. The output from running the command goes into a log file safely stored in an Amazon S3 bucket in your account.

Although AWS provides you with ready-to-go documents, you can also build your own. So the service is incredibly flexible and extensible. This great blog by AWS's Stefan Minhas will show you how to go about this: `https://aws.amazon.com/blogs/mt/writing-your-own-aws-systems-manager-documents/`.

Run Command (Figure 3-24) is actually used by a lot of other AWS services. If you specify an Active Directory domain in the configuration of an EC2 Instance, it's actually Run Command that does the domain join task during the EC2 launch sequence.

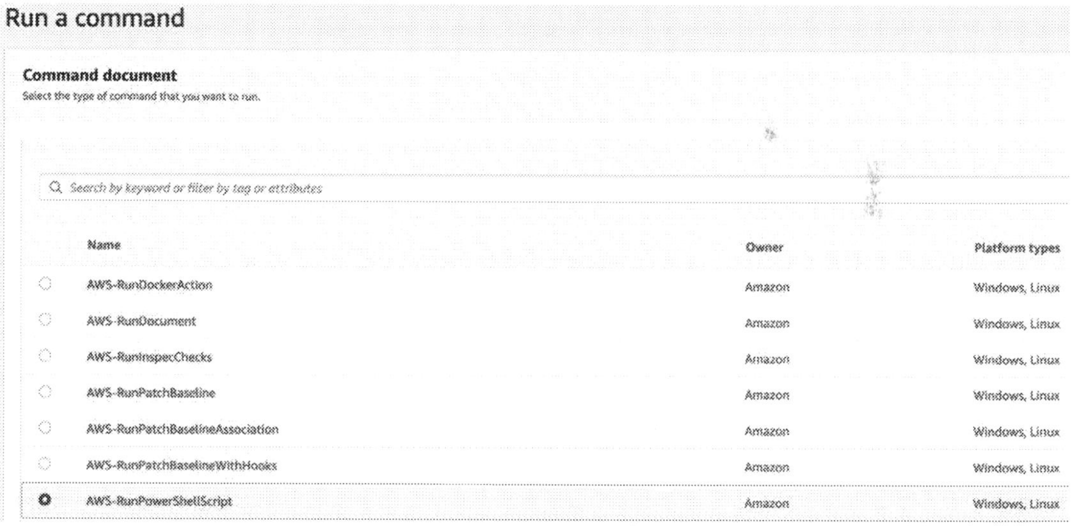

Run a command

Command document
Select the type of command that you want to run.

	Name	Owner	Platform types
○	AWS-RunDockerAction	Amazon	Windows, Linux
○	AWS-RunDocument	Amazon	Windows, Linux
○	AWS-RunInspecChecks	Amazon	Windows, Linux
○	AWS-RunPatchBaseline	Amazon	Windows, Linux
○	AWS-RunPatchBaselineAssociation	Amazon	Windows, Linux
○	AWS-RunPatchBaselineWithHooks	Amazon	Windows, Linux
●	AWS-RunPowerShellScript	Amazon	Windows, Linux

Figure 3-24. Run Command

The next AWS Systems Manager capability is one that even the born-in-the-cloud-devops-gurus use, Parameter Store. This capability, like Run Command, is deliciously simple but incredibly effective. Quite simple Parameter Store stores parameters that you'll use in scripts or configuration.

Maybe in your career you've seen a script that has a clear-text username and password built into the script. It's rare these days to see that, thanks to an increased knowledge of security and the relentless threat of hackers. But it still happens.

Maybe you've seen a clear-text license key or a connection string to a database or some clear-text configuration that you really wish wasn't so visible. All of these configuration items can be stored in Parameter Store which will encrypt them and make them available to you via a unique key.

Having these parameters in one place means you can update things quickly. Imagine needing to change the local administrator password on 1000 machines every month. You can store and update the password using Parameter Store and then refer to it via a PowerShell script, scheduled to run every month via Run Command that updates the password on each machine. Once this is set up, the only task to do every month is update the Parameter Store value, and the rest is fully automated. In Figure 3-25, I've created a parameter called LocalAdminPW, and I can refer to this in scripts like the following:

```
Net.exe user administrator {{ssm:LocalAdminPW}}
```

This will change the local administrator password with the value I store in the LocalAdminPW parameter.

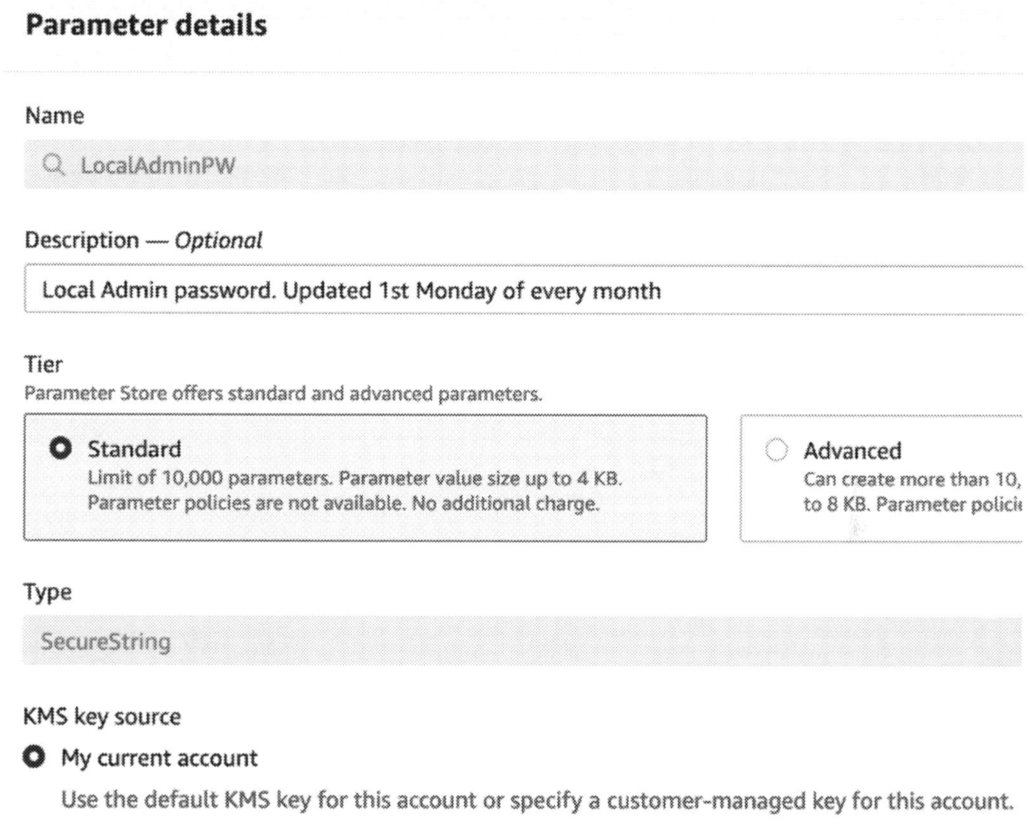

Parameter details

Name

Q LocalAdminPW

Description — *Optional*

Local Admin password. Updated 1st Monday of every month

Tier
Parameter Store offers standard and advanced parameters.

⦿ Standard
  Limit of 10,000 parameters. Parameter value size up to 4 KB.
  Parameter policies are not available. No additional charge.

○ Advanced
  Can create more than 10,
  to 8 KB. Parameter polici

Type

SecureString

KMS key source

⦿ My current account
  Use the default KMS key for this account or specify a customer-managed key for this account.

Figure 3-25. *Parameter Store*

Before we move on, you may be wondering what the difference is between Parameter Store and AWS Secrets Manager. They both store data, can both encrypt that data in a similar way, and are both able to be read via the command line and AWS CloudFormation. The use case for AWS Secrets Manager is to store and manage secrets such as passwords, whereas Parameter Store stores any kind of string value you want it to. While both can be used to store passwords, AWS Secrets Manager also has additional features to manage secrets and should generally be preferred over Parameter Store, unless you have another mechanism for managing and rotating secrets. AWS Secrets Manager has functionality to generate and rotate passwords that Parameter Store does not.

Patch Manager updates your Amazon EC2 instance with the latest patches. It can patch not only Windows Server but also SQL Server, SharePoint, or from a huge range of Microsoft products.

With Patch Manager, you'll need to set up Patch baselines which include rules for auto-approving patches within days of their release as well as approved or not approved patches. Patch Manager integrates with maintenance windows, another capability of AWS Systems Manager, to schedule when to patch your EC2 instances. You can also patch according to tags because it's common that companies patch development or nonproduction environments before they update their production environment.

Patch Manager retrieves a list of available updates that Microsoft regularly publishes to their Windows Update site and is made available for their Windows Server Update Services (WSUS) tool. AWS manages the WSUS tool on behalf of its customers. You don't need to provision a WSUS Server in your account.

Patch Manager (Figure 3-26) then uses Run Command to install patches and log the output to a local logs folder as part of the patching schedule.

You can use one of the AWS-created patch baselines, or you can create your own from scratch. You'll need to select the product (OS or Application) and the severity of what you'd like to patch (Critical, Important, Moderate, or Low).

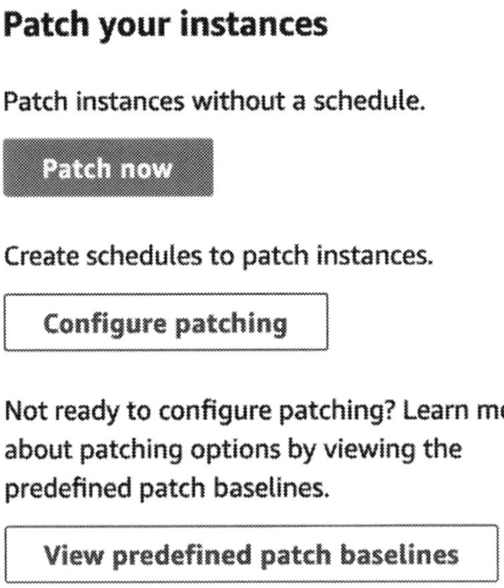

Patch your instances

Patch instances without a schedule.

    Patch now

Create schedules to patch instances.

    Configure patching

Not ready to configure patching? Learn more about patching options by viewing the predefined patch baselines.

    View predefined patch baselines

Figure 3-26. *Patch Manager*

I mentioned earlier about the immutable DevOps dream of not ever logging on to a server and pushing whatever changes you want via a full CI/CD pipeline which updates your infrastructure several thousand times a day. That sounds wonderful, but for those of us who are not there yet and who may still need to securely log in to an actual server, there's AWS Systems Manager Session Manager capability to help us.

Prior to Session Manager, everyone used bastion Hosts or jump boxes to springboard them from the corporate LAN to their VPC where they could RDP (remote desktop protocol) to the servers they manage. There were also more secure and auditable privileged identity management systems available that tied accessing servers into a full workflow that requested permissions from managers before access was approved. All access sessions were recorded in case they were needed by the business. These systems are expensive, tricky to set up, and still require open RDP and SSH ports. However, they do contain some useful functionality.

Session Manager has most of the useful functionality built in, is totally free to use, and does not require RDP or SSH ports to be open.

Session Manager creates a remote session to your Linux or Windows Server inside your browser, as long as the server is one of the managed instances we discussed earlier, meaning that it has the SSM Agent and an IAM instance profile and role attached.

Session ID: rypoth-0e74d9a64b44ed376   Instance ID: i-04a535a432d

```
Windows PowerShell
Copyright (C) Microsoft Corporation. All rights reserved.

PS C:\Windows\system32>
```

Figure 3-27. *Session Manager*

You'll have noticed that Figure 3-27 doesn't look like the Windows Server remote desktop that you are used to seeing. Session Manager gives us a PowerShell command-line session, not the GUI session.

Every command is logged and stored in an S3 bucket, so you'll have full insight into what your administrators are doing.

One final capability I'd like to cover is Distributor (Figure 3-28). For me, it was the missing piece between what I used to use when running Microsoft's System Center Configuration Manager and AWS's Systems Manager.

As the name suggests, Distributor helps you distribute agents and AWS or third-party applications to your Amazon EC2 instances. What Distributor actually does is help you create an AWS Systems Manager document that you can then use with other AWS Systems Manager capabilities like Run Command or State Manager.

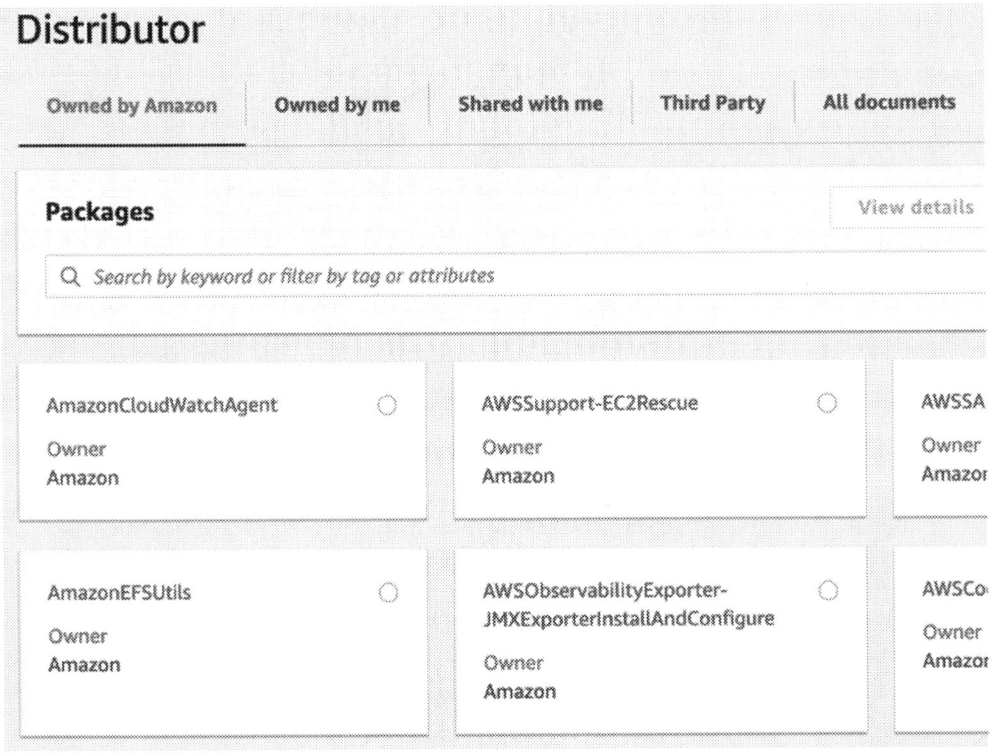

Figure 3-28. *Distributor*

Distributor accepts MSI, DEB, or RPM install packages; you can add a specific platform or architecture that is compatible with your application, and then Distributor creates the package manifest for you automatically. As an advanced option, you can specify Install, Update, and Uninstall scripts to use for this package. The scripts would use standard Windows command line or PowerShell.

After uploading your install package to a designated Amazon S3 bucket and once complete, you have the option of installing the Distributor package one time only or on a schedule.

We've barely touched the surface of AWS Systems Manager capabilities. Maybe you are yet to place it at the top of your favorite AWS Services, but I hope you have a newfound respect for how impactful AWS Systems Manager is, and I hope that you'll take a look yourself.

AWS Systems Manager is part of AWS's management and governance services – a group of AWS services that deserve a full book to themselves. As we approach the end of this section, there is one more service I'd like to bring to your attention.

When problems arise in our application stack, what do we do? We step through the application stack piece by piece until we find the issue. AWS DevOps Guru is a service that uses Machine Learning to constantly analyze data from your application stacks to determine the normal operation of your application. It needs to know what "good" looks like because that helps it quickly alert you when "bad" happens.

If we suffer an application issue in real life, our server and application engineers trawl through the application stack layer by layer looking at log files for clues to the issue. Amazon DevOps Guru uses Machine Learning insights via Amazon SageMaker to precisely pinpoint where the error is.

Using ML to assist in operational issues, this is a perfect example of how AWS innovates on behalf of their customers with every service they launch.

AWS End-of-Support Migration Program (AWS EMP)

One common challenge for customers is what to do with those unsupported servers that still live within their on-premises data centers. I often ask the same question to customers, partners, or students: "What is the earliest version of Windows Server you still have running?" I love this question; the answers always come with a look of resignation that says "yes... I know, I know...."

And I've had every kind of possible reply. From those who tell me Windows Server 2016 – nice, very good, extended support ends in 2027, which is a lifetime away. To those who say 2012 – that's not too bad; they'll have until 2023 to replace those servers. Then we have those customers still running Windows Server 2008, a very popular version which went out of support during 2019. I've heard worse of course – 2003, 2000, even those who tell me they are still running Windows NT. They say that with slight pride in their voice. They have reached a level of acceptance in the risk of running software that is not being security patched that it no longer gives them sleepless nights.

The reasons why customers run out of support versions of Windows Server are usually similar. The server is running an application that for one reason or another can't be moved or upgraded.

It's pretty frustrating when you are working with customers who want to clear out a data center and move to AWS only to find that they've identified a few servers that they can't migrate. Not being able to close that data center means that they are losing out financially on their move to the cloud.

In 2019, AWS acquired technology from UK company CloudHouse that formed the basis of a new service called AWS End-of-Support Migration Program, or AWS EMP (Figure 3-29). Yes, I agree, maybe EMP is not the most comforting abbreviation to use when it comes to safeguarding and protecting data. But the service itself is brilliant.

AWS EMP is a service that allows you to package any out-of-support application you may be running and then gives you the ability to run those out-of-support applications on fully supported versions of Windows Server like 2016 and 2019.

Using AWS EMP, you can decouple those out-of-support but still critical applications (32 bit or 64 bit) from the underlying operating system and run them without any code changes.

At long last, you'll have the ability to empty those data centers!

You'll not find AWS EMP in the AWS Management Console; it's a service you'll find here: `https://aws.amazon.com/emp-windows-server/`.

When first launched, it required you to engage with AWS EMP service teams who would work with you or ask you to engage with AWS EMP Partners who would help you to package your applications. After AWS re:Invent 2020, AWS EMP was open to everyone and free of charge. You can download the tools needed to run the packaging components on Windows Server from the preceding website which also links you to the documentation you'll need to understand the tools and the process.

AWS EMP snapshot's an application installation for all the application components that are reliant on the operating system and also any changes that the applications make during the first time it is launched. AWS EMP brings all this together in what it calls an EMP Compatibility Package.

The EMP Compatibility Package does not include any aspect of the original operating system, so there is no danger of polluting a new OS with legacy components. AWS EMP Compatibility Package also handles any communication or redirections from the application to the OS including network ports or hardcoded drive paths like `C:\WINNT\`.

The whole process is shown in Figure 3-29 but has four main sections:

1. Discovery

2. Package preparation

3. Packaging

4. Deployment

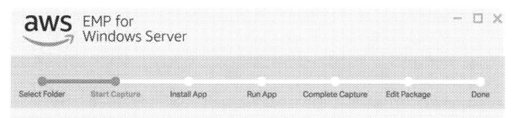

Figure 3-29. AWS EMP process

AWS EMP supports Windows 2003 upward and cannot package applications with low-level drivers like antivirus and so on.

When you download the AWS EMP Package, it installs a number of files onto your server. A full description of these files can be found here: `https://docs.aws.amazon.com/emp/latest/userguide/emp-components.html`.

Once installed on the Amazon EC2 instance that is running your legacy piece of software, you'll click the Compatibility Packager Builder icon to start the process. You'll be asked to select or create an EMP folder before starting the first part of that process which is the "before" system capture. AWS EMP will look at your machine and store information in the `SystemSnapshot.json` file to be found in the `InitialSnapshotFiles` folder under your EMP folder.

Next comes the install of your legacy application.

It's common for customers not to have (or to have lost) the original media of their legacy application. If that's the case, don't worry; we can reverse engineer the installation. Right now, let's complete the packaging based on having the install media that you've just installed.

Stage 4 is to run the application for the first time. A lot of applications make configuration changes during their first launch, and we want to make sure we capture that.

The fifth stage is to complete the capture where AWS EMP compares your "before" and "after" snapshots, and the differences will make up our package (Figure 3-30).

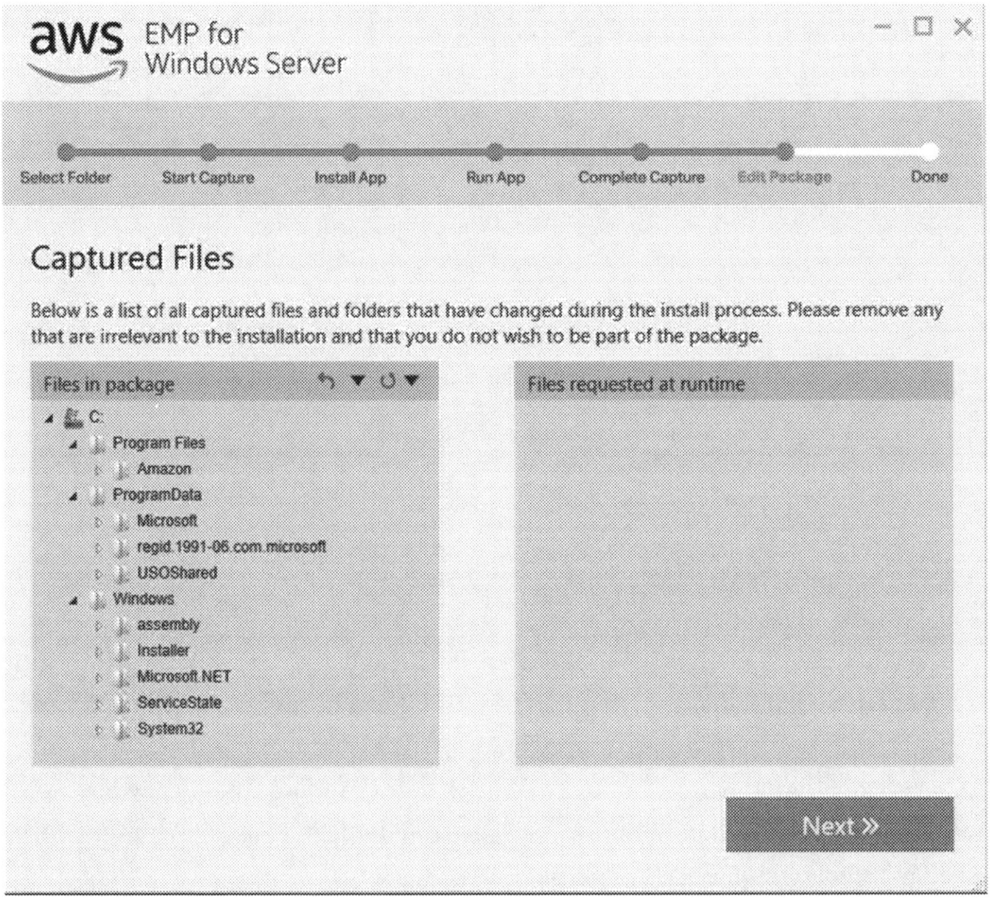

Figure 3-30. *Captured files that will make up your AWS EMP Package*

It's common for the capture process to pick up changes going on inside the operating system at the time of your application install. It's always best practice to review the captured files and remove any that are clearly not part of the installation process. Of course, it's sometimes difficult to know exactly what is and isn't part of an application install. This is where testing the package becomes invaluable.

Once we review the files that have been captured, we will click next and look at the registry keys that were captured during the install process. Same advice here, review them and remove any keys that are clearly not part of your application because there's a lot of changes going on inside your registry, and it's common for the process to pick up stray keys.

The final step in the process is to give your application a name, APP ID, and what to run when launched. You'll then click "Package App" to complete.

You'll find a folder with your application name under the EMP folder you specified at the start of the process.

There is a file here called Compatibility.Package.Deployment.exe which will deploy your legacy application in the new fully supported Amazon EC2 Instance.

The AWS EMP team has put together some great tips on how to reverse engineer your legacy application if you don't have access to the media:

```
https://docs.aws.amazon.com/emp/latest/userguide/emp-getting-started-
packaging-no-media.html
```

It requires you to have access to the SysInternals Process Monitor (Procmon) tool that you can find here: `https://docs.microsoft.com/en-us/sysinternals/downloads/procmon`.

You will use Procmon to detect what processes are being used by the application and to detect the process tree to ensure that you capture all of the files and components.

As with any application packaging tool, testing is critical, and the whole process requires some trial and error to ensure that you get a good quality package that will run without issue.

AWS EMP has significant benefits to businesses and will at last help you overcome those last few legacy obstacles that have stopped you moving fully into AWS.

Summary

I mentioned at the start that this is an important chapter to digest, and we've covered a lot of ground to take us from Amazon EC2 to AWS EMP. On that journey, we've touched upon Amazon Machine Images, AWS Image Builder, Amazon EBS, Amazon FSx, and how to save money on EC2 by using Reserved and Spot Instances.

We discussed Amazon EC2 Dedicated Instances and Hosts and looked at how licensing and bringing your own licenses can really add a lot of value and further cost savings. To manage all your licenses, we looked at AWS License Manager, and that led us neatly on to AWS Systems Manager (it's my favorite service you know) and finally some solutions to the challenge of unsupported workloads via AWS EMP.

This chapter has not been an exhaustive look at all things Server in AWS; later on in the book, we have chapters on containers and serverless to cover those elements. I hope, however, that this chapter has given you reason to explore further and maybe shown you some services you weren't familiar with.

CHAPTER 4

Databases

In a book focused on Microsoft Workloads, you'd be excused for thinking that a chapter dedicated to databases would focus on Microsoft SQL Server. You'd be right of course. I've certainly used MySQL and Oracle in a Windows Server environment without issue, but we need to keep in mind that there are certainly *options* of other database engines for your Microsoft Workloads inside AWS, because the area of databases has evolved over the last 5 years to embrace nonrelational databases as well as database engines created for specific use cases.

While it's increasingly popular to choose particular types of database for specific workloads, since Microsoft SQL Server is the predominant database server used with traditional Microsoft workloads, this chapter will concentrate on SQL Server, and AWS has been supporting it since 2008. An Amazon Machine Image (AMI) running Microsoft SQL Server 2005 was released on October 23, 2008, the very day that a little service called Amazon Elastic Compute Cloud (EC2) was made available to the public. Microsoft SQL Server came preinstalled onto that AMI with the operating system running Microsoft Windows Server 2003.

Versions and Editions

SQL Server 2005, the first version on AWS, was launched in November 2005 and was a significant step forward in features from SQL Server 2000. SQL Server 2005 introduced features that were to be a mainstay for years to come – Database Mirroring, Integration Services, Analysis Services, and Reporting Services.

Microsoft SQL Server 2008 was launched to the world on August 6, 2008. An Amazon Machine Image was launched shortly after, running on Windows Server 2008. Microsoft SQL Server 2008 was replaced with an R2 edition in April 2010 offering to support more logical processors and Master Data Services (MDS). Resilience features added to what was available before and now came in the form of Database Mirroring, Log Shipping, Replication, and Windows Server Failover Clustering.

© Ryan Pothecary 2021

R. Pothecary, *Running Microsoft Workloads on AWS*, https://doi.org/10.1007/978-1-4842-6628-1_4

Microsoft SQL Server 2012 in March 2012 offered much improved performance benchmarks over the 2008 R2 version and also a new option when it came to High Availability – Always On SQL Server Failover Cluster Instances and Availability Groups (see Figure 4-1).

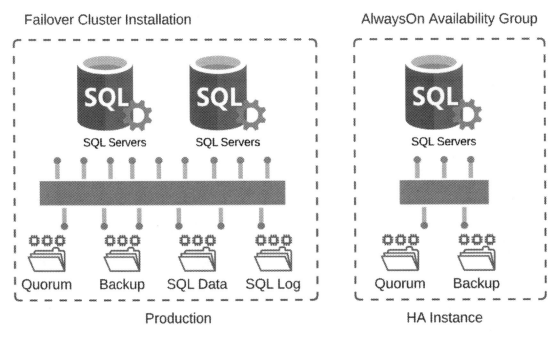

Failover Cluster Installation

SQL Servers   SQL Servers

Quorum   Backup   SQL Data   SQL Log

Production

AlwaysOn Availability Group

SQL Servers

Quorum   Backup

HA Instance

Figure 4-1. *WSFC and Always On Availability Group*

Microsoft SQL Server 2014 added readable secondary replicas to its Always On feature. It also added for the first time the capability to provide disaster recovery with Microsoft Azure. 2014 was the last SQL Server version to be compatible with X86 processor architectures and was launched in March 2014.

Microsoft SQL Server 2016 was launched in June 2016, and a mere year later, Microsoft SQL Server 2017 was launched in October 2017 and became the first Microsoft SQL Server version that you can run on Linux operating systems, removing the products' long-lasting dependency on Microsoft Windows Server and providing an opportunity for customers to run their SQL Server databases without additional operating system licensing.

SQL Server 2019 added new features upon its launch, most of which focused on internal database updates including Intelligent Query enhancements. One I did like was the in-memory TempDB which makes perfect sense than writing this to a slow disk.

We've discussed the versions, but we can't forget to mention that each version of SQL Server comes in a number of editions. Microsoft SQL Server 2008, for example, came in eight separate editions all with slight variations in functionality. The latest version of SQL Server 2019 comes in eight editions, including versions for Linux, Windows, and Docker images for Windows and Linux that also allow hosting in Kubernetes.

SQL Server Licensing

Typically, we see new editions of SQL Server released as an Amazon AMI within a week of their general availability to the public. If the AMI is released by AWS, then it'll be *License Included*. We covered licensing as part of the previous chapter, but in this section, we dive a little deeper on licensing SQL Server.

You have a number of options when it comes to licensing Microsoft SQL Server on AWS: *License Included*, which leaves the licensing worries to AWS, and *Bring Your Own License (BYOL)*, which allows you to reuse licenses that you already own. Microsoft SQL Server comes under the *License Mobility* group of products that can be used in the cloud if you've got active *Software Assurance* on your licenses from Microsoft.

License included covers the option of starting up an Amazon EC2 instance which already has Microsoft Windows Server and SQL Server already installed and licensed for you. You are charged hourly for the Amazon EC2 instance, and that charge includes the SQL Server license. As soon as you stop the EC2 Instance, the license is no longer yours. This may seem an expensive option, but it doesn't tie you to any lengthy contracts and gives you the ability to use and not use SQL Server at any time.

Bringing your license to AWS gives you the responsibility of making sure you comply with your Microsoft Licensing agreement, but you do save a significant amount of money by reusing licensing rather than purchasing new licenses via the *License Included* method. Microsoft SQL Server has a large cost, especially the Enterprise Edition of the product, and I've seen a lot of companies save cost, not only by moving away from SQL Server to one of the open source competitors such as MySQL but by simply revising what edition of SQL Server they actually need for the workload.

Microsoft Licensing practices can be quite dynamic, something which we discussed in Chapter 3, and this can have an effect on how best to run SQL Server. Typically, AMIs come in either Standard or Enterprise edition; the exact version, service pack, and edition will be detailed in the AMI description.

Availability and Resilience in SQL Server

How important is your data?

A vital part of any SQL Server implementation is an understanding of how important the data is. This will give us a view on what our Recovery Time Objective (RTO) and Recovery Point Objective (RPO) will be. In other words, if something goes very wrong, how quickly do we need that data back and how much data can we afford to lose?

Let's talk about what options SQL Server gives us to protect our data.

Transaction Log Shipping

Since SQL Server came into existence, we've had the ability for resilience thanks to Transaction Log Shipping. Transaction Logs contain all the changes to a database since the last Transaction Log was taken. The recovery of a database using Transaction Logs is very simple:

- Restore the last good backup of data onto a working system.

- Replay the changes from the Transaction Logs that have been copied to a safe location or secondary database server.

This is a very easy way to provide a form of resilience or disaster recovery. But there is a lot that can go wrong here, such as corrupt backups or missing transaction logs. The advantages of Transaction Log Shipping are that it's simple and cheap and can be used to recover databases over large geographic distances. You are not required to have a super high-speed connection between the database servers, which is why this method was so popular in the early 2000s when high-speed network connectivity was so expensive.

Database Mirroring

Microsoft has given us Data Mirroring since SQL Server 2005 Service Pack 1. It remedies the issues that constrain Transaction Log Shipping for production environments. When data is about to be written to the primary database server, the same data is sent over to a secondary server first via Log Shipping, and both servers commit data at the same time. Both databases are therefore a mirror of each other at any single point in time. If a failure occurs in the primary server, then the Database Mirroring process makes the secondary server the primary automatically, and little, if any, downtime occurs.

Database Mirroring gives you complete confidence that your data is safeguarded – but at quite a cost. Not only the financial cost of having a server sat there not being particularly useful unless a failure occurs but also a performance cost in having to commit data to the secondary server first. Also, network costs because you'll need high-speed connectivity between servers and finally a cost in having to manage the fact that you need both these servers to be a mirror of each other in terms of security patching, operating system levels, and so on.

The Database Mirroring feature has been deprecated since SQL Server 2012 where it was replaced by Always On Availability Groups, which we explain shortly.

Replication

Mirroring is perfect if you just have a single primary database server that you want to protect, but in this age of huge amounts of data, distributed across the globe, mirroring has some drawbacks. That's where replication comes in handy. SQL Server creates a Replication Publisher, our primary database source, and then a number of subscribers which are the secondary database servers.

The huge benefit of replication is that the subscribers can help offload some of the load from the publisher by taking care of reads from users or applications.

SQL Server offers a number of different replication methods.

Table 4-1. *Replication methods and description*

Transactional	Changes at the Publisher are sent to the Subscriber in real time and applied in the same order
Merge	Data can be changed on both the Publisher and Subscriber and managed via triggers
Snapshot	A moment in time replication of current data
Peer-to-Peer	Similar to transactional replication, but to multiple servers in real time
Bidirectional	Allows two servers to both publish and subscribe to each other
Updateable	If data is updated at a Subscriber, it is sent to the Publisher and then replicated to other Subscribers

Windows Server Failover Clustering (Always On Failover Cluster Instances)

Clustering is actually an operating system process, and SQL Server is just a cluster-aware application. With clustering, multiple servers (either physical or virtual) operate as a single server behind a virtual machine name (VMN). If a server fails, then the VMN moves to an available server. It's important here to describe the failover configurations since they affect how our AWS design will look.

Imagine four servers all clustered together. We have two data centers, and we place two of our clustered servers in each data center. A network switch goes wonky, and we've lost network connectivity between the data centers. At this stage, each pair of servers could think that they are primary and continue writing to the database. This example is called split brain. A million times worse than having no servers writing to the database would be a scenario where we have multiple servers thinking they are primary and each of them writing to the database.

To resolve this kind of conflict, clustering gives you options on what to do when a server fails. A number of these options include something we call a *Witness Server*. This server's role is to vote when there are an even number of nodes in a cluster and therefore decide on which server is the primary.

We know that clusters have multiple servers, but where does the actual data reside? Here, we have the concept of *shared storage*. In our data center days, this would have been a single SAN or multiple SANs with replication if we had multiple data centers. We need to keep this shared storage concept in mind during our AWS design discussion.

Since SQL Server 2012, SQL Server Clustering has been rebranded as Always On Failover Cluster Instances.

Always On Availability Groups (Enterprise Edition Only)

Launched with SQL Server 2012 at the same time as Database Mirroring was deprecated, Always On Availability Groups (AGs) is an amalgamation of Mirroring, Failover Clusters, and Log Shipping all in one.

AGs work at the database rather than the server layer. The database or databases form a group that is replicated using traditional Log Shipping methods from a primary replica to a maximum of eight secondary replicas using synchronous or asynchronous data synchronization. With the synchronous method, the log file is committed to every secondary replica *before* it is committed to the primary. On the plus side, it guarantees against data loss but with a negative impact on performance.

With asynchronous data synchronization, the log file is committed to the primary replica and then replicated to the secondary replicas. So there is an ever-so-slight chance of data loss if a failure were to occur in the time between the primary and secondary replicas being committed.

That ever-so-slight chance is going to keep you up at night, which always comes back to our original question. How important is your data?

Always On AGs aren't only about providing a higher form of availability. They can also be used to scale the use of the database across more than a single database server. When a database is replicated to a secondary replica server, it can be used in a read-only form. Depending on what your application does, this could be really useful and increase performance to your users.

If the primary replica fails, then a secondary is promoted to primary within a few seconds. The advantage of having Always On AGs on AWS rather than your own data center is the low-latency networks already in place between availability zones. Your business might not be able to run Always On AGs across multiple data centers simply because you've not got a good enough network connection in place between them. Therefore, you are limited to Always On AGs in a single data center, giving you protection against server failure only.

Basic Availability Groups (Standard Edition)

To prove that Availability Groups are not only an option for those who can afford Enterprise Edition but can be used with Standard Edition SQL Server also, Basic Availability Groups have a fair amount of constraints over their Enterprise Edition bigger brother. The use of only a single database for instance as well as not allowing the secondary replica to be used for read-only access of backups means that Basic Availability Groups are useful for HA only. In its favor is the fact that it does give you HA at Standard Edition pricing which would give you a significant saving over Enterprise Edition.

Distributed Availability Groups

Distributed AGs can span separate Availability Groups on two separate Windows Server Failover Clustering (WSFC). These clusters can be geographically distant from each other, and the clusters can even be running different operating systems (Linux and Windows) as long as we have network connectivity.

Microsoft details three use cases for Distributed Availability Groups:

1. Disaster Recovery or multisite scenarios

2. Migration to new hardware

3. Increasing the number of read-only replicas

SQL Server on Amazon EC2

As customers, we have a number of options when it comes to running Microsoft SQL Server on AWS. We can use Amazon EC2 instances as virtual machines and create environments which are a mirror of what we have in our own data centers today.

It's a popular design, and there wouldn't be anything different in this kind of solution than what we have already in our data centers. Therefore, it's a discussion around ease of use and supportability vs. manageability and costs. We will discuss this further in Chapter 8.

Let's look at what high availability/resilience solutions we can create using AWS Availability Zones and Regions. Since we are using SQL Server on EC2, the implementation of these designs is the responsibility of you, the customer (see Table 4-2).

Table 4-2. *Replication options*

HA Option	Multiple Databases	Multiple Secondary	Readable Secondary	Automatic Failover	Downtime During Failover
Log Shipping	Yes	Yes	Yes	No	Variable
Mirroring	Yes	Yes	No	Yes	<30 seconds
Replication	Yes	Yes	Yes	No	Variable
Failover Cluster	No	No	No	Yes	<30 seconds
Always On	Yes	Yes	Yes	Yes	<30 seconds

AWS Quick Start

We discussed AWS Quick Starts in the previous chapter, and there is an AWS Quick Start available for Microsoft SQL Server (Figure 4-2). See `https://aws.amazon.com/quickstart/architecture/sql/`.

This provides the template to automatically create a multinode SQL Always On Availability Group using Windows Server Failover Clustering (WSFC) over two Availability Zones within a single AWS Region.

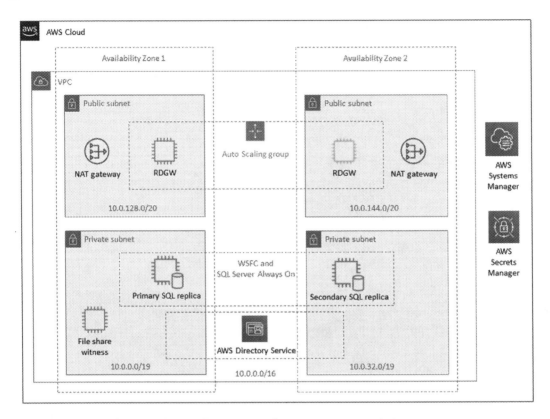

Figure 4-2. *Multinode EC2 Always On cluster via a Quick Start*

The solution includes a number of other AWS Services such as AWS Directory Services (Chapter 10) and AWS Systems Manager (Chapter 3). It also gives you options of having the File Share Witness Server in a separate Availability Zone for added resilience.

Just for completeness, the Quick Start includes NAT Gateway and Remote Desktop Gateway Servers to provide external access to manage the environment. Of course, the template can be changed to include or exclude any of these elements. There are better ways to manage the environment than over Remote Desktop Connections, and in Chapter 3 we looked at AWS Systems Manager's Session Manager capability that provides command-line remote access in your browser.

You have two options when it comes to implementing this Quick Start: either in a brand-new VPC or in an existing VPC. If you choose a brand-new VPC, the Quick Start will create everything in Figure 4-2. But if you choose to run the Quick Start in an existing VPC, then the Quick Start will deploy the SQL Server nodes only.

AWS gives you the ability to provide the maximum amount of resilience for your data without the huge capital expenditure this would otherwise cost you.

AWS Launch Wizard

At AWS re:Invent 2019, we saw the launch of AWS Launch Wizard, a guided deployment mechanism for enterprise applications. Its first application on launch was Microsoft SQL Server although it was closely followed by SAP and now encompasses Active Directory also with more to follow.

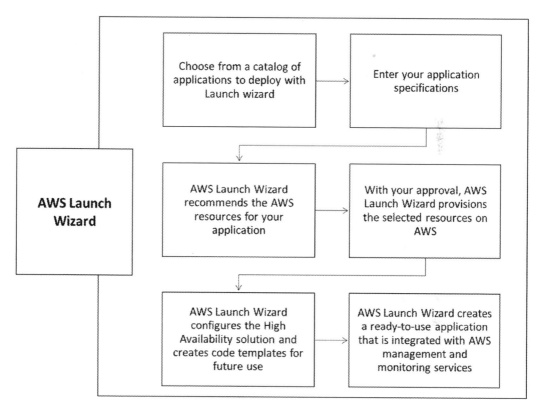

Figure 4-3. *AWS Launch Wizard*

AWS Launch Wizard (Figure 4-3) gives you a best practice way to launch SQL Server into your AWS Account while setting up Amazon SNS notifications and CloudWatch monitoring to your existing or new Active Directory domain. It's the Quick Start feature but with a lot more options and even allows the ability to bring your own license to the party or use *license-included* EC2 Instances if you don't want to go down that route.

Creating a SQL Server Always On Availability Group Cluster

If the Quick Start doesn't give you the flexibility you require, then AWS support has published a step-by-step guide to walk you through the process of creating an Always On AG Cluster in a single region but across two Availability Groups. See `https://aws.amazon.com/premiumsupport/knowledge-center/ec2-windows-sql-server-always-on-cluster/`.

There's no need to repeat the whole guide here, but I'd like to provide a high-level view of the process to demonstrate how easy it is to re-create a very common SQL Server HA design on AWS.

Our prerequisites for this design are as follows:

- A VPC with private subnets in separate Availability Zones.

- EC2 Instances with an Instance Type to support your workloads. Running Windows Server and SQL Server Enterprise Edition 2012 or higher.

- Add additional EBS volumes to each EC2 Instance to store databases, log files, and backup files. AWS recommends the Io1 provisioned IOPS SSD storage type, but it really does depend on your workload.

- An Active Directory (AD) Domain and permissions to be able to create AD objects – we discuss Active Directory in depth in Chapter 10.

- RDP Console access to the EC2 Instances to be able to complete the installation.

- Join the EC2 instances to the Active Directory domain.

- We need two additional IP addresses on each EC2 Instance Eth0 network adaptor. These IP addresses should be valid for the subnet you are using. Why do we need three addresses? First address for Windows Server, second for the Windows Cluster core, and finally a third address for the SQL Server Group Listener.

Here are the steps needed to complete the implementation:

- You'll need to check "Append Primary and Connection specific DNS Suffixes" which you'll find in the Network Adaptor settings on each EC2 Instance.

- Install the Cluster Feature on each EC2 Instance using the Install-WindowsFeature PowerShell cmdlet.

- On one EC2 Instance Run `CLUADMIN.MSC` the Cluster Administrator Console as an Administrator.

- In Cluster Administrator, create a new Cluster, add both servers, and validate the Cluster on the next screen. One tip here – uncheck the **Add All Eligible Storage to the Cluster** box.

- Add one of the additional IP addresses into each node in the Cluster Core Resources section. Bring the Cluster Core online.

- Open SQL Server Configuration Manager and enable Always On Availability Groups from the SQL Server Properties. Do this on both EC2 Instances.

- Open SQL Server Management Studio (SSMS), create a new database, and take a full backup of that database.

- Run the New Availability Group Wizard from the Availability Group section in SSMS. The wizard is very straightforward, prompting you to choose a database to protect and configure replicas and so on.

- Validate the configuration in SSMS.

- Add a SQL Listener via SSMS using the secondary IP address you assigned to the EC2 Instance.

- Finally, test a failover, and you're done.

Always On Availability Groups are ideal within a single Region across multiple Availability Zones, but what about HA across Regions?

This very much depends on what regions you plan to use. It's certainly possible to have Synchronous Replication across regions, and I've seen customers implement this between Ireland and London or London and Frankfurt. But it wouldn't be something I'd recommend between London and Tokyo due to the huge distances and latency you'd expect to see, which is often around the 200-millisecond range. The best practice for multi-region deployments is to use Asynchronous Replication, which offers the best geographic distance.

My advice here, depending on what RTO/RPO requirements you have, is to implement Always On Distributed Availability Groups combining a Multi-AZ approach with multi-region where you have immediate recovery and minimal data loss if an Availability Zone were to fail combined with protection against a full Regional outage. The beauty of Distributed AGs is that you can have multiple read replicas, so depending on your app's write profile, this might be ideal for users that are geographically split.

As with every high-availability solution, there is a cost to bear in terms of AWS usage and SQL Server Licenses, but what value do you hang on your data?

Performance of SQL Server on EC2

So much of a DBA's skill and effort goes into making sure that SQL Server is as performant as it can be. Sometimes, the onus of performance management is pushed to the database layer in a standard multitier application architecture to improve a poorly streamlined application. Either way, a poorly performing SQL Server is going to cause you concern.

SQL Server performance is focused primarily on four components: CPU, memory, storage, and network.

Both CPU and memory can be allocated by the use of the right Amazon EC2 Instance Type. Instance Type is critical and plays a large part in ensuring that the main components specified earlier are available to you in the option you need. For instance, only certain Instance Types have enhanced networking, only newer generation Instance Types are EBS optimized for storage, and so on.

SQL Server tends to be far more memory hungry than CPU intensive. The most popular Instance Type for SQL Server workloads has been the Memory-Optimized R5 Type, currently offering up to 768GB of memory with 96 vCPU.

Remember that you also have the ability to change Instance Types for EC2, but the instance will require an EC2 stop and start. This is a great feature, meaning that you can act on performance test results without having to rebuild the server each time.

Typically, the more memory you have in a server, the more CPU you have to have. This gives us a challenge when it comes to SQL Server, which is licensed on a per-CPU basis. In 2017, AWS gave you the ability to switch off CPU hyperthreading during an EC2 launch. This could effectively halve the number of CPUs the Instance thinks it has and therefore halve the number of SQL Server licenses that are required while still giving the maximum amount of memory.

AWS gives you some options on networking too. Depending on your Instance Type, you can have network interface speeds of up to 10GB to 25GB. AWS provides the ability to use Placement Groups when launching your EC2 Instances that ensure that all EC2 Instances launched in that Placement Group are physically close to each other to reduce latency between Instances. Placement Groups also have another interesting feature: you can use them to ensure that workloads are as far away from each other as possible (within the same Availability Zone), useful if you've got a distributed application where you don't want multiple Instances on the same hardware.

In 2020, third-party marketing and benchmarking company Principled Technologies ran SQL Server performance tests comparing the Amazon EC2 R5b 8xlarge instance type against a similarly spec'd Azure E64-32s-v4 virtual machine. They were looking at the balance between raw performance and cost.

They found that running SQL Server on an R5b delivered two times the performance of orders per minute compared to its Azure counterpart.

The full report and its conclusions can be found here:

`www.principledtechnologies.com/Amazon/EC2-R5b-OLTP-competitive-0321-v3.pdf`

Storage design is a large topic when it comes to SQL Server. We learned in Chapter 3 about the different types of storage available to EC2. Now let's talk about some popular storage configurations and the benefits of them.

Note   Storage design is focused on capacity, speed, and resilience. We can "mirror" disks so that data written to one disk is also written to another, and should one fail, we've not lost any data. Simple enough, but we've doubled the storage cost without any additional benefit other than resilience. We could also "stripe" a number of disks together to form a larger single logical volume. It would be a lot faster than mirroring because you have multiple disks reading and writing in parallel. The downside is that if a single disk fails, you've lost the whole set.

Fortunately, with AWS, EBS volumes are replicated within the same Availability Zone, so there is no need for additional RAID levels for protection. It is recommended by AWS to use striping on EBS to increase performance of your SQL Server database.

EBS volumes are elastic and therefore can be increased up to a maximum size of 16TiB per volume without affecting the EC2 Instance it's connected to. Not even a reboot. AWS also offers a number of other storage options such as object storage via Amazon S3, archive storage via AWS Glacier, and shared file storage via AWS FSx for Windows.

It's common practice with SQL Server to take the different file types and place them on different types of storage. For instance, databases need to be located on EBS SSD fast storage if they are being used a lot by applications. Backup data and Transaction Logs can be placed on slower EBS disk types, while TempDB is placed on the fastest possible disks since it's constantly writing.

A good solution here is either PIOPS or Striped GP3 EBS volumes for your databases (dependent on workload) and ST1 volumes for faster backup and reduced cost over SSD disks, then use Instance Store NVMe disks for TempDB. It's a configuration that AWS recommend and gives great performance.

Just to reiterate here, Instance Store disks are not available on all Instance Types and are not persistent if the server fails or reboots. This is not an issue for TempDB.

In terms of backups, you can either use Amazon Data Lifecycle Manager to automatically create and delete snapshots of a SQL Server Native backup on your backup volume or perhaps use AWS Backup which is a fully managed backup service.

Amazon RDS

Another option for running SQL Server on AWS is to use the Amazon Relational Database Service (RDS) which provides a fully managed service where customers consume their databases and AWS manages the infrastructure supporting that. We discussed the Shared Responsibility Model in Chapter 2, and fully managed services such as Amazon RDS move the boundaries of this ever so slightly. But even though AWS takes on the management responsibility of ensuring the servers running your database are available and secure, at the end of the day, the database and all its data are yours, and you are responsible for configuring the Amazon RDS server with the right instance type, backups and restores, and so on. Here are some additional facts about RDS:

- Amazon RDS comes in all the SQL Server editions that you currently use, Express, Web, Standard, and Enterprise up to SQL Server 2019.

- It can handle Windows and SQL Authentication, Transparent Data Encryption (TDE), Encrypted Storage, and SSL encryption in transit.

- When it comes to Availability options, Amazon RDS provides a single-click Multi-AZ HA option using Database Mirroring. Newer RDS SQL versions also offer Always On Availability Groups.

- Management of SQL Server is the same using SQL Server Mgmt Studio or SQLCMD.

Whereas SQL Server on EC2 gives you ultimate flexibility at the cost of having to manage everything yourself, Amazon RDS is a managed service and therefore has some constraints at the cost of you not having to manage the database servers. We need to understand these constraints further:

- Some services that are not available include SQL Server Analysis Services, Integration Services, and Reporting Services, although you can use Amazon RDS as the data source and run these services on individual EC2 Instances, which is a common pattern.

- Because Amazon RDS is a fully managed service, therefore, the SA root account is not available nor certain root-level groups.

- Amazon RDS requires you to use AWS Directory Services for Active Directory which we will discuss in full during Chapter 10.

- Microsoft Distributed Transaction Coordinator (MSDTC) is not supported at this time.

Let's stop here, grab a coffee, and discuss two important items.

Firstly, as I've stated in Chapter 2, new features for AWS Services are added daily, and I'm sure that all of the constraints I've listed here are already on the road map to be added alongside a whole host of new additional features. Regularly checking the AWS "What's New" site is an important start to your day.

Secondly, it's a natural reaction when you've worked with access to a root-level account that enables you to do anything you want to feel slightly hard done by when using a fully managed service that doesn't give you the same level of access. I certainly felt that way when first using AWS services some years ago, and if you feel strongly about it, then go down the EC2 route and have as much freedom as you want.

However, there's a balance to be had from using a fully managed service above running that same service on EC2 Instances that have to be managed by someone. I certainly don't miss having to manage a fleet of SQL Servers, and I much prefer the ability to be able to switch on an Amazon RDS service when it's needed while I concentrate on tasks that have a higher value.

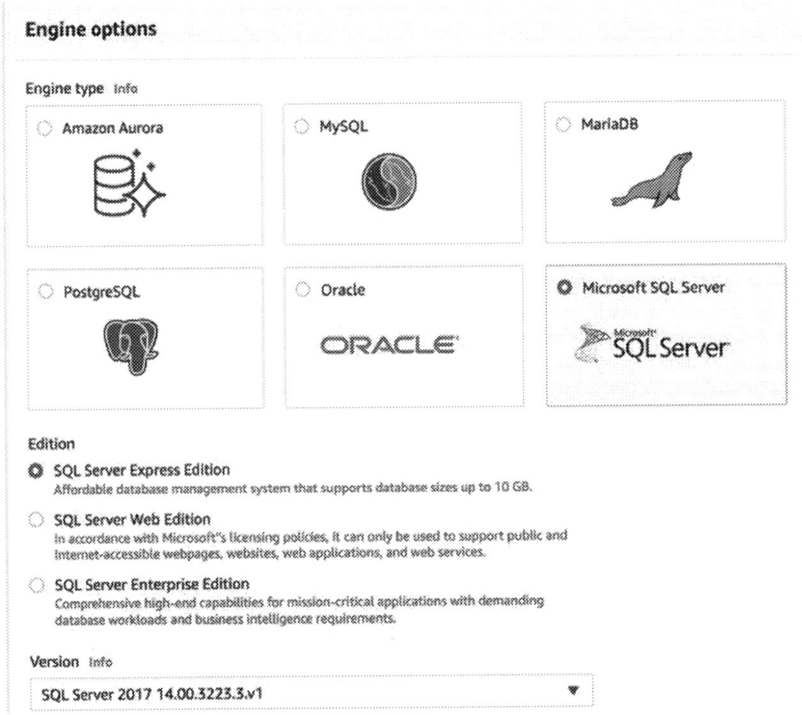

Figure 4-4. *Amazon RDS Database options. You are not limited to just SQL Server*

The Amazon RDS console allows you to not only use many different database engines (Figure 4-4) such as MySQL, MariaDB, Postgres, and Oracle as well as SQL Server. You have the option of step-by-step configuration using the Standard Create method or the ability to create a database with just a few clicks using predefined templates with Easy Create.

Choosing the edition and the version of SQL Server from 2012 through to 2019. You no longer have the ability to use your own SQL Server licenses with newly created Amazon RDS instances due to license changes made by Microsoft. All new Amazon RDS instances have licensing included.

After you've entered some standard information such as database name, user password, and what Instance Type you want to use, you can select to have the database deploy to a Multi-AZ deployment or not. That single click implements a full Multi-Availability Zone database environment which will set up mirroring and automatic failover for you. Lastly, select an AWS Directory Services directory to use and then confirm the additional settings, such as collation, encryption, backups, and so on.

Another AWS Service, Amazon RDS Performance Insights, is enabled during the database creation process by default and gives you a visual reference to what's happening with your database at any one time. It can be used to quickly find issues such as high CPU utilization and then show you what caused that issue inside the database. The cause of the issue could be a SQL procedure that isn't tuned correctly. With Amazon RDS Performance Insights (Figure 4-5), you know the exact state of your database health and where the bottlenecks are.

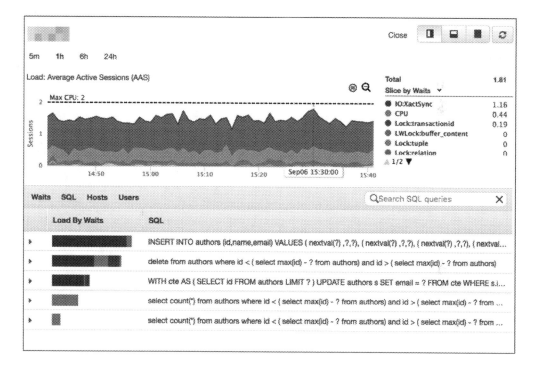

Figure 4-5. *Amazon RDS Performance Insights*

Amazon RDS Parameter Groups help you change the configuration of your selected database engine within RDS. Each additional database you create will be associated with the new Parameter Group and pick up the changes in that to override the default settings. With Parameter Groups, you can change engine settings such as collation or character set.

RDS Option Groups give you three settings to choose from which you assign to your database instance such as Use Native Backup and Restore, TDE, and SQL Server Audit. More information can be found in the documentation.

Migrating Your Database to AWS

Congratulations, you've decided to move your SQL Server databases to the AWS Cloud, but what now?

What tools are available to migrate your databases to AWS? Will the migration require downtime? Will I be able to test the new environment before I switch over, and more importantly, how can I switch over?

Thousands of AWS customers have asked themselves the same questions over the last decade or more, and AWS have created not only the necessary tools to migrate with ease but also the best practice strategies you'll need to make this a success.

We discuss general migration strategies in more detail during Chapter 9, but there are some specific SQL Server tasks we should look at in this section.

Understanding your dependencies is the most critical task; you should have **as complete a picture as possible** of what systems use your databases and what systems your databases use, including storage, notifications, reports, monitoring, backup systems, and so on. SQL Servers are never built in isolation; they are at the heart of application stacks, and a whole operations infrastructure is built around them.

I was very deliberate when I stated "as complete a picture as possible"; if your organization is large enough, then having a 100% complete understanding of anything is difficult, and this unattainable goal will hinder, delay, and derail your migration to the cloud.

The other point that's worth making is rather obvious. Although AWS and third parties have great tools for migrating your database, you've also got the tried and true native SQL backup and restore method that you've no doubt used a hundred times before. What you choose depends on what the business requires from the migration.

Planning

Here are a few best practice suggestions to add to your own migration plan:

- Understand your authentication requirements. In most cases, the SQL Servers will be in mixed mode requiring access to an Active Directory infrastructure. This will need to be in place before we migrate anything and can be designed a number of ways, all of which we discuss in detail during Chapter 10.

- Investigate what SQL Server features you use and then understand what edition of SQL Server you need. Consolidating databases onto servers running specific editions can reduce the number of very expensive SQL Server Licenses. Please do not discount Web, Express, and Developer editions; they all have a role and are extremely cost effective.

- Can you Bring Your Own License (BYOL)? Even though Microsoft made significant changes to their licensing agreements in 2019, BYOL is still an option if you have Software Assurance or your license was purchased prior to October 1, 2019. Reusing expensive licenses could secure your next promotion due to the significant cost savings it'll make to your cloud journey.

- What will the design be? How critical is this database? Do you have any business-led RPO/RTO targets? If you don't currently have High Availability (HA) requirements, then why not? Was this decision based on cost savings, and if so, is now the time to rethink this if you can provide a full HA solution for significantly less than was available to you before? We've discussed the HA solutions available to your SQL Server workloads inside AWS. Another solution could be to rely on traditional backup and restore and create the secondary HA environment via CloudFormation templates when they are needed. Or have the instances created but switched off. You can be very imaginative with your HA designs within the AWS Cloud.

- Understand what recovery model you are using on each database as well as the compatibility level you are using.

- Finally, ensure that you have a good understanding of the performance you require. Remember you have the ability to switch EC2 Instance Types which will mean a reboot of the Instance and therefore not something that can be easily completed within a full 24/7 production environment. Therefore, performance testing is important. The SQL Server Performance Dashboard as well as a combination of T-SQL commands, Database Engine Tuning Advisor, and Open Activity Monitor will provide you a good set of data. Microsoft recommends a small tool called DiskSpd.exe to report on what your current storage performance is, and you can match that using the Amazon EBS figures for different types of EBS volumes.

AWS Database Migration Service

AWS Database Migration Service (DMS) allows you to create a seamless database migration into the AWS Cloud from your on-premises databases. It uses the concept of a **Replication Instance** running inside your AWS VPC that it then synchronizes with your original (source) database while the database is still running. You can then switch over without data loss or downtime. DMS has been used by hundreds of thousand companies to migrate their databases to AWS. It'll even let you perform a Multi-Availability Zone migration to ensure there is no possible chance of loss of data should one Replication Instance fail during migration.

Your data is secured during migration using encryption via AWS Key Management Service (see Figure 4-6).

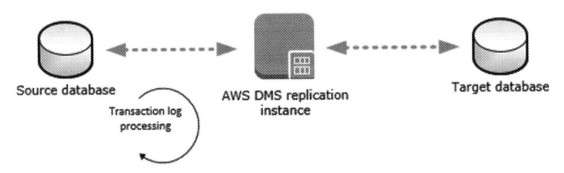

Figure 4-6. *AWS Database Migration Service*

Database Migration Service (DMS) can be used to migrate from on-premises or cloud databases to AWS. DMS can replicate your whole database in a single go, not the best option for a production database that needs to keep running. The other options are to replicate the database and set up a continuous synchronization of data, allowing for a zero-downtime migration. However, if your database is significantly large, then perhaps use another method to perform a bulk upload of the database and set up replication only. You can perform an initial bulk upload using AWS Services such as AWS Snowball, which we will discuss in Chapter 9.

It's important to understand that DMS migrates data, tables, and primary keys; no other database objects are migrated. This is acceptable when migrating to the same database engine (homogeneous migrations), but what about views, stored procedures, functions, and any custom code? And what if you are migrating to a different database engine (heterogeneous migrations)?

Then you'll also need to use the AWS Schema Conversion Tool (SCT).

The Schema Conversion Tool

The purpose of the Schema Conversion Tool is to make it easier to migrate from one database schema to another. It will analyze your database schema and clearly show where significant changes need to be made to your database code to ensure it works with the new database engine.

SCT runs as a downloadable application which you store on your original source SQL Server. Running it allows you to choose the target database engine, and it will report on its analysis of your source database while offering suggestions on how to correct any issues.

The Schema Conversion Tool offers options on converting SQL Server to the following: Amazon Aurora with MySQL compatibility, Amazon Aurora with PostgreSQL compatibility, MariaDB 10.2 and 10.3, Microsoft SQL Server, MySQL, and PostgreSQL.

Download and run SCT via `https://aws.amazon.com/dms/schema-conversion-tool/`. While you're on this website, download the JDBC Drivers for SQL Server which we will need later.

After the install, you are then asked to create a project with the following options: report on a different database engine, the same database engine with cost options, or a report with both those options (see Figure 4-7).

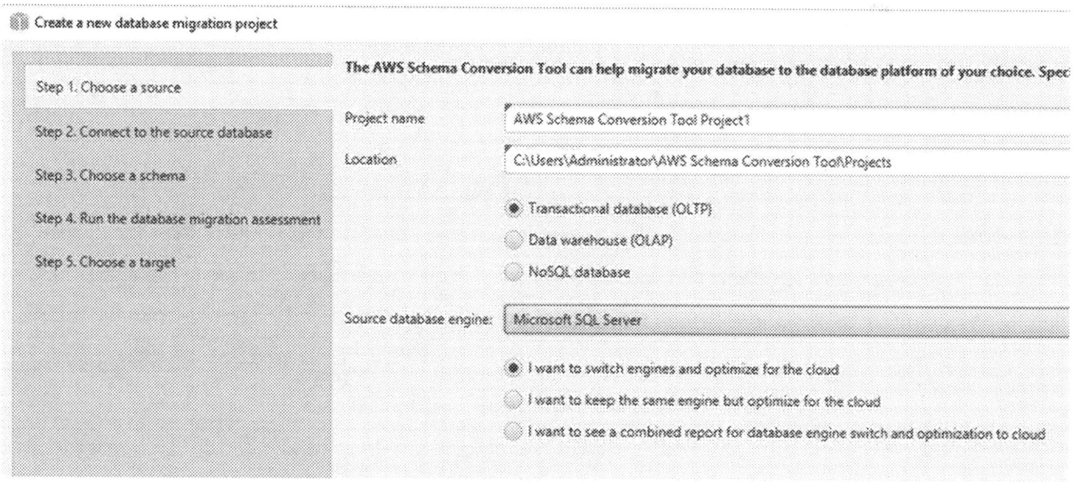

Figure 4-7. *AWS Schema Conversion Tool*

Enter your source database parameters in the next screen, making sure you click Test Connection; otherwise, you cannot move forward. You will also need to enter the path of the JDBC Drivers during this section.

The AWS Schema Conversion Tool has some great features such as

- The ability to use Data Extraction Agents to extract data warehouse data and migrate it into Amazon Redshift.

- You can use SCT to create AWS Database Migration Service tasks and monitor these tasks via SCT.

- Using the SCT Extension Pack, you can begin converting any database features that weren't successfully converted into AWS Lambda functions.

- Analyze cost savings when using SCT to copy your on-premises database into AWS with the same database engine.

One final thing to note on the topic of migrations is that AWS have created step-by-step lab guides that allow you to run through a SQL Server migration using various tools from your own AWS account. There will be a cost incurred from running any AWS CloudFormation stacks that create resources, so please keep that in mind. But I do think it's valuable to familiarize yourself with the different approaches before you take on your own production databases. It can be found here: `https://ms-workloads.workshop.aws/6-rds-sql-server.html`.

AWS Babelfish

AWS re:Invent 2020 was a very different event than the re:Invents we've seen over the previous 8 years. The world was in the middle of a pandemic and mostly locked down, so travel was impossible. AWS changed re:Invent 2020 to a fully online virtual event and did so very successfully. Foregoing the ticket prices and they ran the event for free to all attendees. There was the usual mixture of sessions and keynotes to keep us glued to our screens, and there was a new service release that made me go "Wow!".

If you've ever read or watch any of Douglas Adams' *Hitchhiker's Guide to the Galaxy* books or films, then you'll be aware that a Babelfish fits into the ear of our lead character Arthur Dent and translates in real time every alien language into simple English.

The AWS service does the same thing. But rather than alien languages, it translates SQL Server's T-SQL into PostgreSQL in real time using its own translation layer. The implication of this is that you'll be able to run your Microsoft SQL Server–based databases and code on PostgreSQL with minimal changes.

It's still in prerelease, and you can register for the preview at https://aws.amazon.com/rds/aurora/babelfish/.

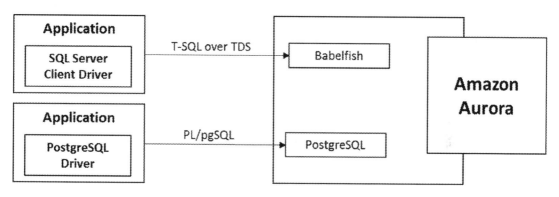

Figure 4-8. *AWS Bablefish for Aurora PostgreSQL*

AWS are quick to highlight that Babelfish won't completely eliminate the need for changes to your code, but it will reduce the amount of code changes significantly, and one thing we know for certain is that AWS will continue to iterate on this service to make it easier for their customers to move away from SQL Server and the license costs and lock-in it attracts.

Babelfish will initially focus on translating Microsoft SQL Server code to run on PostgreSQL which will run inside Amazon Aurora which we discuss next.

Amazon Aurora and Other Database Services

One of the many targets for your database in the AWS Cloud is Amazon Aurora. This addition to the database engine arena was purpose-built to run on the AWS Cloud.

It's a relational database that runs via the Amazon RDS service and is fully compatible with both MySQL and Postgres.

The benefits of Amazon Aurora are speed, cost, and resilience. All of the current database engines such as SQL Server or Oracle were built to run in very static data center environments, whereas Amazon Aurora was designed from the ground up to run in the cloud. One of the compelling features is the automatic scalability, whether that's scaling performance or storage. It also automatically creates six copies of your data across AZs and backs it up to S3 buckets with encryption in transit and at rest.

Multi-region capability comes in the form of regional replicas, and it's fully managed via Amazon RDS, so there's nothing new to learn or manage day to day. One feature that has the potential to be very powerful for you is the ability to trigger AWS Lambda functions via Amazon Aurora stored procedures. It's a feature that makes possible a completely serverless application stack.

AWS now has ten different database services to serve your needs. Most of them are purpose-built for specific workloads whether that be relational, NoSQL, Graph, or Ledger (see Table 4-3).

Table 4-3. *Available Amazon Database services*

Database Type	Use Case	AWS Service
Relational	Traditional applications	Amazon RDS, Amazon Aurora, Amazon Redshift
Key-value	High traffic, web apps, gaming	Amazon DynamoDB
In-memory	Caching, session management, gaming	Amazon ElastiCache (Memcached or Redis)
Document	Content management	Amazon DocumentDB
Graph	Fraud detection, social networking	Amazon Neptune
Time series	IoT, DevOps, industry	Amazon Timestream
Ledger	Systems of record, banking	Amazon QLDB
Cassandra compatible	Performance, scalability	Amazon Keyspaces

At the start of this chapter, we discussed making sure you are using the edition of SQL Server that is right for your workload. Let's take this discussion to its conclusion and discuss using the right type of database for your data.

So the question is no longer confined to: are you going to use Microsoft SQL Server or MySQL or Oracle? This is typically a decision mainly based on available skillset and cost. Now we have so many specific database services to choose from. The question we should ask ourselves is: what does our data look like and what do we plan on doing with it?

Legacy SQL Server Workloads

Microsoft products have a built-in expiration date. It's not a date when everything stops working; it's a date when they finally go out of extended support, and no more security patches are developed or released. It's not a strict expiration date; if there is an important enough issue, then Microsoft returns and releases a patch. Windows XP was released in 2001; its extended support ran out in 2014, and 5 years after that, Microsoft released a security patch in 2019 to address a remote execution exploit.

Running production environments for your company comes with a duty of care which ensures that you have to keep systems up to date with security patches, the consequence of which is a continued cycle of upgrades to latest versions. It's been a fact of life for the last 30 years of running computer systems.

Where the vast majority of computer systems are regularly upgraded and continue to be under support, there are systems that simply cannot be retired due to tightly coupled and badly developed applications that have critical functionality that rely on features found in specific versions of software. And so the business must accept the risk until the application is redeveloped, if ever.

At this current time, SQL Server 2000, 2005, 2008, and 2008r2 are officially out of extended support. Extended support for SQL Server 2012 ends in 2022.

Microsoft launched SQL Server Compatibility Mode in SQL Server 2008 and allows it to run databases from SQL Server 2000 and upward. However, with SQL Server 2008r2 out of support, the next supported version of SQL Server 2012 supports only 2005 and upward, leaving SQL Server 2000 redundant. Compatibility Mode is a good option if it works for you since it doesn't require any changes to your databases.

AWS has numerous options for supporting customers running legacy versions of SQL Server and easing the upgrade path to supported versions of SQL Server or the use of AWS Services or to entirely different database engines. We've discussed AWS Systems Manager already in this chapter. At re:Invent 2018, AWS released another AWS Systems Manager Automation Document that performs a full in-place upgrade of an EC2 Instance running SQL Server 2008r2 to SQL Server 2012. It's a fully automated process that you can leave running without fear of it damaging the original EC2 Instance because it performs the in-place upgrade on a snapshot of the server, not the original.

That still leaves all the customers running pre-2008r2 SQL Server, so how does AWS help these customers? Well, we've already discussed AWS EMP, the End-of-Support Migration Program service that containerized a legacy application, including SQL Server 2000 through SQL Server 2008r2, and allows you to run these on up-to-date versions of Windows Server.

This is a great solution if you don't have resources to spend refactoring applications to work with databases or applications that for one reason or another can't easily be moved.

SQL Server on Linux

One of the most anticipated features of Microsoft SQL Server 2017 was its ability to run on Linux operating systems. For the previous two decades, Microsoft fought against Linux for domination of the operating system arena and won that battle for the majority of that time. But more and more companies are turning to Linux as their server OS of choice, and Microsoft wants to make sure that their premium database product does not get left behind.

As you would expect from a first-generation product, SQL Server on Linux does not have feature parity with its Windows counterpart. There are significant features missing, but none that you can't work around and none that should stop you investigating whether this is a good path for your business moving forward.

SQL Server for Linux runs on Red Hat 7.3, SUSE 12, Ubuntu 16.04, and even a Docker image. Performance is similar if not slightly better than on Windows, and Microsoft has released good documentation on performance tuning when running on Linux.

Features like Reporting and Analysis Services are missing, but can be provided by running these as standalone services via Windows. Replication isn't supported, but HA is covered by Always On which you can have a mixture of SQL Server Linux as primary and SQL Server Windows as secondary replicas.

SQL Server on Linux is available as an Amazon Machine Image (AMI) on Ubuntu and also Amazon Linux 2.

SQL Server 2019 is also available on Linux and has increased the level of functionality over its 2017 version. There are still some basic features that the Windows Server edition enjoys that Linux does not such as Merge Replication and Database Mirroring and also some mainstay functionality like Reporting and Analysis Services, but the functional gap between Windows and Linux versions of SQL Server is shrinking and will continue to shrink in newer versions until Microsoft releases a like-for-like functional service.

I've a feeling that these are three other versions (and therefore 10 years) down the road, but I'm hoping to be surprised by them.

Summary

At the start of this chapter, we asked, "How important is your data?" The answer informs a great many things, from what edition and version of Microsoft SQL Server that we use to how we design and implement our solutions and also whether SQL Server is the best place for our data in the first place.

We started this chapter discussing the various different editions and versions of SQL Server including all the versions that are supported on AWS. We discussed the ever-changing options on Microsoft Licensing and then showed the multiple different ways we can protect our data with the built-in SQL Server HA options such as Always On.

We discussed performance, a vital element for your database environments.

We've shown the many different ways we can run SQL Server on AWS, Amazon EC2, and Amazon RDS and how to get your databases into AWS with zero downtime using AWS Database Migration Service. We discussed a lot of the other options that database administrators have these days, including using AWS Schema Conversion Tool to migrate your database to Amazon Aurora; we also touched upon SQL Server 2017 and 2019 running on Linux.

CHAPTER 5

Developing on AWS

AWS has always been a welcoming home for developers. AWS's first prelaunch services were aimed solely at the development community. Who else has a use for a scalable queuing service if not developers? And have you wondered why Amazon S3 is an object storage service rather than block based like traditional storage solutions?

AWS was designed to make life easier for developers.

From being entirely API driven to creating disruptive services like AWS Lambda which has gone on to form the basis of an entirely new form of IT solution: Serverless Computing.

In its Management Console today, there are ten services grouped under the Developer category. But that doesn't tell the full story, since there are very few of its near 200 services that a modern developer wouldn't make use of.

But what has the AWS experience been for Microsoft-centric .NET developers? If they tell you that they've felt slightly left behind, certainly in the earlier years, in favor of the Python and JavaScript crowd, I would understand their gripe, but I would also argue there's good reasons as to why.

AWS develops its services and new features based in large part from feedback it receives from its customers in the form of Product Feature Requests (PFRs). These PFRs are prioritized based on requests coming from customers, and therefore just by the size of the communities, you are likely to see more weight on one rather than another. However, that changed several years ago when AWS made its "First Class Citizen" vow to ensure that every new service would either on release or within the first 6 months have full support for Microsoft workloads. And you can see the realization of this over the last 2 years by the increasing number of services supporting Microsoft technologies or services entirely focused on Microsoft workloads.

© Ryan Pothecary 2021
R. Pothecary, *Running Microsoft Workloads on AWS*, https://doi.org/10.1007/978-1-4842-6628-1_5

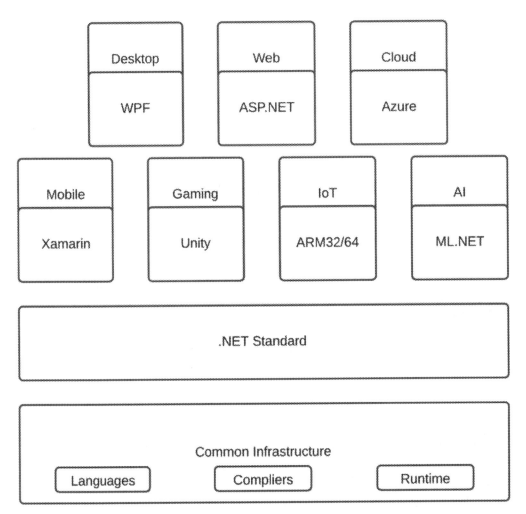

Figure 5-1. *The Microsoft .NET Framework*

Development under Microsoft Windows is also undergoing an evolution itself, with Microsoft introducing .NET Core in 2016 which built upon the standard .NET Framework by providing cross-platform support for Linux and Mac as well as being fully open sourced. This has been a significant departure from the last 20 years of only developing on Microsoft Windows operating systems. And it's going to get even broader in 2020.

.NET 5 (Figure 5-1) was released by Microsoft in November 2020, and although it fell short of the promise of .NET and .NET Core reunification, it took a step toward this and laid the foundations for .NET 6 to follow in late 2021. Microsoft's reunification plan can be found here: https://devblogs.microsoft.com/dotnet/introducing-net-5/.

AWS has supported every previous version of .NET since its Amazon EC2 Service launched in 2008, and they fully support .NET 5 and will do so for subsequent yearly releases after that.

AWS provides full .NET support via its Software Development Kit (SDK) for .NET (see Figure 5-2), which can be found here: `https://aws.amazon.com/sdk-for-net/`.

Providing libraries that are familiar to .NET developers and making it easier to build solutions that use the AWS platform. The AWS SDK for .NET was one of the early releases from AWS focusing on its .NET-based customers.

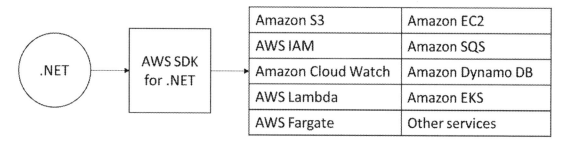

Amazon S3	Amazon EC2
AWS IAM	Amazon SQS
Amazon Cloud Watch	Amazon Dynamo DB
AWS Lambda	Amazon EKS
AWS Fargate	Other services

Figure 5-2. *AWS SDK for .NET*

Porting Assistant for .NET

In Chapter 9, we discuss migration, and over the last 5 years, there has been a huge amount of companies large and small migrating into the AWS Cloud. There are numerous approaches to moving into the cloud, and AWS typically suggest using the *Seven R's of migration strategy*; this is an approach created by Gartner in 2010 to categorize and prioritize workload migrations.

One of the seven approaches is to redevelop or refactor applications to work in a more cloud-native manner.

But only around 5% of Cloud workloads are redeveloped before they are migrated. This makes logical sense since redevelopment of applications is not something to be taken likely and, depending on the application scope, can be a project that can last a significant time.

Where I've seen redevelopment occurs is in parallel to other methods of migration such as rehost or replatform. These terms are discussed in detail in Chapter 9.

I mentioned that AWS has a host of services that help developers, and in 2019 it launched a brand-new service called the Porting Assistant for .NET which helps move .NET code to .NET Core (Figure 5-3).

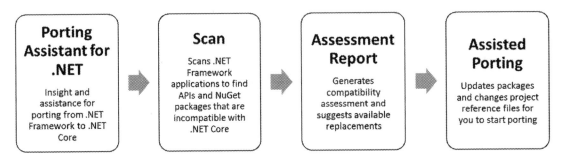

Figure 5-3. *The Porting Assistant for .NET*

The first step in using the service is to download the tools from `https://aws.amazon.com/porting-assistant-dotnet/` and then ensure that the .NET Core SDK 3.1 or later should be installed.

The Porting Assistant looks for an AWS account credential profile that you've stored locally on your development machine. If you don't already have these, then install the AWS tools for CLI (`https://aws.amazon.com/cli/`) and run `aws configure`.

Next, you find the .SLN solution file that contains your code and click Assess. This shouldn't take long to assess, but depends on the size of the application. You will receive a Portability Score along with the number of incompatible NuGet packages and APIs that your code uses.

You'll be able to see a graphical representation of the project references used in your project, which shows you the hotspot packages that have the most dependencies.

You can also see a list of NuGet packages your code uses next to an indication of whether they are .NET Core compatible or which version of the package is compatible.

This gives a straightforward view of what you need to do to get your code working. But you can also dive deeper into each package, and Porting Assistant will give you a line-by-line advice on where in your code you have incompatibilities and what the replacement strategy might be.

There are also two other important Microsoft tools that I need to mention that will help you with your move to .NET Core: Microsoft's .NET Portability Analyzer (`https://github.com/microsoft/dotnet-apiport`) and the Windows Compatibility Pack for .NET (`https://github.com/dotnet/docs/blob/main/docs/core/porting/windows-compat-pack.md`).

Microsoft's .NET Portability Analyzer runs as an extension inside Visual Studio and will report on the portability of your code inside Solution Explorer and gives you a percentage based on each Assembly within your project.

The Windows Compatibility Pack for .NET adds a significant number of additional APIs to your .NET Core project. Microsoft also has documentation guidelines on porting existing applications to .NET Core – `https://docs.microsoft.com/en-us/dotnet/core/porting/`.

The AWS Toolkit for Visual Studio

The primary tool for .NET development is Microsoft's own Visual Studio. It's so well respected as a development environment that many traditional open source developers in other languages prefer to use it as an Integrated Development Environment.

The AWS Tools for Microsoft Visual Studio is installed a number of ways – either as a standalone executable or searching the Visual Studio Marketplace for AWS in Extensions ➤ Manage Extensions (Figure 5-4).

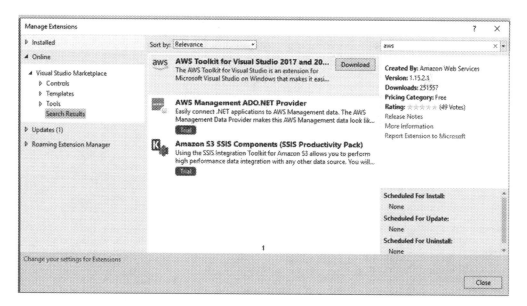

Figure 5-4. *The AWS Toolkit for Visual Studio 2017 and 2019 in Visual Studio Marketplace*

Take a look at `https://aws.amazon.com/visualstudio/` for the latest version and updates. AWS also have a separate AWS Tools for Visual Studio Team Services or Azure DevOps Services as the product is now called.

The AWS Toolkit for VS setup screen requires you to enter information about your AWS account such as profile name, access key ID, and secret access key. The account details you provide must be an IAM user with the Power User managed policy attached. The use of a profile name means that you can tailor the access based on the role of the person using Visual Studio and also access multiple accounts via different profiles.

Once installed, it integrates into Visual Studio in a number of different ways. The most obvious is the new templates you'll see when you create a new project. You can choose from a host of Lambda Serverless and CloudFormation templates (Figure 5-5).

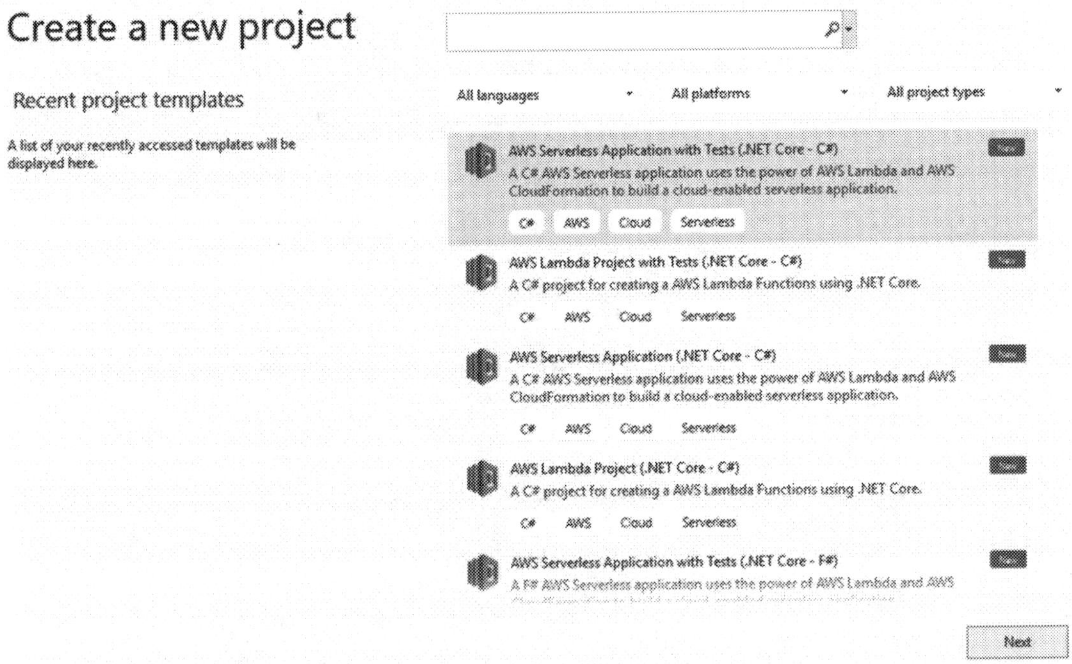

Figure 5-5. *AWS project templates*

If you choose an Amazon Lambda Serverless template, you have the option of starting your project using prebuilt Blueprints (Figure 5-6). These offer precoded examples that you can base your own project on.

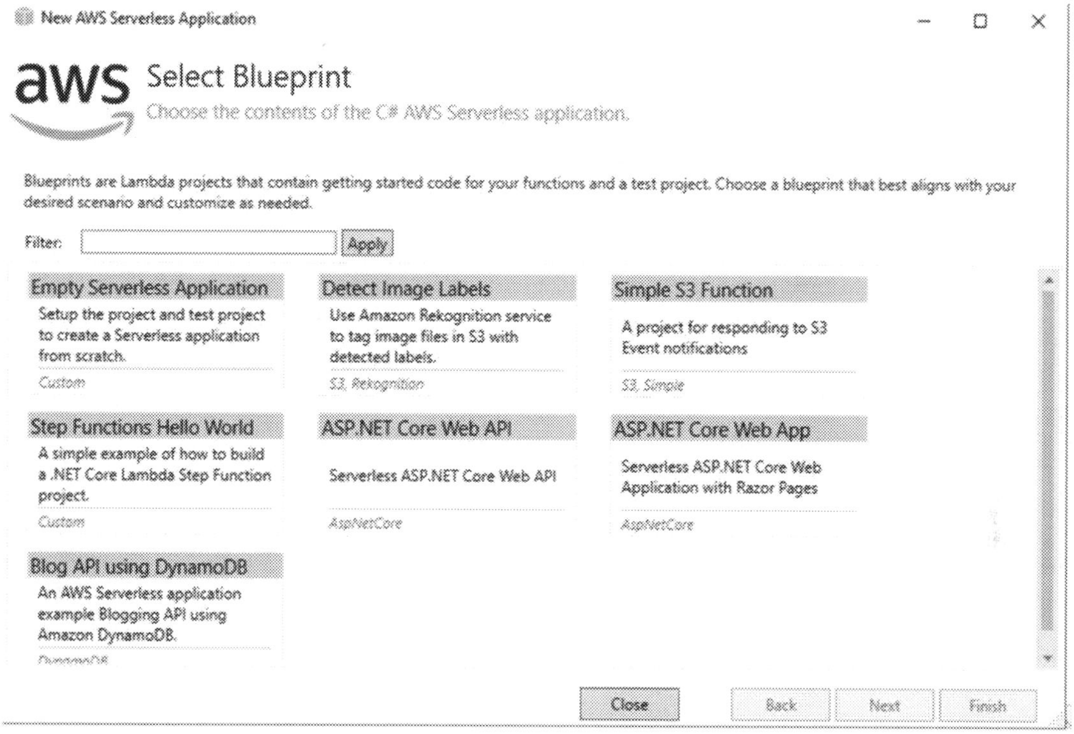

Figure 5-6. *AWS Serverless Blueprints*

You'll also see additions to Visual Studio (VS) Explorer. You'll see a number of AWS Services where you can deploy code or even use the VS Explorer as a substitute for the AWS Management Console to manage your AWS environment. See Figure 5-7.

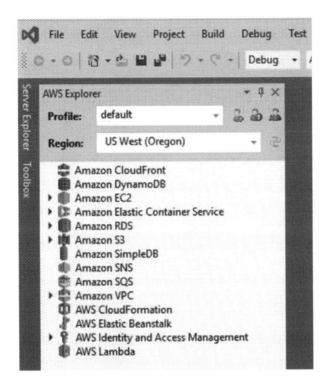

Figure 5-7. *AWS Toolkit additions to Visual Studio Explorer*

Right-clicking your development project in the Solution Explorer gives you the option to **Publish to AWS Elastic Beanstalk**. We will discuss Elastic Beanstalk shortly. But this gives you an example of how easy it is to deploy into AWS once the AWS Toolkit for VS is installed.

Going back to VS Explorer and selecting the AWS Region to which you are deploying, as well as the service you are using, will show you what applications are running on what service in the selected region. Choosing **View Status** gives you additional information on the application running on that AWS Service including some AWS CloudWatch Monitoring metrics, the ability to change the instance types running your code, what resources are in use, as well as configuring Load Balancers and Auto Scaling Groups. All from within your Visual Studio screen.

To store your code, you have the option of committing directly to an AWS CodeCommit repo that you can set up and share with your team. Again, all from within Visual Studio.

As mentioned earlier, you can create and deploy directly to AWS Lambda via the **New Project** wizard (Figure 5-8) which also provides several Serverless Blueprints on which to base your application.

You've also got the option to deploy your code directly to a Docker Container running via AWS Elastic Container Service (ECS). It's also a great way of creating AWS CloudFormation templates inside the most popular developer IDE. The CloudFormation editor includes some neat features such as auto-completion and JSON validation as well as prebuilt templates (Figure 5-8) covering a host of solutions such as SharePoint farms.

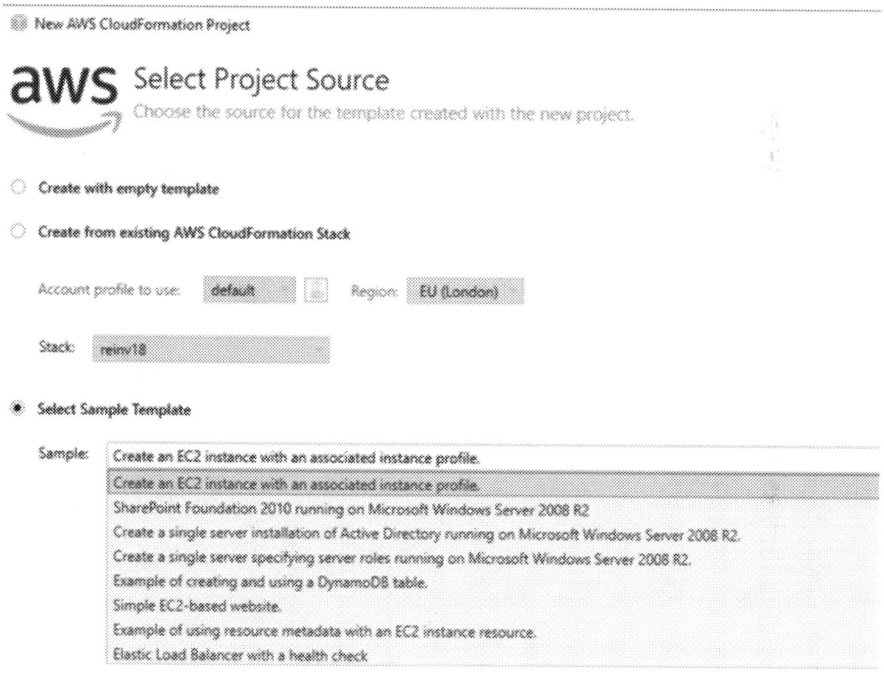

Figure 5-8. *AWS CloudFormation sample templates*

One of the features that I think is invaluable is the Cost Estimator.

Once you've completed your CloudFormation template, you can select **Estimate Cost** from the **Template** menu (Figure 5-9). This starts the Cost Estimator wizard which requires you to input any parameters your CloudFormation template might require. The wizard then uses the resources from your CloudFormation template alongside the parameters you entered to launch the AWS Simple Monthly Calculator and pre-populate all the fields. AWS pricing is incredibly dynamic, so using the AWS Simple Monthly Calculator as the single source of pricing truth allows an accurate estimate and allows you to save and share those costs inside your business.

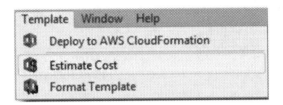

Figure 5-9. *AWS Cost Explorer inside Visual Studio*

AWS Tools for PowerShell

As a .NET developer, you have a lot of support on the AWS platform; there's the AWS SDK for .NET, but if you also use PowerShell, and it's commonplace for developers to do this, then there is also the AWS Tools for PowerShell.

You can get started here (`https://aws.amazon.com/powershell/`) and download the tools from the PowerShell Gallery (Figure 5-10).

aws

1,216,750
Downloads

25,666
Downloads of 4.1.10.0
View full stats

3/23/2021
Last Published

Info

Project Site
License Info
Contact Owners
Report

AWS.Tools.Common 4.1.10.0

The AWS Tools for PowerShell lets developers and administrators man
scripting environment. In order to manage each AWS service, install th
AWS.Tools.S3...).
The module AWS.Tools.Installer (https://www.powershellgallery.com/pa
install, up
+ Show more

Minimum PowerShell version
5.1

˅ Installation Options

| Install Module | Azure Automation | Manual Download |

Copy and Paste the following command to install this package us

```
PS> Install-Module -Name AWS.Tools.Common
```

Figure 5-10. *AWS Tools for PowerShell*

Once installed and configured to use your AWS account, you'll have access to several thousand cmdlets covering the vast majority of AWS services.

If you also use the standard AWS CLI (command-line interface), then you could try the `Get-awscmdletname -Awsclicommand "<name of cli command>"` to provide you with the name of the equivalent PowerShell cmdlet to use.

Infrastructure as Code

Although not strictly *Development*, we need to discuss our Infrastructure as Code options such as AWS CloudFormation, HashiCorp's Terraform, and AWS's Cloud Development Kit. We learned from the previous section that we can easily create and deploy AWS CloudFormation templates in Visual Studio.

But what do we mean by Infrastructure as Code?

Taking you back to Chapter 2 where we provided an AWS 101, we mentioned that one of the benefits of the AWS Cloud is that it's a fully API-driven web services platform. This allows you to issue a command from your machine that can create or change one of the AWS Services in your account.

```
for region in `aws ec2 describe-regions --output text | cut -f3`; do
echo -e "\nInstances in: '$region':"; aws ec2 describe-instances --query
'Reservations[*].Instances[*].InstanceId' --output text --region $region; done
```

The preceding code uses the AWS command-line tools to call the `Describe-instances` API for the AWS EC2 service in every region, giving us an output of every EC2 instance running in every region within our account. I run this command locally, which sends the API call to one of the AWS EC2 endpoints over the Internet. The AWS command-line tools encrypt this call, and I use the access ID and secret key for my IAM user to ensure I'm hitting the right AWS account.

If we can create, read, and describe things programmatically in our account, then we can create an entire infrastructure using just a few lines of code.

Think about this for a second.

If I can *program* my cloud infrastructure, then that opens up a whole host of possibilities for how I build, deploy, and manage my cloud. We will touch upon the unlimited potential of using the AWS .NET SDK shortly, but right now let's discuss how we can programmatically provision multiple data centers worth of infrastructure using AWS CloudFormation.

AWS CloudFormation, in the same way as HashiCorp's Terraform, is a *Declarative* Language. I use the word Language very carefully here since it's not a standard development language like C# or Python. Effectively, it's a clever configuration file that can do some neat tricks.

Both CloudFormation and Terraform have a similar structure, and both can use JSON or YAML syntax.

Inside our template, we describe what **Resources** we require to be built and how they should be configured. The beauty of creating your infrastructure in this way is that, as with all development code, it can be committed to a code control repo and versioned so that I can see a complete history of changes that have been made to our cloud infrastructure by my team. If we strictly use templating to create our cloud environment, then it avoids the issues caused by making small unrecorded changes that lead to configuration drift and increases resolution time when errors occur.

If my template is configured correctly, then I can actually use the same code to create a mirror of my cloud environment in an entirely different Region. I simply run the AWS CloudFormation template in that region and wait for it to complete.

Since CloudFormation is an AWS service, then new AWS services are required to be compatible with it either at launch or within a set time limit afterward. There is no such requirement for HashiCorp's Terraform, and so it tends to play catch-up, but not by much; Terraform is extremely popular and cloud agnostic. Although any template you write is specific to the cloud it was developed for, an Azure template won't run on AWS and so on. As you can see, it's cloud agnostic but in the loosest sense of the word.

Templating your cloud infrastructure has a lot of benefits, but in larger environments, AWS CloudFormation templates can become very long. This is why AWS launched AWS CloudFormation StackSets which modularize those large CloudFormation templates and allow you to use different templates as building blocks for other deployments in your account. StackSets are mainly used in larger multi-account environments.

If direct coding is not your passion, then AWS give you the option of the AWS CloudFormation Designer (Figure 5-11), which allows you to design your environment using only a few clicks of your mouse and will output a full CloudFormation template for you.

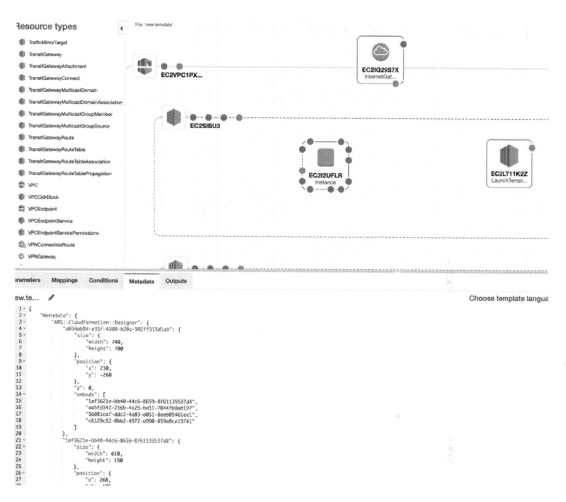

Figure 5-11. *AWS CloudFormation Designer*

There is another option when it comes to Infrastructure as Code. In 2018, AWS released its Cloud Deployment Kit (AWS CDK) which brings all the benefits of Infrastructure as Code to standard development languages such as JavaScript, Python, TypeScript, Java, and also C#. CDK is revelatory in allowing you to create complex cloud environments very easily with a small amount of coding, including .NET.

The example in Figure 5-12 creates a brand-new VPC in our account and an AWS ECS cluster.

```
1  const vpc = new ec2.Vpc(this, 'MyAppVpc', {maxAZs: 2});
2  const cluster = new ecs.Cluster(this, 'MyAppEcsCluster', {vpc: vpc}};
3  const fargateService = new ecs_patterns.LoadBalancedFargateService(this,
4  'MyAppFargateService', {
5                      cluster: cluster,
6                      containerPort: 3000,
7                       image: ecs.ContainerImage.fromAsset(_dirname + '/../app')
8                       }
```

Figure 5-12. CDK example

This small amount of code (Figure 5-12) is the equivalent of approximately 700 lines of the AWS CloudFormation template! This example was taken from a demo by AWS's Principal Evangelist, Martin Beeby, which can be found at the following address: https://youtu.be/bz4jTx4v-l8.

AWS CDK takes cloud deployments to a new level and has .NET compatibility built-in, so there is no need for your team to learn a new language. In late 2019, AWS released the CDK Explorer for Visual Studio Code. This allows you to create CDK apps, directly from Visual Studio Code.

AWS Elastic Beanstalk

AWS Elastic Beanstalk seems to have been around for a long time, and I'm always amazed by how many customers completely rely on it for all of their production deployments, even though its deployment functionality can be found in the newer AWS Code* suite of developer-focused services. My customers love the simplicity of AWS Elastic Beanstalk, and it provides them with all the functionality they require as a complete managed service. You develop the code and leave the cloud deployment to AWS Elastic Beanstalk.

AWS Elastic Beanstalk is so popular because it's so easy to use, but that doesn't mean it's not powerful. You give it your application, and it will create an AWS infrastructure to run it. When it was launched, the benefit of using AWS Elastic Beanstalk over the Chef-compatible deployment service AWS OpsWorks was the native .NET support and the fact that you could easily do Blue-Green deployment option. But the Elastic Beanstalk team has quietly listened to its users and added a whole range of cool features.

It can be used for a whole host of different programming languages and even Docker Containers using either Amazon EC2 for a single container or AWS ECS for multi-container support.

AWS Elastic Beanstalk's beauty is that everything is preconfigured for you. At the welcome screen, you can get up and running within a minute just by giving your application a name and selecting what programming platform it should sit on.

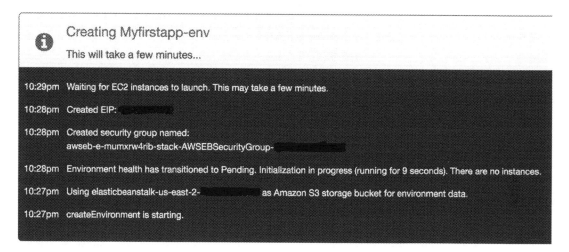

Figure 5-13. *AWS Elastic Beanstalk creates an infrastructure for your application*

Once your application has been deployed (Figure 5-13), you are given a unique URL such as `http://myfirstapp-env.uniqueid.us-east-2.elasticbeanstalk.com/` (Figure 5-14).

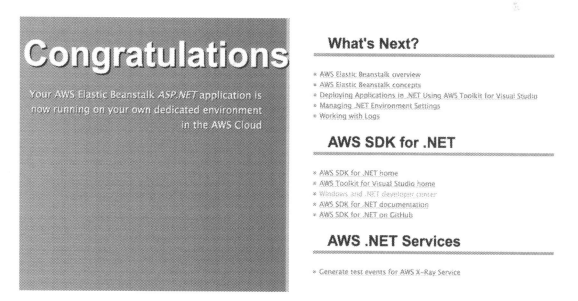

Figure 5-14. *Our published ASP.NET application*

Even though the whole infrastructure has been created for you by the AWS Elastic Beanstalk service, that doesn't mean that you are stuck with the defaults it sets for you. You can actually configure a whole host of components that make up your application infrastructure. You can also monitor your AWS Elastic Beanstalk applications from this single screen, check log files, and create and monitor events and alarms (Figure 5-15).

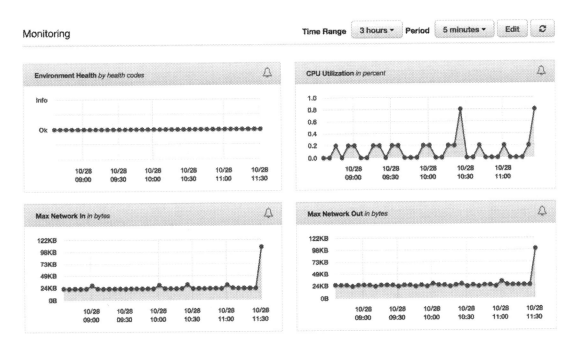

Figure 5-15. *AWS Elastic Beanstalk monitors the application we've just published*

AWS Elastic Beanstalk has its own command-line interface (CLI), and you can also connect to other AWS Services via it, for example, if you need a database, then you can create an Amazon RDS instance from within AWS Elastic Beanstalk, and it will integrate the RDS instance with your application environment.

There are no costs associated with using the actual AWS Elastic Beanstalk service, but you will incur costs for the resources that are used by your application such as EC2 or RDS.

Application Architecture

.NET was released in 2002 when the IT world thought about application architecture a lot differently than it does today. Let's not beat ourselves up about this. It was a different time, and IT infrastructure was implemented in a different way than it is today, so it made sense that application architecture followed that pattern.

Following the design principles used by mainframes in the Jurassic era, applications were typically created as monoliths with all available functionality added to a very large, single package, to be run on a very large single server, in a very singular single data center. Client/server architectures moved some of the processing to the application client running on a workstation. Web Services moved the processing to the browser, but back-end application systems and the application architecture they served did not change significantly during this time.

Distributed Systems as a concept is rooted in the early 1980s, but it took the AWS Cloud platform to realize this benefit for the average business.

We discussed High Availability in both Chapters 3 and 4, and we have to also approach the subject in this chapter but from a development perspective.

It's a long-established AWS mantra to advise developers to create loosely coupled software. This messaging can be found in everything that AWS produces that is aimed at the development community – whether it's whitepapers, presentations at summits, or their YouTube channel as well as in the AWS Certifications that are available.

The move from applications being tightly coupled to loosely coupled, in theory, doesn't need to be too complex and should be relatively pain free – using Amazon Elastic Load Balancers (ELB) and Amazon Simple Queue Service (SQS) as services between the layers in an application architecture. AWS provides lots of advice on this topic such as this blog post: `https://aws.amazon.com/blogs/compute/building-loosely-coupled-scalable-c-applications-with-amazon-sqs-and-amazon-sns/`.

As you can see in (Figure 5-16) the comparison of a standard three-tier application stack, the left-hand side design has single points of failure, giving us concern not only in availability but also performance bottlenecks. Moving to the right-hand side design, you can see the use of Amazon Elastic Load Balancers at the Presentation layer, which are now also part of an AWS Auto Scaling Group using the number of web connections as a metric for the ASG's expansion.

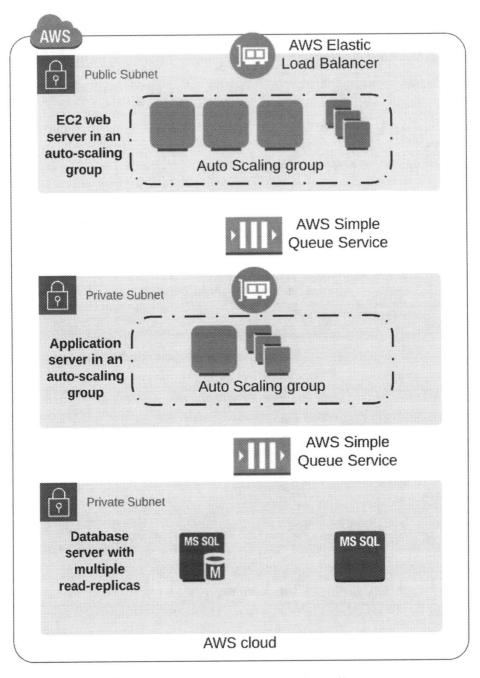

Figure 5-16. *Using SQS to loosely couple a customer ordering system*

We are also using Amazon SQS to provide communication between Web and Application tiers. To complete this design, we have implemented Read Replicas on our Database layer.

If we are really embracing the potential that AWS offers, then we can include a few more AWS Services in the preceding design to improve performance, such as AWS ElastiCache for local web server caching or maybe Amazon CloudFront to deliver static web content globally via the AWS CDN network. Are we doing complex queries at the database level? Would a move to Amazon Aurora, a relational database, or DynamoDB, a highly available NoSQL database, be a better fit and more performant at a lower cost?

Immutable Infrastructures

If the way we think about developing software has changed with the advent of Public Cloud Platforms, then we must acknowledge that the way we implement the application infrastructure has also undergone a substantial shift since the rise in popularity of AWS.

Pre-cloud our infrastructure design would have a single goal – to stay up and running for as long as possible.

We would perform maintenance on our infrastructure to ensure it stayed healthy and kept running – security patches, application updates, and so on. This is called *Mutable Infrastructure* because it can change after the initial build.

The benefit of having an API-Driven Cloud Platform enables deployment tools such as Jenkins, Chef, Puppet, and so on and leads to the ability to create an *Immutable Infrastructure* where the developer commits code which then triggers a deployment pipeline workflow and builds an entirely new application infrastructure as part of that deployment pipeline. The previous infrastructure is then removed.

Having the benefit of rebuilding your application infrastructure each time using the latest Amazon Machine Image (AMI), which already contains the latest security patches, means that those common housekeeping tasks don't need to be undertaken, and our infrastructure remains immutable until the next time code is committed.

We discussed in Chapter 3 the use of services such as AWS Image Builder and AWS Systems Manager which coupled together can provide a full infrastructure build pipeline ready for your latest application version to be deployed using the AWS Code * services we will discuss next.

But is this immutable nirvana just for those environments running Linux? Not at all, it is perfectly possible to use the same methodology for those of us running Microsoft workloads.

Here is a great example of an AWS customer doing just that. Tandem Bank run a full Microsoft stack and moved away from Azure to find a home at AWS to run their fully Immutable Microsoft infrastructure (`https://tech.newstatesman.com/it-leaders/ tandem-bank-goes-all-in-with-aws-and-infrastructure-as-code-in-bid-to- improve-agility`).

AWS Developer Services

During AWS re:Invent 2014, AWS announced three new developer-focused services: AWS CodeCommit, AWS CodePipeline, and AWS CodeDeploy. These were later joined by additional services, AWS CodeBuild, AWS CodeStar, and the acquisition of Cloud9 to give us the cloud-based IDE AWS Cloud9.

In this section, we take a whistle stop tour of each of the AWS Developer Services starting at the beginning with committing our application to a repo.

AWS CodeCommit

Version control is a very important part of the development cycle, and this function has been ably taken care of by the Git command, built into Linux distros since 2005.

AWS CodeCommit implements Git in a scalable, redundant, and durable manner with the focus on ensuring that your projects are secure and accessible. AWS CodeCommit uses encrypted repos, with Access Control provided by Amazon IAM or federated users. AWS CodeCommit is a fully managed service; therefore, scaling resource is automatic and lets you get on with the business of code development rather than infrastructure capacity control (Figure 5-17).

What I find most useful about AWS CodeCommit is the integration, not only with other AWS Developer Services but also the close integration with Visual Studio. From Visual Studio, I can commit my code to an AWS CodeCommit repo via Team Explorer in the same way I can commit to Local Git or Visual Studio Team Services (Azure DevOps).

Setting up AWS CodeCommit within Visual Studio is straightforward. Visual Studio will need access to AWS CodeCommit, and therefore you'll need to create a new IAM User for this task. Always adhering to a policy of Least Privilege, the following URL details a number of IAM Policies that can be used with AWS CodeCommit: `https://docs.aws.amazon.com/codecommit/latest/userguide/auth-and-access-control-iam-identity-based-access-control.html`.

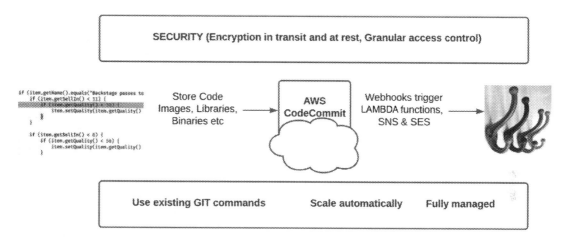

Figure 5-17. *AWS CodeCommit*

AWS CodeBuild

Continuous Integration and Continuous Delivery (CI/CD) are two terms used in modern development practices. Although the concept was around before AWS, CI/CD owes a debt to Cloud Platforms and the way in which infrastructure and services can be created via API calls. Being able to push code updates often is a trait used in our new DevOps development methodology. Almost all tech-savvy companies deploy code several times a day, and it's easy to understand why given their large geographically disperse development teams.

Continuous Integration is a process used after a developer has committed their code to a repository such as AWS CodeCommit. The act of committing to the repo kickstarts an automated process where the code is sent to a *build* server which provides automated building of that source code and then automated testing to ensure that it works.

When you have a large development project with multiple developers involved, then Continuous Integration would be used to ensure that all these separate items of source code can function by themselves and also as part of the larger development project.

This is the job that AWS CodeBuild conducts as part of a full CI/CD pipeline (we will get to pipelines next) and is an integral part of the development workflow. AWS CodeBuild works natively with .NET Core, but can also work with .NET Standard with some slight tweaks which are detailed here: `https://aws.amazon.com/blogs/devops/extending-aws-codebuild-with-custom-build-environments-for-the-net-framework/`.

To create your build, you have to provide AWS CodeBuild with a Build Project via a `buildspec.yml` file. The Build Project details all the environment and commands you wish to run on your source code when the build commences.

AWS CodePipeline

If Continuous Integration provides the process to automatically build and test each committed piece of code, then what happens after that?

Continuous Delivery is used to release that tested code to an environment such as production, UAT, or staging. Facebook releases updates to their platform several times every hour, and they all go via an elaborate delivery pipeline where after internal testing the new code is released to 2% of its user base where they collect any monitoring alerts and user feedback before pushing the release across its platform.

AWS CodePipeline covers the whole CI/CD process and integrates with all the other AWS Development services to ensure that every step can be fully automated.

Creating a pipeline using the built-in wizard requires at least two stages: a Source stage and either a Build or Deployment stage. It uses other AWS Services or third-party services like GitHub or Jenkins as Action Providers to carry out tasks at each stage you define.

Since AWS CodePipeline controls the CI/CD process, it is language independent and can be used with providers that are compatible with both .NET Core and .NET Standard.

AWS CodeDeploy

It's common to struggle with the difference between Continuous Delivery and Continuous Deployment. My understanding is that Continuous Delivery doesn't necessarily mean that your code is delivered to a production environment. It could simply be delivered to staging/pre-prod/UAT or any other environment you run. On the other hand, Continuous Deployment provides an automated mechanism for deployment through all your environments and into production.

Either way, AWS CodeDeploy helps you deliver (and deploy!) your code onto Compute services such as Amazon EC2, AWS ECS, AWS Fargate, or even on-premises servers.

There are multiple deployment methods created over the course of time that help developers deploy their code safely. AWS CodeDeploy chooses the two most popular methods, that is, Rolling and Blue-Green.

AWS CodeDeploy is configured per application. The first step is to decide on which Compute platform you'll deploy to – Amazon EC2 or on-premises servers, Amazon ECS, or AWS Lambda. Next, you create a Deployment Group which specifies where and how to deploy your application. When creating a Deployment Group for the first time, you'll need to specify a **Service role**.

We discuss AWS IAM (Identity and Access Management) in Chapter 11, but briefly an IAM Service Role provides permissions for one AWS service to use another. To use AWS CodeDeploy, you'll need to create a Service Role and assign that new role permissions. AWS CodeDeploy comes with a number of pre-created permissions such as **AWSCodeDeployRole** for Amazon EC2 or **AWSCodeDeployRoleForECS** or **AWSCodeDeployRoleForLambda**. These three roles give a significant amount of access from the AWS CodeDeploy service to the other Compute services. You can limit the amount of permissions AWS CodeDeploy has by using the **AWSCodeDeployRoleForECSLimited** role or creating a bespoke permission set yourself using the details found in the User Guide:

```
https://docs.aws.amazon.com/codedeploy/latest/userguide/getting-started-
create-service-role.html
```

Once you've got the correct Service Role, then you have the options of In-place or Blue/Green deployments followed by a way to filter what EC2 Instances (or containers) to deploy to using Tags or Tag Groups.

Deployment Settings provide a way of tailoring the exact way in which you will deploy your new application. Since In-place deployments take an instance offline in order to deploy your code, Deployment Settings allow you to specify to do that *One EC2 Instance at a time, Half of your instances at a time*, or *All at once*. You can also be very granular by creating your own Deployment Configuration which allows you to specify a percentage or number of healthy Instances to leave untouched while your other Instances are being updated.

AWS CodeStar

So far, we've discussed four separate AWS services (CodeCommit, CodePipeline, CodeBuild, and CodeDeploy) that form the basis of a full CI/CD development process for your code. But that's four services that you have to understand, configure, and manage. AWS CodeStar provides a streamlined interface (Figure 5-18) to configure all of these services at once.

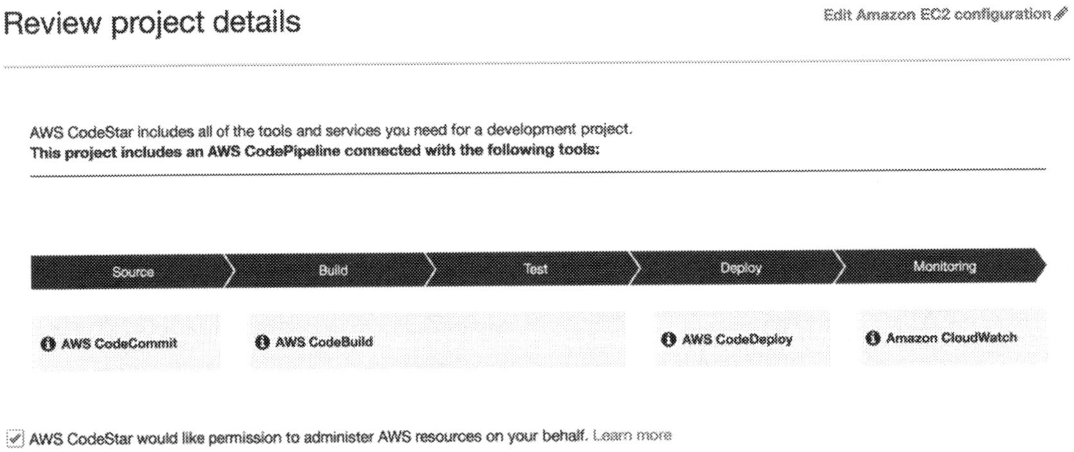

Figure 5-18. *AWS CodeStar project screen*

AWS CodeStar can be used with a number of different programming languages including a C# ASP.NET Core template that comes with the service. Others include Go, Java, Node, Python, Ruby, and PHP.

The *raison d'être* of the service is to make the whole development process very easy to configure so that you can get results fast. And it does this well.

As soon as you give your new project a name, an AWS CodeCommit repo is created with the same name, and all service roles are created for you. You also have the choice of using GitHub as your development repo, and again CodeStar handles the permissions here with a simple **Connect to GitHub** button.

Next, AWS CodeStar needs to know what development IDE you wish to use so that it can configure the service for the right environment (Figure 5-19).

Pick how you want to edit your code

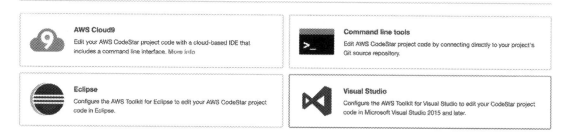

Figure 5-19. *AWS CodeStar needs to know what IDE you are going to use*

As you can see in Figure 5-19, Visual Studio is one of the options you have here, and you are given full instructions on how to configure Visual Studio to work with AWS CodeStar. Within AWS CodeStar, you have full access to each stage which redirects you to the individual AWS service, fully configured, via AWS CodeStar.

One of the main features is teamwork. You can add multiple users to this project and have them all work together (Figure 5-20). It also integrates with Atlassian's Jira product.

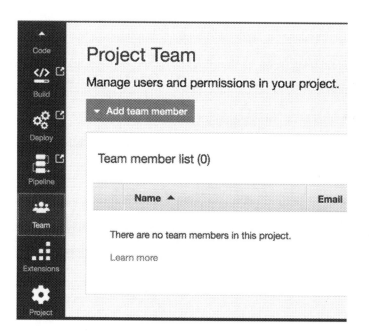

Figure 5-20. *AWS CodeStar allows multiple users to work on the same project*

AWS Cloud9

Cloud9 (`www.c9.io`) was created in 2010 and acquired by AWS in 2016 and launched as a service during AWS re:Invent 2017. It provides a full development IDE (Integrated Development Environment) that can be used by multiple developers at the same time to collaborate on the same project.

AWS Cloud9 provides a full environment from within a browser. This brings a huge range of benefits since there is nothing to install on a local machine and allows the developer to use any device to read and write code.

AWS Cloud9 also integrates with the previously mentioned AWS CodeStar if you decide you rather not use Visual Studio. Although it's been a much requested feature for some time, AWS Cloud9 doesn't natively support .NET out of the box.

However, there is a way around this if you want to use AWS Cloud9 today to develop your .NET Core applications.

The full instructions for this process can be found here: `https://docs.aws.amazon.com/cloud9/latest/user-guide/sample-dotnetcore.html`.

Before we get started, we will need an existing AWS Cloud9 environment, and you can fire one of these up very easily from within the AWS Management Console and search for Cloud9.

Click the Create Environment button, provide a name and answers for some simple configuration questions such as Instance Type and Platform, and an environment will be created for you within a few minutes.

Once the environment is created, then open the IDE (Integrated Development Environment), and you see the console section of the IDE at the bottom of your screen (Figure 5-21).

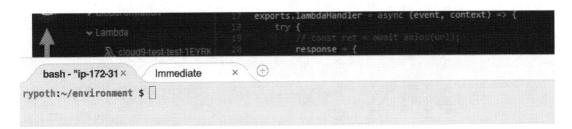

Figure 5-21. *AWS Cloud9 console*

Let's install the .NET Core SDK using the following commands in the console:

```
sudo yum -y update
```

```
sudo yum -y install libunwind
```

```
wget https://dot.net/v1/dotnet-install.sh
```

```
sudo chmod u=rx dotnet-install.sh
```

```
./dotnet-install.sh -c Current
```

In the documentation, the next step is to use VI to append the .dotnet folder to the PATH. One tip here is if VI seems far too confusing for its own good (and it is), then you can do the same using nano ~./bashrc.

Load and test the .NET Core SDK by entering the following in the Cloud9 console:

```
. ~/.bashrc
dotnet --help
```

AWS's instructions continue to create a new C# project, build the code, and create a runner and finally allow you to run your .NET Core C# code inside AWS Cloud9 with success (Figure 5-22).

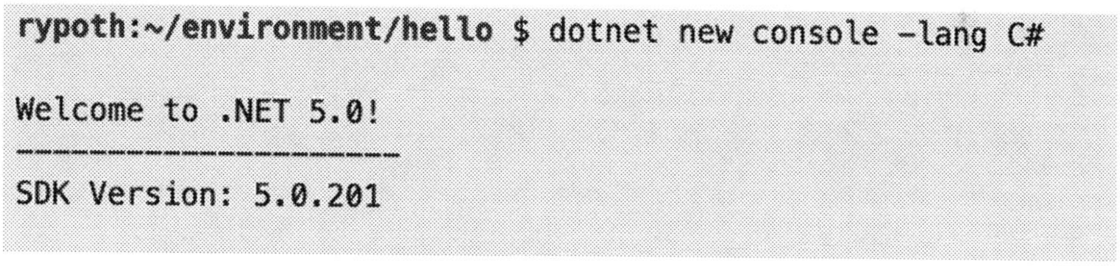

```
rypoth:~/environment/hello $ dotnet new console —lang C#

Welcome to .NET 5.0!
---------------------
SDK Version: 5.0.201
```

Figure 5-22. *Successfully running .NET Core inside AWS Cloud9*

Summary

I hope after reading this chapter you'd agree with me that AWS is not only the best platform for developers but also the best platform for .NET developers.

AWS has shown a strong commitment to the .NET community, recently becoming a corporate sponsor of the .NET Foundation (dotnetfoundation.org) which is an independent organization made up of members of the .NET community.

"Developing for the Windows platform" has evolved to become "Developing using Microsoft tools and languages" as Microsoft slowly becomes far more platform agnostic than ever before in its existence.

2020 and 2021 will see the biggest changes to .NET since it was created, and AWS is perfectly placed to help its customers develop cross-platform applications using .NET 5.0 today and .NET 6.0 when it is finally released.

If you attend the many virtual or physical AWS Summits and Conferences AWS holds globally, you'll find helpful .NET developer advocates and evangelists who are happy to share their experience with you.

AWS continues to create services aimed at developers, and in this chapter, we've learned about its Toolkit for Visual Studio, AWS Elastic Beanstalk, and the Code Suite of services from AWS CodeCommit through to AWS CodeStar via CodeBuild, CodePipeline, and CodeDeploy.

Build on!

CHAPTER 6

Serverless

In retrospect, it was an obvious thing to do; AWS had for a long time developed services that abstracted the user or application away from the underlying infrastructure, such as the database service Amazon RDS.

But the repercussion of introducing an AWS Service that simply ran your code without the need for a server is slowly but surely changing the IT industry and is certainly seen by all as the way forward for traditional application development.

For the last 30 years, we've bought, built, run, and managed servers – physical servers, virtual servers, LPARs, desktops, virtual desktops. And the whole concept of a server over traditional desktop PCs is focused on availability and performance. All in aid of one thing. To run your code.

Just take a moment to think of all the tasks we do to make sure that our servers run the application code we need them to – monitoring, availability, backup, performance, and so on. All of these tasks have a hundred subtasks, capacity management, data synchronization, restoration playbooks, application performance management.

AWS Lambda does just one thing. It runs your code.

And this simple service has ushered in a whole new area of IT, with countless businesses now looking at their legacy applications and questioning whether to develop them to run on traditional servers/EC2 Instances or as part of a Serverless solution architecture. There is a growing community of Serverless Champions covering not only AWS Lambda but also Azure and Google Functions, which are similar services on the other two large cloud platforms.

© Ryan Pothecary 2021
R. Pothecary, *Running Microsoft Workloads on AWS*, https://doi.org/10.1007/978-1-4842-6628-1_6

AWS Lambda completely isolates your code from the underlying infrastructure it uses, ensuring you have no servers to manage. Considering that costs are in the ballpark of $0.20 for 1 million requests per month and you are charged per 1ms of compute you use, then you realize that moving to this Serverless nirvana can be very cost-effective. Just a few years ago, companies bought physical servers which lasted 3 years and kept them running 24/7; now they are running Amazon EC2 Instances which are billed per hour (or per second), and you stop paying when they are stopped. Finally, with AWS Lambda, they pay only for the milliseconds that our code takes to execute. Companies never pay for idle CPU cycles, no servers to manage, no worrying about security patches. Don't you agree that this is revolutionary?

Let's look at the benefits:

- No infrastructure to provision or manage

- Automatic scaling to give you performance when you need it

- Never pay for idle CPU servers

- High Availability and security built-in

- The fastest way to get code running

- Perfect for innovation

Event-Driven Architecture

AWS Lambda's ability to connect with other Services and respond to Events has led to a resurgence in Event-Driven Architectures, an application architecture that aligns with the loosely coupled mantra that guides AWS and drives businesses like Netflix and Amazon.com.

AWS Lambda can be the *Action* triggered by an *Event* from another service.

In Event-Driven Architectures, code from state are separated and decoupled from one another. Integration between functions is done with messaging services like Amazon SQS which create asynchronous connections.

Apart from full-scale application architectures, AWS Lambda can be used to proactively manage your cloud infrastructure. From a Microsoft workload's perspective, AWS Lambda has been able to run .NET Core and PowerShell Core for quite some time and continues to be a part of its road map with recent additions of custom runtimes which allow runtime libraries, not natively supported to be added, including C++.

Under the Hood

AWS Lambda completely abstracts the compute layer from running code. But what's underneath it all?

AWS has been quite forthcoming in what is behind its Lambda service. Although there isn't a single whitepaper that explains everything, you can find insights provided by AWS presenters during global summits and re:Invents. As mentioned, there is a growing Serverless community and User Groups which AWS Evangelists often attend to share and answer questions.

AWS Lambda has evolved considerably since its introduction in 2014. At first, each AWS Lambda service used a private EC2 Instance in order to run the users' code. This was a first step or minimum viable product (MVP) as they describe; it met all the goals of the service and ensured that one customer's code would remain private and secure. However, it's true to say that AWS had not imagined the number of users who took up the service and the way customers are using it today with trillions of Lambda function executions per month and hundreds of thousand active customers.

After launching the service, AWS set about to make AWS Lambda more efficient while also ensuring security remained a top priority. AWS used Kernel-based Virtual Machine (KVM), a Linux virtualization technique created in 2006 and bought by Red Hat in 2008. KVM is entirely open sourced and has been part of the Linux Kernel since 2007. AWS used this technology to create its own microVM virtualization called Firecracker which was released during re:Invent 2018.

Firecracker lets you launch microVMs in a fraction of a second and is the power behind both AWS Lambda and AWS Fargate. It's a fully managed Container service that is incredibly efficient using low-overhead virtualization technology that consumes only 5MiB of memory and can start VMs in 125ms.

Rather than keep this technology proprietary, AWS open sourced the service.

Why use AWS Lambda and not just Firecracker?

AWS Lambda is a mature service and runs code in response to events created by services such as AWS CloudWatch, AWS API Gateway, and Amazon SNS. There is a lot of support for AWS Lambda, and the service is firmly integrated with Microsoft Visual Studio via the AWS Toolkit for VS.

Although Firecracker runs underneath the AWS Lambda hood, its use case is for businesses needing to use that technology rather than consume the fully managed and fully integrated AWS Lambda. If you are going to use Firecracker, you'll need more effort to achieve the same effect as creating a quick AWS Lambda function.

Amazon API Gateway

In most Serverless architectures, you'll see the use of Amazon API Gateway providing the input to your Serverless solution. This section describes Amazon API Gateway so you are familiar with it before we start to use the service.

API (Application Programming Interface) is the phrase used to describe a function that can be called to return some form of data from an external service or to execute an action. For example, if I send a request with my geographic coordinates to an online weather service such as AccuWeather, then they will send back a forecast based on my location – very much in a microservices fashion which we discuss in the next chapter.

Amazon API Gateway is a fully managed service which handles API requests (calls) from clients both internal and external. Amazon API Gateway is fully integrated with both AWS Lambda and also the AWS monitoring service CloudWatch. For access and security of your APIs, Amazon API Gateway provides a full Amazon CloudFront infrastructure to ensure protection against DDoS (Distributed Denial of Service) attacks as well as authentication security via AWS IAM, Amazon Cognito, or the recent addition of AWS Lambda Authorizers.

Amazon API Gateway manages the scalability that you'll need when your serverless application is receiving thousands of API calls by scaling up and down as needed. Amazon API Gateway Endpoints can be configured in one of three ways, which depend on where your Client API calls are going to come from:

- Edge optimized – To help you reduce client latency from anywhere on the Internet via some help from AWS CloudFront distributions

- Regional – To help you reduce latency when calls are made from the same region as the API Gateway

- Private – Used to expose APIs only from inside your Amazon VPC

Amazon API Gateway also has the ability to cache API calls from your clients in order to return often used information back to them faster.

Amazon API Gateway handles both REST APIs and WebSocket APIs, and a new feature released during re:Invent 2019 called Amazon API Gateway HTTP APIs allows for a huge reduction in cost for the customer as well as significant performance benefits and a much easier development experience.

More information on HTTP APIs with Amazon API Gateway (Figure 6-1) can be found here: `https://aws.amazon.com/blogs/compute/announcing-http-apis-for-amazon-api-gateway/`.

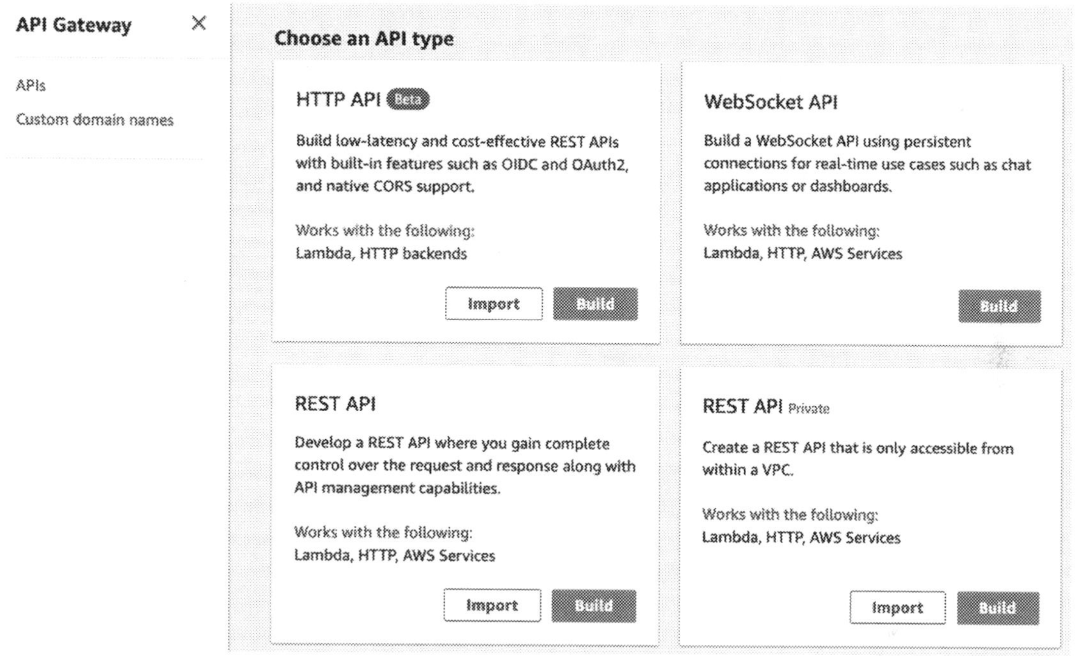

Figure 6-1. *Amazon API Gateway*

AWS DynamoDB

An important aspect of Serverless solutions is making sure there is a way to store and keep data after your Serverless function has run. Think about an AWS Lambda function that gets called every time you score a point in a video game; you'll need somewhere to store that new score after the function has ended. AWS DynamoDB is typically the service to do this.

AWS DynamoDB is a fully managed NoSQL database; availability and scalability is managed for you. There are no servers to manage. AWS DynamoDB was designed to handle OLTP (online transaction processing) workloads where the request patterns are known.

As we discussed in Chapter 4, AWS has many different types of database services, and although from a Microsoft on AWS's perspective we may be more familiar with Microsoft SQL Server, AWS certainly has options available to you should a structured relational database not fit your workload. AWS DynamoDB, for instance, is well suited to serverless workloads due to its performance and NoSQL, key-value, storage. The structure of a NoSQL database isn't a million miles away from traditional relational SQL databases; we have tables, partition keys, sort keys, the concept of a partition key, and so on. But it's the type of data that is referenced by these keys that is the difference, because each key value can be of any data type, and we don't have to specify it before we start storing the data in the database.

As with other AWS database services such as Amazon Aurora, your items within an AWS DynamoDB table are replicated with an AWS region automatically to ensure durability and availability.

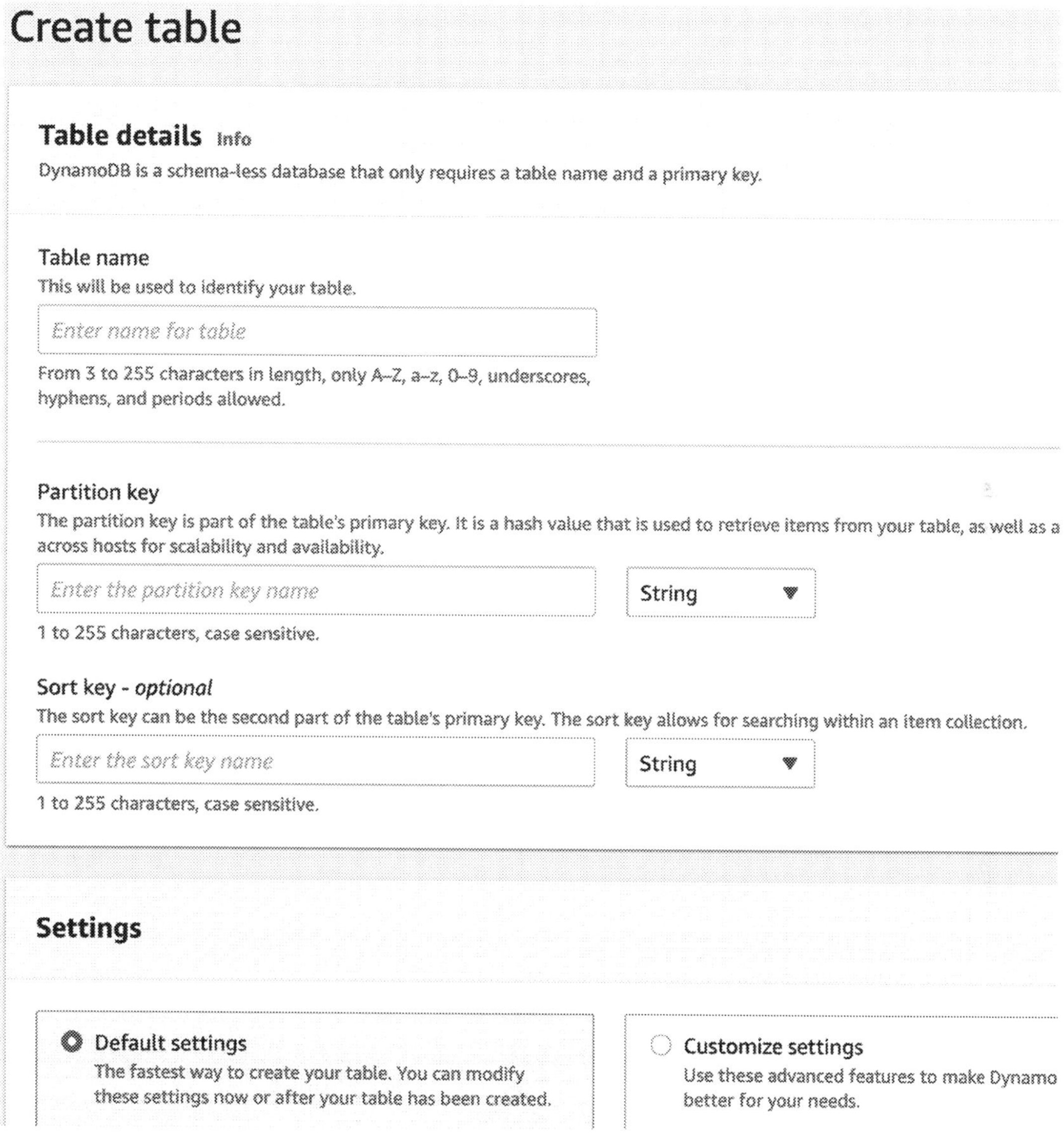

Create table

Table details Info

DynamoDB is a schema-less database that only requires a table name and a primary key.

Table name

This will be used to identify your table.

> *Enter name for table*

From 3 to 255 characters in length, only A–Z, a–z, 0–9, underscores,
hyphens, and periods allowed.

Partition key

The partition key is part of the table's primary key. It is a hash value that is used to retrieve items from your table, as well as a
across hosts for scalability and availability.

> *Enter the partition key name*   String   ▼

1 to 255 characters, case sensitive.

Sort key - *optional*

The sort key can be the second part of the table's primary key. The sort key allows for searching within an item collection.

> *Enter the sort key name*   String   ▼

1 to 255 characters, case sensitive.

Settings

⊙ Default settings	○ Customize settings
The fastest way to create your table. You can modify these settings now or after your table has been created.	Use these advanced features to make Dynamo better for your needs.

Figure 6-2. *Creating a table in AWS DynamoDB*

Table 6-1 compares a structured relational database with an unstructured key-value
database such as Amazon DynamoDB.

Table 6-1. *Comparison of SQL and NoSQL databases*

	Relational (SQL)	Key-Value (NoSQL)
Data storage	Rows and columns	Key value, document, graph
Schema	Fixed	Dynamic
Query	Using SQL statements	Focused on a collection of documents
Scaling	Vertical	Horizontal

Amazon RDS Proxy

With Amazon DynamoDB, you've got a purpose-built, high-performance, scalable database that integrates really well with AWS Lambda. But what if your AWS Lambda function needs to read or write data to a more traditional relational database?

One of the biggest issues seen when connecting to relational database servers from serverless applications is the high number of potential connections from AWS Lambda to Amazon RDS. As every new function is run, a new connection is required, so the database server spends a lot of overhead just managing connections from our application. Amazon RDS Proxy allows serverless applications to share the connections that previous serverless functions have already established between AWS Lambda and Amazon RDS.

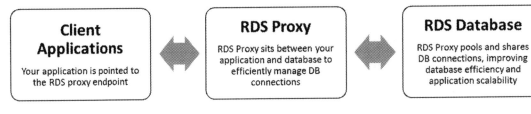

Figure 6-3. *Amazon RDS Proxy*

Amazon RDS Proxy (Figure 6-3) isn't just limited to its work with AWS Lambda, its use case covers any service or application making a high number of database connections. Serverless fit really well with this functionality.

Another nice part of this service when used with a Highly Available Multi-AZ RDS solution is that Amazon RDS Proxy will maintain all those database connections should you need to failover from your primary database server to the secondary.

To ensure that database connections are being made in a secure way, Amazon RDS Proxy integrates with Amazon IAM to authenticate each connection using a centrally managed secure connection string repository using Amazon Secrets Manager.

The Basics of a .NET Core AWS Lambda Function

AWS Lambda has the ability to run functions created in either C# .NET Core or PowerShell Core. These different Microsoft options give us a lot of breadth when it comes to how we use AWS Lambda. For instance, I can use C# to write Event-Driven Applications, whereas functions written by PowerShell Core can be used to automate the management of your AWS Cloud.

Whatever I choose to do, Microsoft Visual Studio is the best starting point.

Let's run through the creation of an AWS Lambda function via Visual Studio Professional. The first step is to create a new project using the traditional Visual Studio interface. You will then see a list of templates to use, including a large number using AWS Lambda (Figure 6-4).

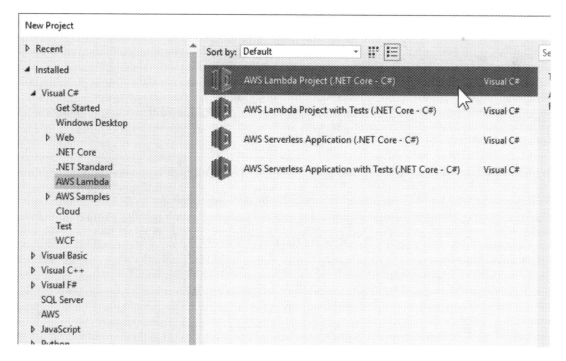

Figure 6-4. *Creating a new project using Microsoft Visual Studio*

For this example, we can select a project type of `AWS Lambda Project .NET Core C#`, and on the next screen, we can select the type of serverless application we wish to create using one of the many serverless Blueprints that are available to be used within Visual Studio (Figure 6-5).

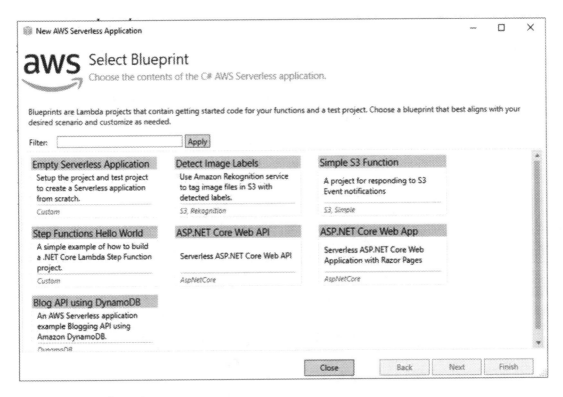

Figure 6-5. *Blueprints*

For this example, we will choose the ASP.NET Core Web App which will provide us with a fully functional ASP.NET Web App ready for us to configure. Once you select the Blueprint and click Next, Visual Studio will populate with all the files you require in the Solutions Explorer window. You can then make whatever changes you need to the code at this stage before completing the final deployment step which is to right-click the project and **Publish to AWS Lambda** (Figure 6-6).

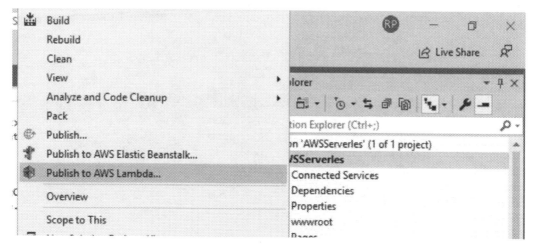

Figure 6-6. *Publish to AWS Lambda*

You are then presented with an additional two screens as part of the Publish to AWS Lambda wizard (Figure 6-7). The first screen prompts for details about the deployment such as what profile to use, what framework to use, and the name and S3 location for the CloudFormation template the wizard will create and deploy for us.

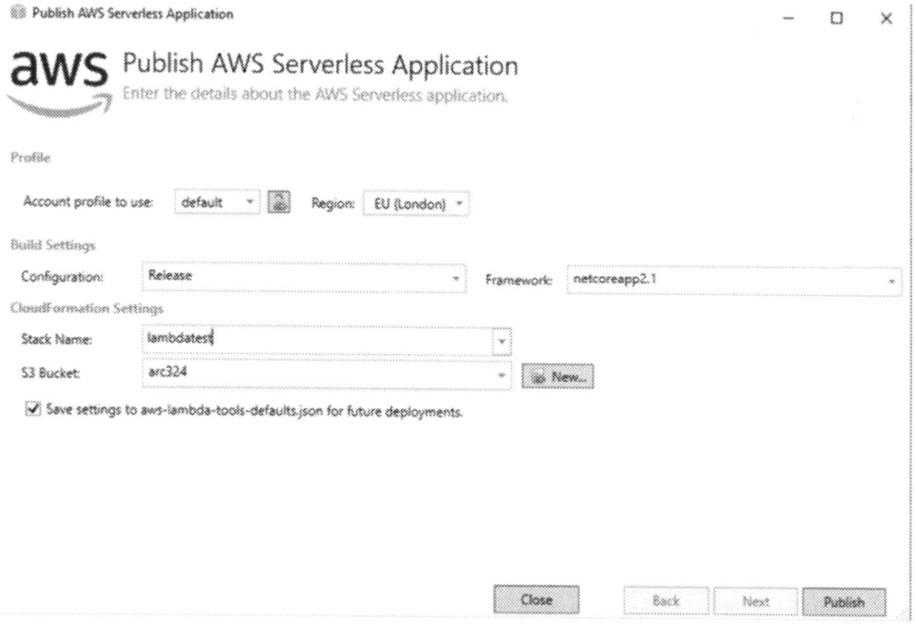

Figure 6-7. *Publish AWS Serverless Application wizard*

Once we click Publish on this screen, then the wizard will create and deploy a standard AWS CloudFormation template using all of our configuration options and our code correctly packaged ready to be run by AWS Lambda (Figure 6-8).

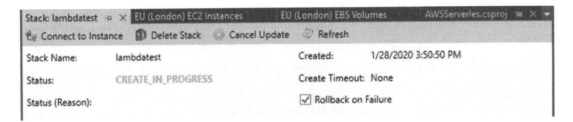

Figure 6-8. *Creating the serverless stack*

Finally, once complete, our ASP.NET Core website is available (Figure 6-9).

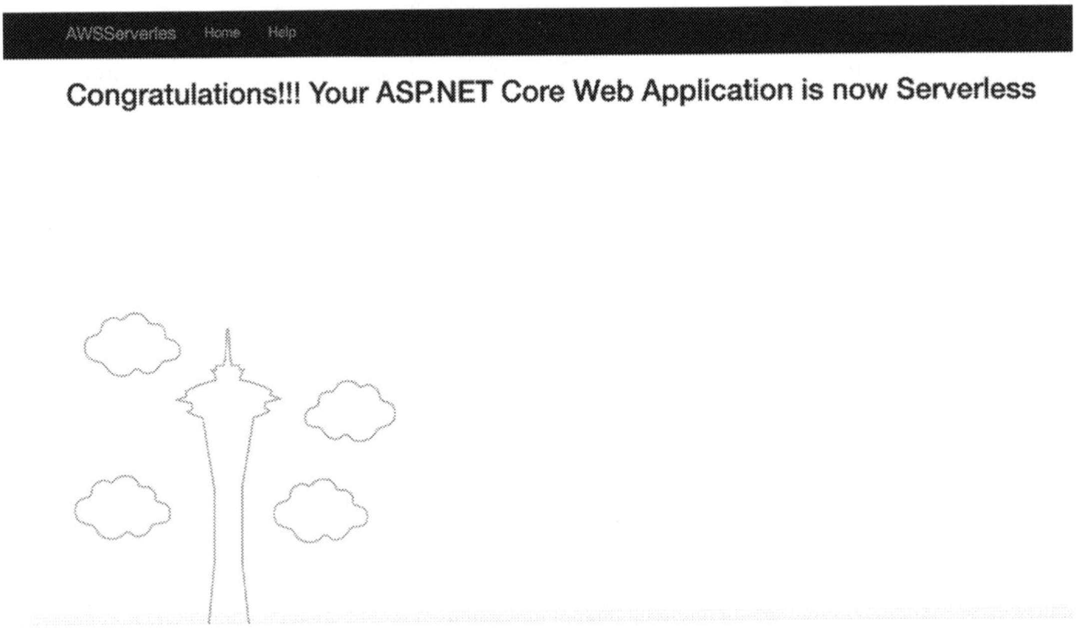

Congratulations!!! Your ASP.NET Core Web Application is now Serverless

Figure 6-9. *Our serverless ASP.NET Core web application*

The Performance of Your Function

AWS Lambda's unit of scale is concurrent executions – how many functions can run at the same time. Incoming requests need to be in line with the concurrency limits in place in the AWS Region where you create the function; otherwise, throttling can occur. But throttling is no bad thing, and you may well need to throttle requests to prevent overwhelming downstream systems.

The first time that a function is invoked, behind the scenes AWS Lambda creates an instance of the function and processes the event. Once the function has run and returned a response, it stays active and waits for similar requests to occur for this function.

There are limits to the amount of burst concurrency you can have, and the current limits are

- 3000 – US-West-1 (Oregon), US-East-1 (Virginia), EU-West-1 (Ireland)

- 1000 – AP-Northeast-1 (Tokyo), EU-Central-1 (Frankfurt)

- 500 – All other Regions

Now, imagine that you've got multiple requests coming in to run this function. AWS Lambda creates multiple instances or routes the requests to existing AWS Lambda instances that are running. After the initial burst, AWS Lambda will add a further 500 Instances every minute until you hit the concurrency limit. This is typically 1000 but can be raised with a support request.

When your function scales up, the first request served by each new instance is impacted by the time it takes to load and initialize your code. There is significant documentation, blog pages, and forum questions that tackle the subject of making your function package as streamlined as possible.

The maximum time that a function can run is 15 minutes.

Back in 2018, a blog post on behalf of the awesome cloud trainers A Cloud Guru benchmarked AWS Lambda performance against all available development languages that it supported, not including custom runtimes; you can read the full feature and follow-ons here: https://read.acloud.guru/comparing-aws-lambda-performance-of-node-js-python-java-c-and-go-29c1163c2581.

It certainly caught a lot of interest due to the results, which showed that against languages like Node.js and Python, .NET Core functions ran the fastest.

Serverless performance is incredibly important and is typically focused on the area where the Bootstrap is loading and the function is run. While there is often a lot of focus on the startup/bootstrap time, the time it takes to execute the code is also critical. Not only does execution time directly affect cost, but faster execution can reduce the level of concurrency needed.

The reason this is important is .NET Core executes Lambda faster than Node.js and Python, but its cold start time is greater. Therefore, it's good to use .NET when execution time matters, but if cold start time is really important, it either makes sense to avoid .NET Core or instead to use Provisioned Concurrency (Figure 6-10).

Download your code	Start new container	Bootstrap the runtime	Start your code
Cold Start			Warm Start
AWS optimization		Your optimization	

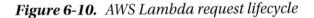

Figure 6-10. *AWS Lambda request lifecycle*

Understanding what modules you need to run your function is critical as is removing any unneeded modules – anything to reduce the time that AWS Lambda is going to need to unpack your code and start executing it.

A new feature arrived at re:Invent 2019 – AWS Lambda Provisioned Concurrency.

This really helps performance if you have functions that suffer with cold start issues. With Provisioned Concurrency, AWS Lambda keeps functions initialized and ready to respond with millisecond latency. It does this by pre-creating execution environments all the way through the Bootstrap/Init phase. There is a very small charge for using this feature, but the additional cost is often outweighed by having functions run faster overall.

There are a few things to keep in mind. Firstly, there is a soft limit of 500 provisioned executions per minute, and as mentioned earlier, the whole process is still limited to the overall burst concurrency limit per account per region.

Secondly, AWS assign less CPU burst to Provisioned Concurrency than to normal on-demand functions during the bootstrap/INIT phase, so code could take longer to execute. Finally, in order to maintain availability and help with scaling, AWS actually provision more resources than you've actually requested. You don't pay for these execution environments.

Pulling It All Together with AWS Step Functions

AWS Step Functions is a standalone service that lets you orchestrate and coordinate multiple AWS services to accomplish a task. The output of one step becomes the input for the next step.

AWS Step Functions has a nice graphical interface which lets you visualize the whole task easily. The benefit, apart from ease, of using AWS Step Functions rather than scripting a workflow is that AWS Step Functions handles errors in the subtasks intelligently. It can retry subtasks and offers tracking for each step.

AWS Step Functions works on "state" and "transitions" which are created in Amazon States Language which is JSON based. One of the challenges of using Serverless functions to run everything is handling the state between these functions. AWS Step Functions can do this for you.

Without the use of AWS Step Functions, it would be difficult to scale the development of a full-blown Serverless application using just AWS Lambda alone. AWS Step Functions orchestration is vital to pull all the individual functions together.

It also integrates with a host of services that are used regularly within a serverless solution, like Amazon DynamoDB, Amazon SNS and SQS, Container services such as Amazon ECS and Amazon Fargate, and finally Amazon SageMaker, the machine learning service. It can also integrate with other services by the use of custom connectors (Figure 6-11).

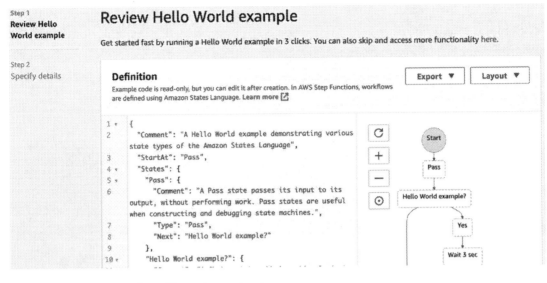

Figure 6-11. *AWS Step Functions start screen*

Let's give an overview of the specific AWS Step Functions State Language. As soon as you understand the basic commands and see some examples, I'm sure you'd agree that it's not very daunting.

```
{
        "Comment": "State Language Example",
         "StartAt" : "FirstState".
         "States" : {
                "FirstState": {
                "Type": "Task",
                "Resource": "arn.aws:lambda:us-east-1:
                012345678:function:FUNCTION_NAME",
                "End": true
                        }
                }
}
```

This will run a simple task invoking an AWS Lambda function and then exiting. There are a few other AWS Step Functions States that you can add to provide choices and so on:

- "Choice" – Provides branching logic to decide on the next State

- "Parallel" – Performs tasks in parallel

- "Pass" – Passes the input to the output without doing any work, used primarily for testing

- "Wait" – Causes the state machine to wait before commencing the next State

- "Succeed" – Terminates the state machine as a Success

- "Fail" – Terminates the state machine and marks it as a Fail

- "Map" – Processes all of the elements of an array, independent of each other

A new feature for 2020 has been AWS Step Functions Express Workflows which automatically start with events from Amazon API Gateway, AWS Lambda, and so on. Its use case is for high-volume request processing such as streaming data or IoT device ingestion. It uses in-memory processing for high-event workloads of up to 100,000 state transitions per second for a total duration of 5 minutes.

You can combine these new Express Workflows with Standard Workflows which can handle events for a longer duration. An example might be to use Express Workflows to process a stream of IoT data followed by a longer running State Machine to handle the output of that.

One thing to note with Express Workflows, whereas Standard Workflows display their history and visual debugging in the AWS Step Functions console, Express Workflows send its history to Amazon CloudWatch Logs.

Table 6-2. *Comparison between Express and Standard Workflows*

	Express Workflows	Standard Workflows
Supported execution start rate	Over 100,000 per second	Over 2000 per second
Max runtime	5 minutes	1 year
Execution guarantee	At least once	Exactly once
Execution history	Available in CloudWatch Logs	In Step Functions service

AWS Lambda Layers

AWS Lambda Layers (Figure 6-12) allow you to package a part of your function as a ZIP file, then upload it as a layer. The immediate benefit of this was to allow users to package application dependencies or even custom runtime components as an AWS Lambda Layer which you can then refer to in other Lambda functions.

If you are using multiple functions, each of which has dependencies that are common across the functions, then using AWS Lambda Layers you can separate out those dependencies into individual layers, giving you a much reduced and streamlined original Lambda function.

You can choose from up to five layers, each of which has to already be a published function in the AWS Region from which you are creating your new function, as long as your total unzipped package does not exceed the package limit of 250MB.

To do this with .NET Core, you have to use a feature that came with .NET Core 2.0 called "Runtime Package Store" which lets you package apps with links to packages that exist in the target environment. More information on Runtime Package Store can be found at https://docs.microsoft.com/en-us/dotnet/core/deploying/runtime-store.

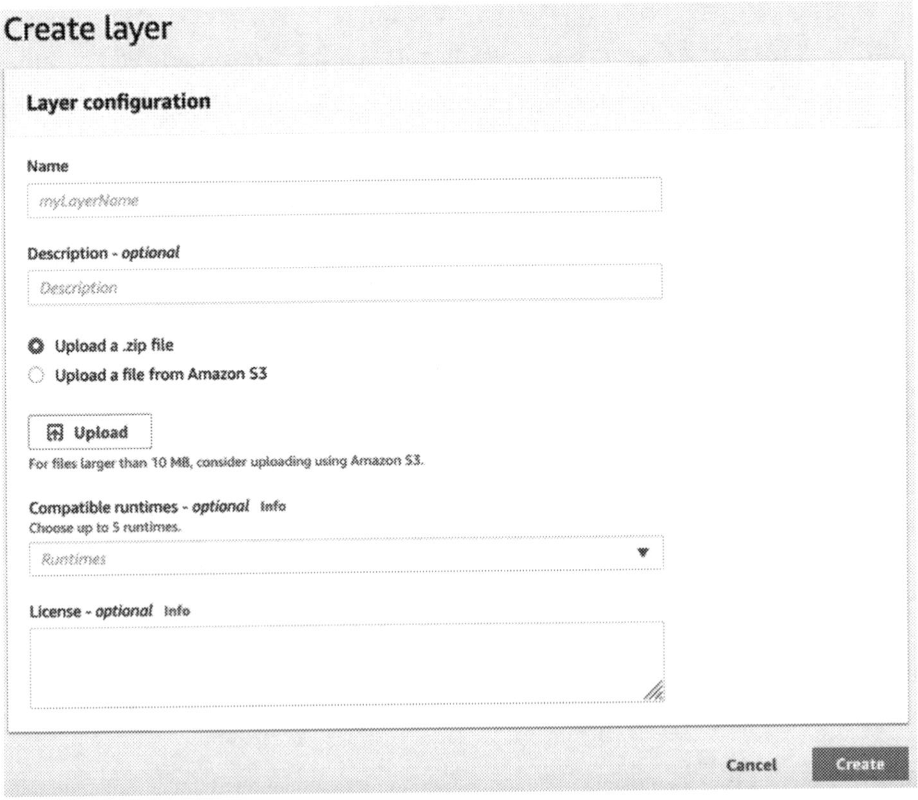

Figure 6-12. *AWS Lambda Layers*

Integrating Your Applications Using AWS EventBridge

Amazon EventBridge is a Serverless event bus that allows you to take streaming data from multiple providers such Software-as-a-Service (SaaS) applications, custom applications, and AWS Services and route that data to services like AWS Lambda, Amazon Kinesis, AWS Step Functions, Amazon SQS, Amazon SNS, and so on.

To do this, Amazon EventBridge uses the concept of Rules to provide the routing logic between the source and the target. When an Event occurs, it's evaluated against the current set of Rules, and if there is a match, then that Rule action is triggered and the Event sent to the specific target or targets. Amazon EventBridge will provide all the retry and wait services should your target not respond as expected.

The following is an example of a custom application rule:

```
service: event-bridge

provider:
 name: aws
 runtime: nodejs10.x

functions:
 notify:
   handler: handler.hello
   events:
     - eventBridge:
         eventBus: marketfeed
         pattern:
             source:
                 - feed.news.shareprice
```

We use the **NOTIFY** function to create a **Marketfeed** event bus which looks at a source of **feed.news.shareprice**.

Further information about Amazon EventBridge rules, examples, and syntax can be found here: https://docs.aws.amazon.com/eventbridge/latest/userguide/create-eventbridge-rule.html.

When Things Go Wrong – Amazon X-Ray

We discuss monitoring on AWS in Chapter 8 where we mainly focus on monitoring Amazon EC2 and Storage services. But let's take a moment to discuss how we provide insightful monitoring data across your new landscape of Serverless and containerized applications where microservices and Serverless functions run at high rates for subsecond durations.

Amazon X-Ray is the service that will help you identify latency and performance bottlenecks within your Serverless applications to help you pinpoint the issue to a specific service in your application (Figure 6-13), letting you identify the impact on users of these application issues. Using the SDK, the Amazon X-Ray library needs to be integrated with the code you are running (Figure 6-14). This library works in conjunction with the X-Ray daemon which acts as a local buffer and sends X-Ray data to the service every second.

Figure 6-13. *Amazon X-Ray service map visualization of a current trace*

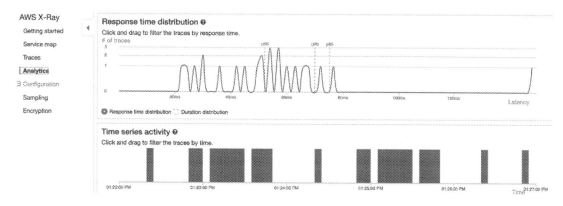

Figure 6-14. *Amazon X-Ray performance data of a web application*

Summary

AWS developed an entirely new way of providing compute resource and by doing so ushered in a new application development methodology supported by some of the most passionate development communities throughout the world. You may be using Serverless approaches for your business today, or this may be something that you'll decide to investigate further after your move to the cloud is complete.

Either way, this will be something you'll be investigating further, and the more you learn about it, the more of a convert you'll become.

In this chapter, we've taken a small step into the world of Serverless from a Microsoft .NET Core perspective. We've shown how easy it is to begin your first function using Visual Studio Serverless Blueprints and the ease in which you can simply "Deploy to AWS Lambda."

We've discussed the various accompanying services being used today by Serverless practitioners such as Amazon/AWS – API Gateway, DynamoDB, RDS Proxy, Step Functions, Lambda Layers, EventBridge, and X-Ray.

This is a huge subject; books devoted simply to each of these individual services are available. Hopefully, this chapter has given you an overview and a look into what is possible. This is an area that is worth your time and effort in pursuing some further learning. AWS has some excellent guides and documentation as well as support for the Serverless communities running meetings and workshops every month. Enjoy.

CHAPTER 7

Containers

Docker emerged in 2013 with their Container technology, although the term Containers can be traced back as far as 2006 with Google's Process Containers or 2008 with LXC (Linux Containers). In reality, the idea of abstracting and isolating processes and user environments from each other can go back to the mainframe days of yore.

So, why Containers (Figure 7-1)?

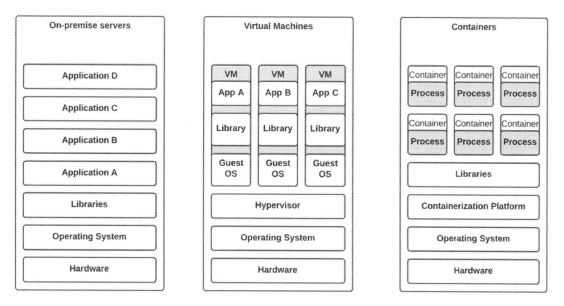

Figure 7-1. *Containers vs. virtualization*

Let's go back to our application developer who works inside a large distributed development team and is creating components of an application that will need to be brought together to make a final working application. He's creating his part of the application in his development environment and regularly pushes this code to his teams' code repository which then triggers a whole automated build pipeline to deploy in a development environment for testing.

© Ryan Pothecary 2021
R. Pothecary, *Running Microsoft Workloads on AWS*, https://doi.org/10.1007/978-1-4842-6628-1_7

All good so far. That working application then needs to go to a user acceptance test environment and after that a pre-production environment before finally ending up in its final home, a production environment.

In the past, each of these environments was either manually built by engineers or put together with automation, but either way, they were not immutable, and changes were allowed to happen. This gives us the reason why applications can be buggy or just downright fail by the time they are run by actual users.

Containers abstract the operating system and configuration away from the application, which allows a containerized application to work in exactly the same way in each environment.

A container consists of the application, the complete runtime environment, and all of the dependencies, configurations, and libraries all bundled in one single package. In terms of scale, a container is significantly smaller than a virtual machine, and therefore a physical server host could run a lot more containers than it could virtual machines. Obviously, considering that the container contains the application and not a whole operating system, it means that containers can be started very quickly. This lets us use them only when they are needed to run their bit of code in a true "just-in-time" manner. Similar to what we just learned about AWS Lambda, once a container's code is run, they can be terminated quickly, freeing up the Host server to run more containers.

Containers came into fashion at the perfect moment when large enterprises were redeveloping their large monolithic applications into new microservice architectures.

But let's not forget. A container is just a way of presenting compute power to an application. If your business or customer tells you they want to use containers, that's a good time to challenge them and ask why. What are the goals?

You find that potentially what they really want is to use microservices.

Microservices

Microservice architectures decouple, or deconstruct, application components by separating them into independent services. Each service runs in its processes and communicates externally – and with other microservice-based components in that same application – through APIs. Containers and microservices are a natural fit. Containers provide process isolation that makes it easy to break apart and run applications as independent components.

Modern applications are distributed, cloud native, and built with microservices. A modern application can scale quickly to support millions of users, provide global availability, manage petabytes and potentially exabytes of data, and respond in milliseconds. Applications built with microservices can have a faster release velocity because changes to an individual component are easier to make.

The key rules for microservices are

- Loosely coupled

- Testable and independently deployable

- Structured around business capabilities

- Owned and maintained by a single small team

- Responsible for their own data management

As you can see, they fit very nicely to our cloud tenets and lend themselves for high velocity development and deployment which cloud is perfect for. Being loosely coupled means that we can now think about scaling and resilience. The popularity in developing microservices is directly aligned to cloud adoption. Containers are also a key construct to deliver microservices for cloud-native applications.

Practicing what they preach, or eating their own dogfood (personally, I prefer the former), Amazon switched to small DevOps teams that each own a microservice which they deploy to containers as part of a full CI/CD pipeline. As far back as 2014, it meant that they could reach over 50 million deployments per year.

Another benefit of application development using microservices is that it lends itself to *polyglot programming*, allowing each microservice to be developed in a programming language that is most appropriate for the *task the microservice performs*.

A UI or User Interface microservice could be developed in JavaScript, whereas a microservice handling application logic could be developed in C#. While that may sound inefficient from a skill's perspective for your teams, it would actually be beneficial for the application – with the right language being used for the right task.

There are still challenges however. Moving to a microservice architecture invariably leads to a large increase in the complexity of services and APIs, often referred to as "container sprawl." Also, we are now moving further away from traditional server technology, and how does that affect our operational processes such as monitoring for instance? Monitoring and visibility of our microservices is vital as there are now more watchpoints.

Moving to a microservice architecture approach is a significant cultural and organizational change for most businesses.

It Works on My Machine

You've just been given a new application to deploy into an environment, and you hit problems. The application doesn't work. So, you go back to the development teams and get the all too familiar "Well, it works on my machine."

There are many reasons why an application can work in one environment and not in another. Typically, it's due to the configuration of a system or some underlying dependency that one system has and the other does not. The challenge of making environments the same is as old as when we first started using these systems themselves. Firstly, if you've ever tried to manually build more than a couple of servers, you'll invariably find that one system will give you an issue causing you to provide a workaround that the other systems don't have. Or you're tasked with updating systems with security patches or application updates, and for one reason or another, you'll get an error on an individual system, whereas the same process worked fine on the rest of the server farm. You'll have configuration drift which is a term used to describe the differences between one system and another. It's a challenge that has provided us with tools like DSC (Desired State Configuration) and system imaging and naturally leads us to where we are today with CI/CD pipelines and immutable workloads.

Containers are designed to solve the problem of "It worked on my machine" at scale, by isolating software from its environment and ensuring that it works uniformly, despite any differences in deployment locations.

A container image is a super lightweight executable package of software which will include everything required to run an application. This will include the application code, any runtimes required, any libraries, and also system tools and configuration settings. A container is created by running a container image. Once built, the container image is immutable; therefore, we see containers as the target for application deployments via CI/CD pipelines. Portability ensures that a container image can be run on many hosts. We can therefore have different container images with different versions of our application all happily running on the same host and allowing true Blue/Green deployments of our apps.

Speed is also a key characteristic of using containers. The ability to start a container within seconds provides huge benefit when it comes to application deployments.

This leads us to a question. How do containers work in our Microsoft landscape? We will be discussing this, but first let's look at the AWS container services.

Amazon Elastic Container Service (ECS)

AWS launched their first container service, Amazon Elastic Container Service (ECS), in November 2014, providing Docker containers on AWS as part of a fully managed service. AWS ECS is a container orchestration service that handles the Docker cluster management, allowing users to focus instead on building and running your container resources.

Amazon Elastic Container Service is a fully managed container orchestration service that supports container workloads at production scale with a high level of automation that can handle thousands of hosts running millions of containers.

Amazon ECS gives you the option of running containers on Amazon EC2 which offers you more flexibility or using Amazon Fargate which completely manages your container infrastructure.

In Figure 7-2, we can see a number of different layer objects; let's discuss each in turn.

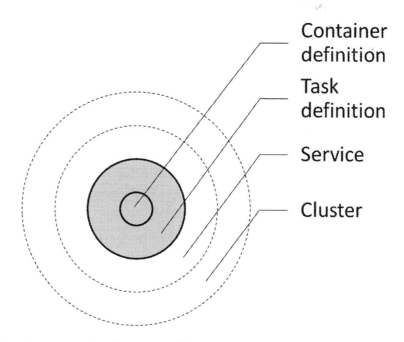

Figure 7-2. *Amazon ECS objects and how they relate*

Starting with the ECS cluster which is a logical grouping consisting of services and tasks which once configured and deployed allows us to run containers using task definitions. Generally, it's best practice to have different clusters for different environments, so test, development, production, and so on. You can scale the clusters up and down via the Amazon ECS console.

Next comes the service layer which allows you to run and maintain a specified number of simultaneous instances of a task definition. If any tasks were to stop or fail, the service scheduler launches a fresh Instance to replace them.

Then the task definition defines which image to use for a container and how much memory, CPU, networking including subnet placement and security groups to attach. Also, it includes any commands to run and what storage should be allocated. Task definitions can be affected by constraints and strategies which can be added when a task is run.

Last is the container definition which is the container image and the application that you want to use.

Scheduling and orchestration are the key capabilities of Amazon ECS (Figure 7-3), and the cluster manager and placement engine are its main components. The cluster manager monitors the health of the host instances in a cluster. The hosts are the Amazon EC2 instances that our containers are running on. The cluster manager integrates with EC2 Auto Scaling Groups to provide scaling operations for the host servers in an Amazon ECS cluster.

One of the side effect benefits of Amazon Auto Scaling Groups (ASGs) is their ability to ensure that the number of instances running in an Auto Scaling Group matches the minimum number we configure when they are created. Sounds logical so far, but the effect of this logic is that should an Amazon EC2 Instance fail or terminate for some reason, the Auto Scaling Group will automatically provision a replacement, effectively giving us a self-healing container cluster.

What if you want to run specific containers on specific Instances? For example, if you have containers that require specialized hardware such as graphic processors or maybe you are placing container hosts across multiple Availability Zones, the placement engine handles all these requests for you.

A daemon called the Amazon ECS Container Agent runs on each Amazon EC2 host in a cluster. This agent enforces resource allocation at an EC2 level and provides monitoring metrics.

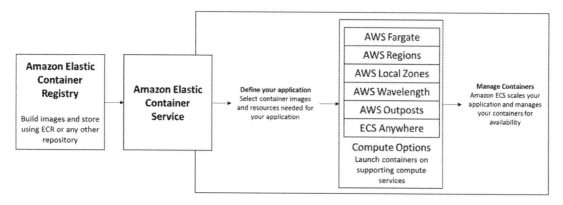

Figure 7-3. *Amazon Elastic Container Service*

AWS Elastic Container Registry

We can't really discuss Amazon ECS without understanding Amazon ECR (Figure 7-4) and how the two services are tightly integrated with each other. Amazon Elastic Container Registry is a fully managed service that allows us to store, deploy, and manage container images. This service integrates with Amazon IAM to allow you to be very granular in what you allow your users to do. We can also share the repositories that we create using Amazon ECR across multiple accounts, meaning that our entire organization and all its AWS accounts can share and use a defined set of container images.

Adding images to Amazon ECR doesn't mean I have to use them with Amazon ECS or EKS (Amazon Elastic Kubernetes Service). I can actually call on the container images from multiple sources including bare metal EC2 or even on-premises.

Amazon Elastic Container Registry isn't the only register of container images. There are also public registries such as the official Microsoft Container Registry (MCR) on dockerhub (`https://hub.docker.com/publishers/microsoftowner`).

Amazon ECR, on the other hand, is a completely private container registry fully controlled via Amazon IAM which encrypts all images automatically.

As is normal with AWS Services, Amazon ECR is fully managed and highly available by default. A great feature is something called Amazon ECR lifecycle policies which allow you to define a set of rules that remove and retire older container images automatically. You can create rules based on tags, so you can pinpoint different environments or different versions of an image. This saves a huge amount of housekeeping when you have a large number of images.

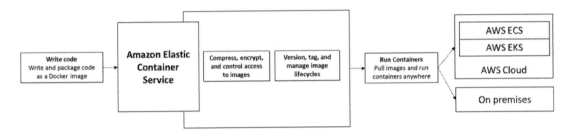

Figure 7-4. *Amazon Elastic Container Registry (Amazon ECR)*

AWS Fargate

You'll often hear reference to AWS Fargate as "a serverless container service." The key reason it's earned that title isn't due to its fully managed nature or the abstraction of hosts or even its ability to scale on demand with built-in high availability. The reason why AWS describes AWS Fargate as serverless is that it scales by unit of consumption rather than by a per-server unit, aligning it far closer to AWS Lambda than to Amazon EC2.

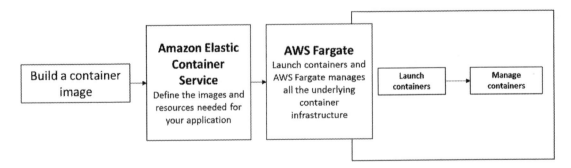

Figure 7-5. *AWS Fargate*

Why do we need another container service? Well, running Amazon ECS in EC2 mode still means we have to manage a few things such as the operating system of the host, the Docker, and Amazon ECS agents. AWS Fargate allows the user to manage only their containers. AWS Fargate handles all of the underlying infrastructure in a complete pay-as-you-go model.

AWS allows you to mix and match how you run containers inside its platform, so you can actually have a number of Fargate Instances and Amazon ECS in EC2 mode inside the same cluster. AWS Fargate (Figure 7-5) is far more specific about Task CPU and memory requirements because that's how it handles billing, but there are a multitude of different CPU/memory configurations to choose from.

AWS Fargate provides ephemeral storage for each running container based on Amazon EBS. Each task is allocated approx. 10GB and also a special 4GB volume of scratch space to share data between containers. AWS Fargate also integrates heavily with AWS IAM to provide fine-grained access permissions at the cluster, application, and housekeeping level.

More information on this can be found here: `https://docs.aws.amazon.com/AmazonECS/latest/userguide/security-iam.html`.

AWS Elastic Kubernetes Service (EKS)

Kubernetes is an open source platform for managing containers, created by Google and now managed by the Cloud Native Computing Foundation (CNCF). Created to allow containers to run at significant scale and developed using a software development lifecycle in mind, Kubernetes handles how your applications work inside the container cluster, which we call container orchestration.

Using the container building blocks provided by Docker, Kubernetes uses a master/worker architecture where the master coordinates the cluster and the workers are the nodes that run applications.

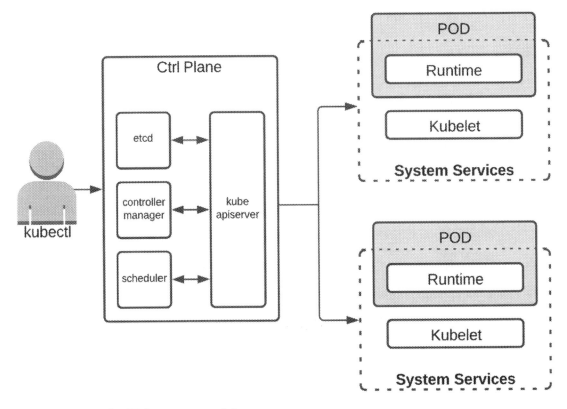

Figure 7-6. *The Kubernetes architecture*

Kubernetes uses the concept of pods (Figure 7-6) to group together services used within a single application; that way, they can share resources. A service is a collection of pods that perform a similar function; services allow for discoverability, scaling, and load balancing.

Amazon EKS creates your Kubernetes clusters and manages the availability and scalability of the control plane across three Availability Zones, allowing users to focus entirely on building applications.

Kubernetes has grown from almost a decade of development, and there are lots of features to understand. The best place to start is the official documentation at `https://kubernetes.io/docs/concepts/overview/what-is-kubernetes/`.

The 6-Gigabyte Elephant in the Room

Now that we understand what AWS Services are available for us to use, where does this leave those of us wanting to run Microsoft workloads on containers?

Let's go back to the launch of Windows Server 2016 when Windows containers were first introduced. Microsoft had to reach out and partner with Docker to make this happen. That's a full 2 years since AWS launched Amazon ECS and 3 years after Docker exploded into our IT universe. It's fair to say that, once again, Microsoft was playing catch-up.

Windows containers are just not the same as traditional Linux containers; since the internal OS architecture is significantly different, there has had to be a lot of effort from both Docker and Microsoft to make Windows containers a possibility.

To make containers lightweight, interoperable, and fast, they use a shared kernel. This also poses a slight security risk when running on Windows Server because of the tight coupling between APIs contained in DLLs and the underlying OS services. So, if a shared Windows kernel is hacked in some way, then all the containers using it are exposed. This is the reason why Microsoft has two versions of its container technology.

The first is very similar to traditional containers and uses process isolation; this is called Windows Containers. The other is very similar to traditional virtual machines and uses Hyper-V to provide full isolation between containers running on a host; this option is called Hyper-V Containers (Figure 7-7).

There's also the question of compatibility with containers running on different versions of Windows and also what the different editions that are available are capable of. As you can see, containers on Windows can be complex!

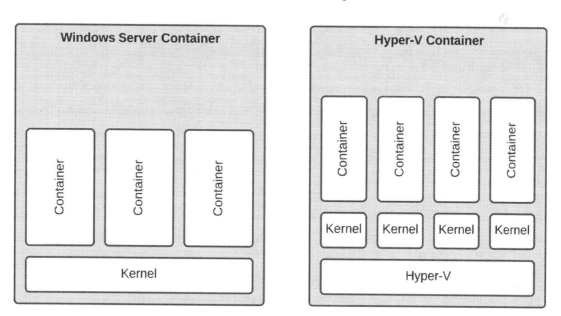

Figure 7-7. *Windows Server Container architecture*

If you want to run a Windows Server container on Server 2016, then that container must be built from a Server 2016 base. Running the same container on the 2016 Semi-Annual Channel releases like version 1709 or 1803 will mean the container will not work. It means you must only run containers on the same OS version as the host.

Even with all this complexity around versions and isolation, the reason that stops companies considering running Windows containers is the size of the image. When it was launched, Windows Server 2016 was a whooping 6GB in size. Compare that to a standard Linux image of between 2MB and 200MB, and you'll see some obvious shortcomings in terms of being able to run Windows containers that start and terminate quickly in order to run a task.

Microsoft is working hard to reduce this footprint. After Windows Server 2016, it released the first version of Windows Nano Server, a container-focused image with a much smaller footprint and a subset of the full functionality of standard Windows Server.

But it's not only footprint alone that Microsoft has to work out a solution for, because the real issue here is not one of image size, and any associated storage that requires, but rather the large size causing delays in both container creation and startup. It makes sense that the larger the container, the longer it takes to run your application.

Windows Nano Server

Microsoft Windows Nano Server was an option during a Windows Server 2016 deployment. It's a 64-bit-only edition with a cut-down amount of functionality but also a number of welcome benefits.

The upside of being able to support a minimal amount of server roles is that only a small subset of security patches need to be applied; this also has a knock-on effect in the amount of reboots required and therefore the amount of uptime you should expect.

The biggest benefit that Windows Nano Server has to offer is in its footprint. The image size of Windows Nano Server was a mere 400MB, which is still double what an average Linux image is but on the other hand is a gigantic 15 times smaller than Windows Server 2016. Smaller footprint means faster setup time, and in comparison to Windows Server 2016, Nano Server is nearly eight times faster during setup.

Managing Windows Nano Servers cannot be done via Remote Desktop Protocol (RDP), SSH, or an actual login to the server. Access is via the Nano Server Recovery Console, Windows Remote Management (WINRM), or PowerShell Remoting.

Apart from having to manage Windows Nano Server differently than the rest of your Windows Server estate, all seem good right? Small, fast, perfect!

Well, that really depends on what you plan to do with your Windows Nano Server once it's running. Windows Nano Server does not support MSI Windows installations, so getting your apps installed is going to require a different approach. Also, there are no GUI features at all, so getting your apps configured and running is also going to require some thought.

Windows Nano Server is also not able to run full .NET applications. But you can run .NET Core.

This really begs the question: if I can only run .NET Core applications, then surely I'd be better off doing that with a more streamlined Linux distro than using Windows 2016 Nano Server?

As we've learned, Windows Nano Server is really a mixed bag of potentials and constraints. But Microsoft has learned lessons, and things do get better with Windows Server 2019.

Windows Server 2019

Microsoft Windows Server 2019 has embraced containers. Certainly, more than its predecessor did. It still gives you the options of Windows Containers or Hyper-V Containers, but Docker now becomes integrated much tighter with the ability to install the containers feature.

By default, only Windows Containers are allowed; an upgrade to Docker Enterprise Edition is needed to also run Linux containers natively from the OS. It's also good practice to keep your Windows and Linux containers on separate clusters.

Another welcome enhancement has been the image size which is 1.5GB for Server 2019 and just 98MB for Nano Server 2019.

AWS's support for Windows Server 2019 containers began in June 2019 with the ability for customers to run 2019 containers on Amazon ECS. This was followed up with Kubernetes support using Amazon EKS in October 2019.

Containers will continue to play a significant role in Microsoft's strategy moving forward. It really has no choice since enterprises have really embraced containers as part of their digital transformations, and Microsoft already faces a very real threat to its enterprise dominance from Linux.

Supporting Containers

Now that we have our Docker and Kubernetes clusters up and running with hundreds of Windows containers, our thoughts turn to exactly how are we going to support these containers operationally? Fortunately, AWS has some great services that can help here.

Let's start with monitoring the health of our containers. Docker and Kubernetes already have services we can use when it comes to container monitoring. Kubernetes has the Web UI Dashboard (Figure 7-8) to provide visualizations of health and performance metrics.

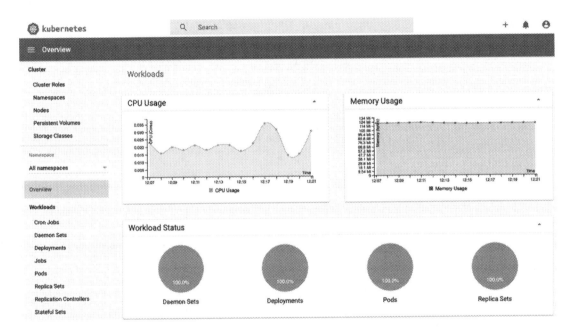

***Figure 7-8.** Kubernetes Web UI Dashboard running on Amazon EKS*

A full tutorial on how to set up this dashboard to run on your Amazon EKS cluster can be found here: `https://docs.aws.amazon.com/eks/latest/userguide/dashboard-tutorial.html`.

Docker has Prometheus which can be run as a ready-built appliance via the AWS Marketplace and also integrated with the monitoring service, AWS CloudWatch (`https://aws.amazon.com/blogs/containers/using-prometheus-metrics-in-amazon-cloudwatch/`).

It's worth reminding ourselves that there are also multiple third-party container monitoring solutions available.

Using AWS CloudWatch allows us to monitor the whole container cluster holistically. We can monitor the EKS worker nodes and Docker hosts, whether they are Linux or Windows, that make up our environment. Pulling metrics from the hypervisor and container level, we can create dashboards focused on our container health as well as our entire AWS estate.

AWS have gone a step further and provided a dedicated container monitoring service inside AWS CloudWatch called AWS CloudWatch Container Insights (Figure 7-9). This service lets you monitor clusters, container services, and tasks and allows you to set alarms that trigger proactive events.

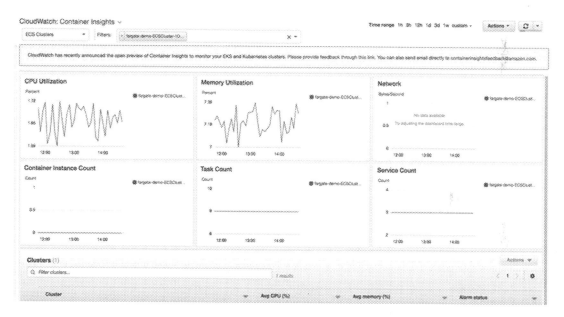

Figure 7-9. *AWS CloudWatch Container Insights*

An often-requested feature from the Windows container community is the ability to join containers to an Active Directory domain. This can be useful in terms of container security and administration or have their container application authenticate to another service.

A school of thought exists that dismisses the requirement of using AD with containers. Containers should be short-lived immutable places to run your microservices, whereas adding them to an Active Directory domain suggests that they will be stateful and long-lived. However, a use case exists where a container might need to be domain joined for authentication or security reasons.

AWS launched this update during AWS re:Invent 2019 using an Active Directory feature called Windows Group Managed Service Accounts (gMSA). This is available for both Amazon ECS and EKS and is implemented by the use of a credential spec file via a task definition.

AWS App Mesh

Let's step back for a second and think about our new way of developing applications using multiple microservices rather than one huge monolith. You can see there are lots of benefits to this approach, particularly in terms of supportability, agility in getting out new features, and ownership from small two-pizza teams who are now responsible for individual microservices rather than a whole department reasonable for the entire monolith.

We mentioned at the start of this chapter there are also disadvantages in terms of complexity. Each microservice needs to be aware of the microservices it needs to communicate with and also understand where those microservices live after being updated since they may well have different IP addresses or DNS names.

This is the problem that AWS App Mesh solves.

AWS App Mesh provides uniformity when it comes to inter-service communication, and this becomes very important if you consider who will use microservices and how you'll deploy your application updates to them via rolling or Blue-Green deployments. AWS App Mesh provides a proxy which sits alongside all microservices, whereas the AWS App Mesh control plane manages all the proxies.

AWS App Mesh works across a large number of AWS's container services such as Amazon ECS, EKS, Fargate, and EC2.

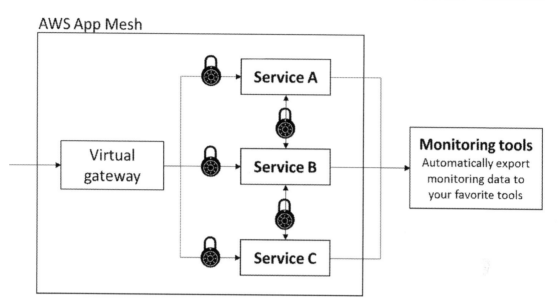

Figure 7-10. *AWS App Mesh*

AWS App Mesh (Figure 7-10) also provides network traffic shaping and routing capabilities between microservices while also integrating closely with another service, AWS Cloud Map.

AWS Cloud Map

One final piece in the container puzzle is the ability to discover new microservices when they are constantly being updated or new functionality introduces them.

AWS Cloud Map provides service discovery for your microservice or CI/CD deployments. Microservices can launch and terminate quickly giving your application the headache of how to manage all of its dependencies. When a microservice runs, it registers with AWS Cloud Map which holds an up-to-date registry of application services.

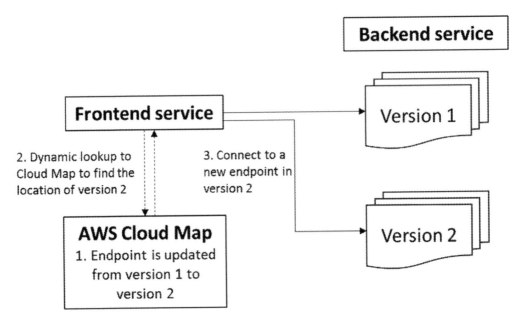

Figure 7-11. *AWS Cloud Map overview*

You start by creating a namespace and then decide how your applications can be found via their endpoints. AWS Cloud Map also integrates with Route 53 and will monitor the health of your services and mark them as unhealthy in the registry if they do not respond.

Summary

We've covered a lot of different technologies during this chapter, and this is very much a high-level view of the world of Windows containers on AWS. There is an awful lot of information to dive deep into if this is an area you'd like to pursue.

Microservices are very much the current phase of application development, and you may already be running containers in your own AWS accounts. We've found the journey to understand Microsoft Windows containers to be confusing at times with lots of options and advantages/disadvantages we need to process to understand what works for us.

It's also very welcome that AWS seems to be leading the way in the field of containers and pouring significant effort into developing services and features to help with this new deployment paradigm – not only improving their Docker and Kubernetes services but also developing a mature ecosystem of services that support us.

A statistic that sums this up and reinforces why we use AWS in the first place is this: 80% of containers running in the cloud run on AWS.

CHAPTER 8

Operational Integration

"Cloud is Different" is a mantra I repeat on a daily basis. I've seriously thought about getting t-shirts made. The reason for banging on about this for such a long time is simple. Businesses have been doing IT in the same way for the last 40 years, and a lot of companies think that they can continue to use the same processes, tooling, and methodologies after they've moved to the cloud.

And they jolly well can't.

Well, that's not *entirely* true. Businesses certainly *could* use existing processes, tools, and methodologies to manage their cloud environments. But it's fair to say that they would lose a lot of the benefits of moving to the cloud and even find the management of their cloud environments to be even more time-consuming than their existing on-premises platforms. This is why *everything* needs to be revisited and revised as we move our workloads into the cloud. This chapter covers the huge changes required through cloud adoption.

Don't be scared though. Every cloud adoption project has a host of lessons learned, and we will be picking through these carcasses throughout this chapter. Although we discuss the unique challenge of operating Microsoft Workloads in AWS, this chapter more broadly shows the impact of moving to the cloud in your organization.

Firstly, what's with the fancy chapter title? What exactly does Operational Integration mean? Operational Integration or OI is the process of modernizing our current IT operational process to be used in cloud environments.

AWS has put a lot of effort into understanding the impact of cloud adoption which has informed the creation of methodologies such as the Cloud Adoption Framework (CAF) to highlight the impact of the cloud in an organization and provides a plan to arm ourselves for some of the challenges that lie ahead of us.

© Ryan Pothecary 2021
R. Pothecary, *Running Microsoft Workloads on AWS*, https://doi.org/10.1007/978-1-4842-6628-1_8

AWS published six advantages of Cloud Computing (`https://docs.aws.amazon.com/whitepapers/latest/aws-overview/six-advantages-of-cloud-computing.html`); here's the list:

- Trade CapEx for OpEx

- Benefit from massive economies of scale

- Stop guessing capacity

- Increase speed and agility

- Stop spending money on data centers

- Go global in minutes

I can probably add a few more to that list:

- Innovation

- More security options

Let's look at the impact of each of these on a traditional IT department.

Trade CapEx for OpEx (Help Me Save Money)

IT budgets have worked on the basis of regular large capital expenditure costs and very linear operational expenditures. It's how IT system integrators and outsourcers usually bid on new projects. There is still CapEx required in a Cloud Adoption, a dedicated network link, reskilling staff, new roles required, and so on, but what's missing is the cost of all that hardware and data center management that becomes part of the per-hour/second/millisecond cost of using an AWS service.

Cost management becomes way more dynamic when applied to a cloud environment. AWS has given us services like Cost Explorer and Trusted Advisor to be able to highlight where costs are incurred and where savings can be made. Running your IT infrastructure for 12 hours a day, Monday to Friday, is only 35% of the week, so the potential is there to save 65% by switching systems off. This is just one action; there are a lot of other ways to save even more money.

A fully holistic view of cloud costs must be attempted during a company's cloud adoption. A good starting point would be your on-premises operational costs and an expected saving of between 20 and 40%. Of course, this will require some common sense during the migration by choosing to right-size server specifications based on actual usage.

A great help in this area is an AWS service we discuss in Chapter 9, but you won't find it in the AWS Management console, AWS Migration Evaluator (Figure 8-1).

Figure 8-1. *AWS Migration Evaluator savings report*

Conversations with IT professionals who are firmly anti-cloud all begin the same way, with them telling me that their internal IT infrastructure is much cheaper than any potential AWS environment. You can present data to argue the case, and you can discuss pricing mechanisms like Spot or Reserved Instances and so on, but I've learned over time that rather than arguing about a per-server price comparison, it's more effective to focus on other areas – most notably, resource efficiency, operational resilience, and business agility.

Resource efficiency covers the fact that your IT teams don't need to cover the tasks that AWS manages for you – procurement, data center management, and so on.

Operational resilience can be found by understanding the cost of an IT systems failure and the impact it would have on your business.

Business agility highlights the benefits of becoming more agile – more product launches, more changes, speed to market, and so on.

Cost is a very large part of every company's cloud adoption journey. Every prospective AWS customer I've met or every AWS partner I've spoken to all say that cost savings is the biggest driver to moving to the cloud. Preparing a business case to inform your company of these benefits against staying in your on-premises data center is mandatory to a successful cloud adoption.

Benefit from Massive Economies of Scale

At AWS re:Invent 2016, there was a session by Amazon principal engineer James Hamilton who finally let the public into the previously secretive world of the AWS global infrastructure. I assigned it as homework in Chapter 2; have you seen it yet? If not, it can be found here: `https://youtu.be/AyOAjFNPAbA`.

A few minutes in, he shows a slide stating that in 2015 AWS deployed enough Server capacity every day equivalent to powering the whole of Amazon.com in 2005 when it was an $8.5B enterprise. Fast forward 5 years and you can only imagine how much capacity AWS has within its 25+ regions. Cloud capacity in general was significantly tested during 2020's Coronavirus pandemic with not only huge increases in businesses using cloud platforms but also an incredible increase in people using services running in the cloud such as Netflix or Zoom. Compared to others, AWS held up incredibly well.

Economies of scale don't only affect the cost of something but also the investment into the quality of that something.

As AWS grows, so does the amount of services it offers, and the cost of running those services reduces.

AWS's 80+ proactive price reductions since 2008 are a good indicator of how large the platform has grown, but also the increases in the number of AWS services over the last 12 years. Now over 200 services and covering some very advanced and sometimes niche use cases.

How does this affect our Operational Integration? Both in terms of cost management and in terms of how we manage the use of AWS Services throughout our organization. Some of AWS services can incur quite a large bill if left unchecked which comes under the remit of general cloud governance and cost management. But what about the ability to use the services themselves? Do your teams have the skills and knowledge to use some of the more advanced services such as analytics or machine learning?

AWS Service Catalog was built for this very use case. Using it, you can enforce policies across multiple accounts and enforce governance by managing what AWS services are available to be used. You can remove the ability to use some of the costly services or services that have an impact on identity or security, for example.

Stop Guessing Capacity

In our traditional on-premises environments, capacity management is an ongoing task that has an impact on several other operational domains such as cost management, release management, asset management, and so on.

We know that cloud platforms have a seemingly endless amount of capacity that we can draw from in terms of compute and storage resources. Being able to use that in our own IT environments is a big benefit in moving to the cloud, and the services that offer this unlimited capacity also have a few additional benefits that we can use inside our cloud environments.

Storage services like Amazon S3, AWS EFS, and AWS FSx for Windows automatically scale the storage you need, and you pay per GB of storage you consume, whereas Amazon EBS does not grow the storage automatically, but certainly lets you manually make changes to what storage you require. An interesting feature of Amazon S3 is S3 lifecycle policies that, once defined, automatically move your files to different S3 storage tiers based on what your requirements are. For example, if I take a snapshot of an Amazon EBS volume attached to my server, that snapshot is placed in Amazon S3 standard tier. In reality, a snapshot backup of a server is only usable within the first week, although there are occasions where we need to go back further to restore some data. After the first week, Amazon S3 lifecycle policies could move the snapshot to Amazon S3 Infrequent Access, which has a lower cost per GB but a cost for access. Since I don't intend to access the snapshot, that's fine by me; I'll take the lower price. For compliance reasons, I have to keep backups for a year, so maybe after 30 days Amazon S3 lifecycle policies will move the snapshot to AWS Glacier, the archiving service, and after a full year will delete the file. Rather than obsolete files using expensive storage, we can constantly reduce the cost by using different storage tiers – automatically!

When it comes to compute capacity, you have the options of both vertical and horizontal scaling. If you need more CPU or memory for your server, then you can stop the Amazon EC2 Instance, resize it to a larger EC2 Instance Type, then restart it. Scaling vertically takes minutes and can be scripted via the AWS CLI.

Scaling Amazon EC2 horizontally involves setting up an amazing service called Amazon Auto Scaling Groups (ASGs). ASGs are part of the Amazon EC2 Instance service and work in conjunction with the monitoring service AWS CloudWatch.

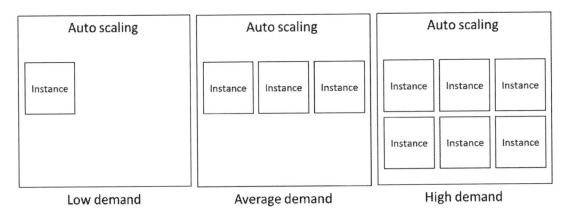

Figure 8-2. *Amazon Auto Scaling Groups in action*

As you can see (Figure 8-2), ASGs can scale the number of Amazon EC2 Instances to a preset maximum and even scale back to a preset minimum depending on how busy your application is. You can scale up/down based on CPU performance and network in/out metrics and even configure custom metrics based on data from your application such as "Number of Users Logged in."

A great side effect of Amazon Auto Scaling Groups' persistence to adhering to the minimum/maximum EC2 instance you set is that should an Amazon EC2 instance fail at some point, ASGs will replace the unhealthy instance with a newly created one.

Traditional on-premises environments had to ensure that they had enough capacity for the busiest periods in their calendar. For a retail business, that tends to happen around the holiday season, and the downside of ensuring that you have enough capacity at that time is that you certainly have way too much capacity and wasted resources during the other 10 months of the year. Cloud does have the ability to fix this overconsumption, but only if you spend time at an application development level to fully understand the impact that automatic scaling has on your application design. Being able to scale the web server/presentation layer up to high numbers may mean that your users get a responsive website, but if that scaling does not continue at the application or data layer, then the end result will potentially be a poorer experience for the user than if the website appeared unresponsive in the first place.

Increase Speed and Agility

Let's try an experiment, shall we? Set a timer on your watch or phone, and when you're done reading this sentence, press GO.

Another huge benefit of the cloud is its self-service nature and the ability to create whatever resource or service you need very quickly. This also presents a challenge for those businesses that don't adapt their operational processes to the cloud.

Let's think of a common situation for many: your internal change management board meets once a week to discuss and approve changes happening to your IT systems. The change management board then approves (or not) the change, and it is scheduled for implementation.

How can this change management process work in our dynamic cloud environment?

Speed and agility are a huge benefit of moving to the cloud and could be the first cloud tenet to be sacrificed to constrictive internal processes, although this need not happen, since a revised cloud-friendly change management process can work very successfully.

Change management is focused on *reducing* the business risk and *delivering* the business value.

If you work in an IT career, then you'll fully understand when and how things go wrong with our IT systems – large application changes that have not been fully tested, unexpected issues that force a server to go offline, or changes being made to our IT systems that cause a system outage. Change management is in place to protect us from these issues, but we can significantly reduce these issues from happening with some standard common sense management of our cloud environments.

Automation plays a key role in this. Using a full CI/CD pipeline via AWS Elastic Beanstalk or maybe AWS CodePipeline, AWS CodeCommit, AWS CodeBuild, and AWS CodeDeploy, we can automate the test and deployment of application updates following the AWS good practice mantra of making small, frequent changes and ensuring that failed deployments are not seen as a bad thing because there is a full rollback mechanism in place to address issues when they happen.

Automation also mitigates the issues that arise from failed implementations. Engineers are humans, well most of them are, and humans make mistakes. Scripting changes and deploying those changes via our CI/CD pipeline can significantly reduce the errors that occur. Deploying infrastructure changes via AWS CloudFormation allows for automatic rollback if errors occur; a full description of why the error occurred will be present in AWS CloudFormation and AWS CloudTrail.

This leaves us with the final issue which we must address, and that is the unexpected failure. Remember, "Everything fails (given enough time) so design for failure" – Amazon CTO, Dr. Werner Vogels.

This design for failure approach could be via using multiple availability zones and AWS Elastic Load Balancers or, perhaps, even AWS Auto Scaling Groups placed on every single point-of-failure application server – not configured to scale out on demand, but rather to replace the application server should it become unhealthy. Multiple availability zone solutions are better of course, but a sub-five-minute outage could be perfectly acceptable to a business that is focused on cost reduction.

Change introduces the business value. It's critical that changes meet customer and business expectations and are able to be supported by IT operations. The business must also be prepared to adapt to the new frequency of releases and the automated deployment methods. Trust needs to be earned in these new methods.

The other impact on our topic of speed and agility is how to manage the self-service nature of the cloud. Giving your IT users the ability to create resources in AWS without the overview of centralized IT could give you a troubled night's sleep. But once again, with common sense AWS best practices around security and the use of AWS Service Catalog and AWS Config, you can provide your IT users with the freedom they require to be agile and fast when delivering projects while always ensuring that they cannot expose the business to security risks and are only able to use the AWS services they need to.

OK, let's stop that timer.

In the time it's taken you to read this section, you could have easily created an Amazon EC2 Instance in an AWS Auto Scaling Group that will scale up and down based on customer demand.

When I speak with businesses thinking about moving to the cloud, the actual time to provision a virtual server is generally 2 to 4 weeks, whereas a physical server would be closer to 10 weeks.

That speed and agility is exactly why you are thinking of moving to the cloud, so let's make sure that we revise those internal processes to allow that to happen.

Stop Spending Money on Data Centers

After spending a significant portion of my working life in and around data centers, I have no intention to go anywhere near one again. Cold, windowless, noisy with no nice vending machines. Why would anyone want to be sat on a cold floor directly plugged into a network switch when they could be working far more effectively in a nice warm place with wifi and access to the AWS Management console?

It puts a smile on my face when talking about TCO comparisons with organizations that are thinking of moving to the cloud to tell them their current infrastructure costs are only one third about the server itself. There are a further two thirds cost associated with facilities, power, and cooling. It's something that many don't consider when looking at cloud costs, and the normal behavior is to just compare physical servers to EC2 Instance costs.

AWS has so many different ways for you to save money or to notify you of the money you are spending compared to on-premises environments, and as we know cost is one of the biggest drivers for your business moving to the cloud. When I first became an AWS customer, what I found completely staggering was the focus on continued cost reduction. I'd come from a background of working with managed service providers whose whole focus appeared to be getting the customer (me) to spend more, not less.

Over time, AWS has developed services and features entirely focused on reducing cost for their customers. These need to be part of your operational toolkit:

- AWS Trusted Advisor

- AWS Cost Explorer

- AWS Budgets

There are other services that we discussed in Chapter 3 that also lend themselves to cost-effectiveness:

- Amazon EC2 Reserved Instances

- AWS Savings Plans

- Amazon EC2 Spot Instances

- AWS License Manager

There are also advanced services that you can use to reimagine how you present and use IT Services, such as containerization with Amazon Fargate or serverless with AWS Lambda. Because the cheapest way to run a server is not to run a server at all.

Go Global in Minutes

At the time of writing, AWS has 25 regions and has announced a further 5 regions for 2022. The AWS global infrastructure has grown at a staggering rate, but still whenever I speak to organizations, I'm sure to get a question along the lines of "When will AWS launch a Region in...."

The fact that AWS's Regions, Availability Zones, Transit Centers, Edge Locations, and all the network circuits that span entire oceans are entirely AWS owned and managed is staggering in its scope. AWS has never announced the cost of its global infrastructure, but I imagine that running a cable from the West Coast of the United States 14,500 km and 3 miles on the ocean floor to Australia does not come cheap.

But AWS knows that its global infrastructure underpins the reliability and performance that its customers need, and it also is one of the key differentiators between itself and other cloud providers. Speaking to companies that have moved between cloud providers, performance and reliability are two of the three main reasons, cost being the third.

From an operational standpoint, your business now has the ability to launch services in other countries, and therefore you need to be aware of all the compliance and data sovereignty ramifications that this has.

Innovation

Here's where things get really interesting from an Operational Integration perspective. Our IT teams' job roles were generally split based on their skills and competences – network, development, security, Windows, Linux, and so on. The DevOps methodology changes all that, creating smaller teams that are capable of building and running their own code.

These teams should be empowered to use whatever AWS Service they need for their solution, but how do we balance that with cost, security, and governance?

How do we ensure that if we give free rein to our teams, we won't receive a huge bill because someone is using very large Amazon EC2 Instances or they've just started a large Amazon RDS Multi-AZ SQL Server deployment? How can we ensure that they are working securely? Security is only as good as its weakest link, and if we have teams, who are not security experts, creating Security Groups or AWS IAM Policies, then should we be concerned? What about which services to use? Do we allow our teams to choose from all 200+ services or only a subset of services that we approve at a corporate level?

If we do that, are we stifling innovation?

There's a dilemma facing every large business that moves into the cloud, and that is in creating a balance between freedom to innovate and the responsibility to protect the business. AWS has some services that can help us here.

Firstly, AWS Identity and Access Management (AWS IAM) is a truly amazing service that provides you with everything you need to provide fine-grained access controls for your teams. AWS IAM is the bedrock of your security controls.

However, rather than wrestling with IAM Policies to give your teams access to some services and not others, or at an even granular level, some functions of services and not others, we can use AWS Service Catalog.

AWS Service Catalog gives your business the ability to create catalogs of IT services that are configured to already be compliant with your IT Security. The catalogs can be individual services or multitier application stacks that get built and configured when they are needed.

AWS Service Catalog is part of the AWS Management and Tools category alongside AWS Config and AWS Systems Manager. We took a very brief tour of AWS Systems Manager in Chapter 3 and found its huge number of available capabilities. More information on AWS Service Catalog can be found here: `https://aws.amazon.com/servicecatalog`.

Security

If "How much can I save?" is Question #1, then "Is cloud secure?" is a closely followed Question #2 from every potential cloud customer. AWS has been very consistent in my time using the platform by always stating that "Security is Job Zero," and it goes to great lengths to ensure that its customers run their platform in a secure way with lots of blog posts, whitepapers, services, and guidance on this important subject.

From an Operational Integration perspective, AWS's security best practices should be appended into your updated security processes and playbooks created that reflect cloud security operations. These will all center around AWS's Shared Responsibility Model.

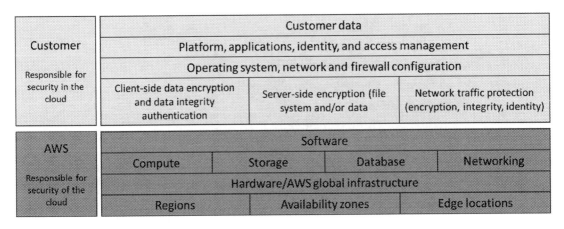

Customer	Customer data		
Responsible for security in the cloud	Platform, applications, identity, and access management		
	Operating system, network and firewall configuration		
	Client-side data encryption and data integrity authentication	Server-side encryption (file system and/or data	Network traffic protection (encryption, integrity, identity)

AWS	Software			
Responsible for security of the cloud	Compute	Storage	Database	Networking
	Hardware/AWS global infrastructure			
	Regions	Availability zones		Edge locations

Figure 8-3. *AWS Shared Responsibility Model*

The Shared Responsibility Model (Figure 8-3) is the cornerstone of security operations in AWS and was developed to provide guidance on where a business needs to focus its security processes. AWS is responsible for Security *of* the cloud, whereas the customer is responsible for Security *in* the cloud. Personally, when speaking with organizations, it's heartwarming when someone has concerns about cloud security; it shows to me that it's something they are worried about, and together we can focus that concern into a security plan to ensure that from day one they operate securely.

On several occasions, I've had the opposite response, where a customer tells me that they've moved to AWS, and now everything is completely secure.

Ouch!

I would never be confident enough for such a statement, because I'm well aware that security is an ongoing job and demands our attention at all times.

It's true that the AWS global infrastructure and internal security teams mitigate security threats, and added on top of that are some AWS services which are available at zero cost and can be enabled on your account, such as AWS Shield which protects against DDoS attacks and AWS GuardDuty which gives us threat detection by continuously monitoring for suspicious behavior using machine learning.

However, this should not mean that you can relax when it comes to security. There have been lots of stories of businesses suffering issues such as loss of data even though they were AWS customers. These normally take the form of unpatched public-facing services such as web servers or not implementing some of the AWS Security Services that are available. A full overview of AWS security processes can be found in this whitepaper: https://d0.awsstatic.com/whitepapers/aws-security-whitepaper.pdf.

The good news is that help is at hand to guide you on security *before* you have an issue with their Well-Architected Framework process, which is a great place to begin (`https://aws.amazon.com/architecture/well-architected/`).

The AWS Well-Architected Framework has been around for some time and comprises five pillars: operational excellence, security, reliability, performance, and cost optimization. Alongside this is the Well-Architected tool which allows a business to discover how to design and operate their cloud environment in a well-architected way.

Another area that AWS helps you is around compliance. AWS holds a large number of compliance accreditations, some global like ISO and PCI-DSS, and others are geographic specific such as HIPAA, ISMS, and GDPR. Knowing that the AWS infrastructure already holds these makes it easier to certify your own AWS solution if it has to comply with any of these accreditations. AWS manages over 2500 security controls as part of its compliance program, allowing you to focus on the ones that you have responsibility for.

For more information about what AWS compliance programs are available in your region, use the AWS Artifact service which is in the AWS Management Console and allows you to download reports provided by AWS and its auditors on the state of each of its compliance accreditations.

Cloud Adoption Framework

AWS developed the Cloud Adoption Framework (CAF) (`https://aws.amazon.com/professional-services/CAF/`) to assist with helping its customers understand that Cloud Adoption transforms the way they work. It's a framework that isn't tied explicitly to AWS; you can use it with other cloud providers. In fact, Microsoft has now developed its own version of CAF (`https://docs.microsoft.com/en-us/azure/cloud-adoption-framework/`) that it released in 2020, a full 6 years behind AWS's launch.

AWS's CAF is based on six perspectives and typically runs over two stages – Envision and Align:

- Business

- People

- Governance

- Platform

- Security

- Operations

The Envision stage takes the form of a workshop with the customer and is typically facilitated by AWS Professional Services or an AWS partner familiar with the process. During this workshop, clear business outcomes are defined.

This is then followed up with the Align workshop in which people from around the business communicate concerns about cloud adoption which are then mapped to one of the six CAF perspectives, and an action plan is produced to tackle these concerns.

It's a great process to follow and very beneficial in demonstrating that a move to the cloud isn't the same as a data center migration; it will have unique challenges for a business, but the best way to overcome these challenges is to be aware of them.

The reason for doing this is that technology issues very rarely cause a cloud adoption program to stall or be unsuccessful; it's almost always what are referred to as "Cultural Issues," and the AWS CAF workshops draw out these issues and provide an action plan to mitigate them.

Cloud Center of Excellence

Adopting a cloud in your organization requires some significant changes not only with your IT department but within the business as a whole. To be successful requires strong stakeholder support and the enablement of an organizational structure that helps the business as a whole understand and equip themselves for this change.

As part of its work on CAF, AWS spent time developing the Cloud Center of Excellence (CCoE) (Figure 8-4) methodology based on feedback from its own professional services teams and the work they did with large enterprises in adopting the cloud. It's the role of the CCoE to provide the cloud governance role normally held by central IT. The CCoE will advise the business on how best to use the cloud securely and cost-effectively.

My advice on creating a CCoE is to start small with some cloud champions from within your business; they should come from multiple different roles and from all around the business, not just IT. These champions can help the team via their influence and knowledge of the business functions. Partners can also be brought in to the CCoE to share their own cloud knowledge which is particularly useful if the cloud is new within the organization.

The initial team should be small, around four to five people, only large enough that two pizzas can feed them, hence the label two-pizza teams. Their role is to set best practices for working with the cloud.

Initially, this will revolve around security, access management, account strategy, and hybrid architectures, but the scope will grow as the team grows due to increased cloud adoption throughout the business.

But rather than grow a very large team, we keep the team small and instead create additional teams based on a mixture of those now experienced in the cloud and those who aren't.

Effectively, we are slowly upskilling multiple teams using osmosis.

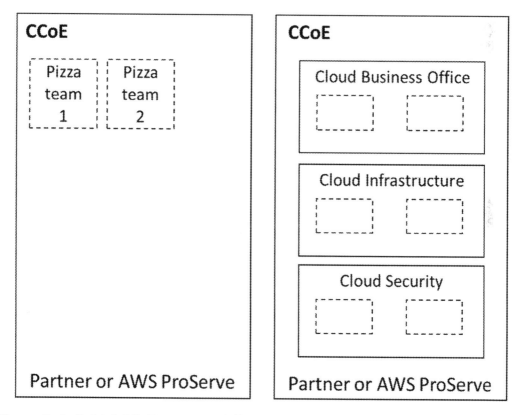

Figure 8-4. *Initial CCoE structure followed by a mature CCoE structure*

Cloud Operating Models

At this point, you've understood the impact of the cloud thanks to the Cloud Adoption Framework and have begun to set up your own Cloud Center of Excellence team to create and share best practices and cloud governance throughout the business.

Before we start moving any workloads or data, we need to understand how we are going to operate and support our cloud workloads once they have been built or migrated. Typically, a cloud adoption takes place at the same time as an adoption of DevOps, which makes sense because the cloud is the enabler of a DevOps structure.

There are numerous nuanced definitions of DevOps; the one I like the best is "You build it, you own it," and it's typically implemented alongside agile workflows and structural changes to the organization.

But how do we get from our traditional Operations model to a pure DevOps model? AWS have developed a number of transitional Cloud Operating Models to help here.

AWS released a whitepaper that covers this changing Cloud Operating Model and what they refer to as the Cloud Enablement Engine. It can be found here: `https://d1.awsstatic.com/whitepapers/building-a-cloud-operating-model.pdf`.

It details six steps that every business should take to introduce their own Cloud Operating Model. They are described here:

1. Work backward from the customer.

2. Reenvision the world as products.

3. Organize teams around products.

4. Bring the work to the team.

5. Reduce risk through iteration.

6. Own your entire lifecycle.

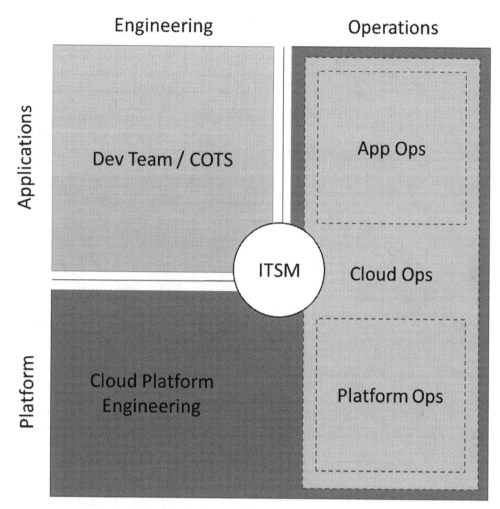

Figure 8-5. *Traditional Ops model when initially adopting the cloud*

You can see in Figure 8-5 a transitional operating model for a business that has started its cloud journey.

You can see that each team is still very compartmentalized, with the developers focused on development and the Operations team covering platforms and operational functions, albeit with a new name now, Cloud Operations and Cloud Platform Engineering.

In this phase, the Development team develops, builds, and packages software which is then released by the Operations teams. There may be a Cloud Platform Engineering team to help codify infrastructure, but this too is controlled and released by Operations. The Operations team themselves may still be using existing tooling to perform its actions including releases and monitoring.

But as the adoption of DevOps and the cloud increases, the Cloud Operating Model adapts to suit the changing ways of working.

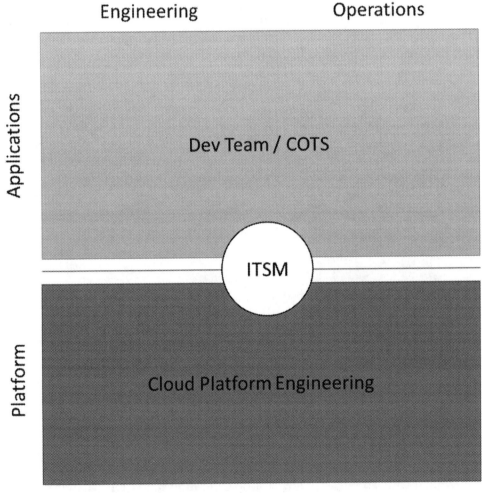

Figure 8-6. *The CloudOps model*

The next evolution is the CloudOps model where application-based and platform-based teams are still separated but now also manage the operational aspect of their roles.

So the CloudPlatform teams now codify and run their infrastructure build, and the Development teams build and release their own software.

In this phase, your teams will be using the CCoE to provide the governance of what services they can use and how best to use them to ensure security and cost-effectiveness.

The goal we want to get to, and potentially one of the drivers of your entire cloud adoption, is a move to DevOps.

DevOps will give us small two-pizza teams working to build and release applications and features for your users and then managed in life by the same team.

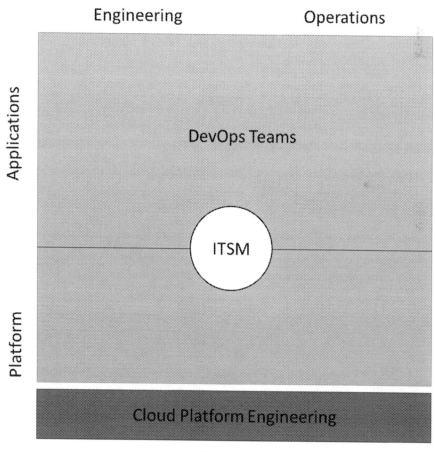

Figure 8-7. *A full DevOps operating model*

As you can see in Figure 8-7, you've finally moved beyond compartmentalized teams into multiple small DevOps teams who are using CI/CD pipelines to build and release software on a far higher frequency than you've previously been able to.

Challenges in Moving to the Cloud

A report from Unisys in 2019 showed the impact that Operational Integration has on your Cloud Adoption journey (`www.unisys.com/offerings/cloud-services/news%20 release/one-in-three-cloud-migrations-fail-unisys-cloud-success-barometer`).

Unisys surveyed over 1000 IT leaders who had completed a full Cloud Adoption, not just to AWS but all other cloud providers were included also.

The headline in the report read that "One-third of organizations have seen no improvement to their organizational effectiveness as a result of cloud adoption."

Delving further, it becomes clear that a lot of companies are migrating to the cloud, but not all are migrating in the right way. A big part of that was how their organizations dealt with a move to the cloud – with only a third saying that their organization has made cloud transformation a core part of their business strategy.

It's little surprise that when asked what challenges, aside from security, that companies find moving to the cloud, they mention "Changing to new processes and procedures."

Traditional operational processes are firmly based on the ITIL framework but need to be revised for cloud adoption. Different migration strategies (the Seven R's described in Chapter 9) offer different challenges and significant levels of change in our current ITIL process depending on the different types of migration and Cloud Operating Model you choose.

There are a lot of challenges moving to the cloud. While this chapter has barely scratched the surface, diving deep on the themes raised in this chapter could be a solid starting point to unlock those cloud advantages.

Summary

In this chapter, we've briefly stepped away from a focus on Microsoft workloads on AWS to consider the wider ramifications of a move to the cloud. We now understand that these challenges are rarely due to technical problems and almost always due to "Cultural Issues" within your business.

If it ain't broke, don't fix it may have been our guiding principle for the last 20 years (a close second place is "Never make changes on a Friday afternoon"), but with a move to the cloud, changes have to be made; the processes we've written to derisk and protect our business don't need to be torn up. But they certainly need to be reread to see if they still make sense in our new cloud world.

I've been fortunate enough over the last 7 years to see how well a cloud adoption can be managed when you have good stakeholder support, and the cloud is a core part of your business strategy. I've also seen what happens when that isn't the case. Projects take years to complete, and barriers are put up everywhere you turn.

It's human nature that we get such a response because by nature we are creatures of habit, and change causes us to question ourselves. Can I learn this new cloud thing? Do I need to be a developer? What if I'm comfortable as I am, and I don't want to learn anything new?

The AWS Cloud Adoption Framework workshops draw out these concerns, allowing the business to plan for ways to address them with new training, mentoring, and maybe new organizational structures that move into two-pizza teams where we all learn from each other's strengths.

I hope this chapter has given you a cause to think, maybe pause, your full-scale migration to the cloud and consider the impact and operationally how you'll manage once those workloads are migrated.

Get this right, and everything else is smooth sailing.

CHAPTER 9

Migration

This chapter covers the business and technical aspects of migration to the AWS Cloud. From a business perspective, we'll cover the business case, costs, and resources. From a technical perspective, we'll cover the tools and services you'll need to move your Microsoft workloads to AWS.

It may surprise you that a cloud migration isn't a given for most companies.

There are those that are still unconvinced that the benefits of operating in the cloud outweigh the effort it takes to get there. Added to that are businesses that have been unsuccessful with their previous attempts or perhaps companies that only see cloud as a home for all "new development" work and are happy to leave existing application workloads in their data centers.

But for the rest of us, there is the "migration project" to complete – hopefully with some compelling event looming in the not too distant future to help steer our minds away from the infinite possible design architectures or the "We always do things this way" mentality and focus on epics, tasks, and sprints.

Migration projects all have their unique differences. They will challenge us, make us question our career choices, and generally make us scream in frustration, but will also provide us with moments of true pride and achievement, such as when you transition your first app into production or finally get that horrible CRM system with multiple dependencies working and performing perfectly.

Added to the complexity of a Migration are the Microsoft Workload dependencies such as an Active Directory infrastructure, licensing, legacy version support, as well as Monitoring and Management tasks such as patching and Image Management. We've already covered much of this, and we go on to cover Identity and Active Directory in the next chapter.

© Ryan Pothecary 2021
R. Pothecary, *Running Microsoft Workloads on AWS*, https://doi.org/10.1007/978-1-4842-6628-1_9

The Business of Migration

Long before you have that three-hour meeting with your cloud architects on a tagging strategy, you'll need to convince someone in a very senior position that a move to the cloud is going to benefit the business. This will involve creating a Business Case, and AWS offers some guidance in this undertaking.

A section of the AWS Prescriptive Guidance is dedicated to accelerating large-scale migrations, but the advice here will come in useful whatever your business size: `https://docs.aws.amazon.com/prescriptive-guidance/latest/mrp-solution/welcome.html`.

Why do we create a Business Case rather than a standard TCO (Total Cost of Operation) Analysis?

Looking at Figure 9-1, we can see a graphical representation of a normal Cloud Migration. You'll notice that TCO is just a very small part of that, while the Business Case covers the whole Migration, TCO, Cost Optimization, and Business Value.

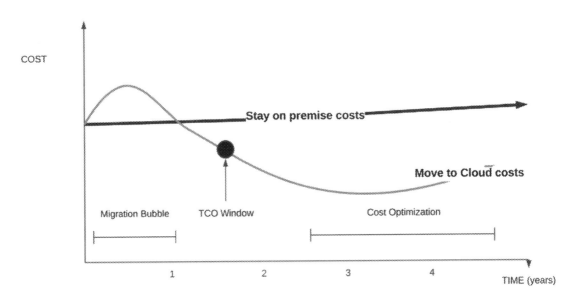

Figure 9-1. *Standard Cloud Migration*

A large part of the business case is going to be focused on the financials of Cloud Adoption.

- Migration Costs
- Operating Costs in AWS

- Costs associated with exiting current data center, including power and cooling

- Estimated cost savings of moving to AWS

- Length of Migration

- Resources required and so on

However, we must also remember to include the intangibles that oftentimes don't have a financial impact we can immediately see, such as

- The impact of doing nothing

- Competitive disadvantage

- Speed to market or business agility

- Innovation

- Operational resilience

- Resource efficiency

AWS suggests that Business Cases are not only prepared for the initial Cloud Adoption and migration into AWS but also for any new workloads that are potentially going to move into AWS. The Business Case will highlight costs associated with bringing those new workloads into AWS and ongoing Operational costs.

Two different types of Business Case are Directional and Detailed. See Table 9-1.

Table 9-1. *Directional and Detailed business cases*

	Directional Business Case	**Detailed Business Case**
Time taken	1 week	Up to 10 weeks
Detail	High level	Low level
Data	Limited customer data	Broad customer data
Output	Presentation	Presentation, documents, spreadsheets
Tools	Simple TCO calculator	Multiple tools
Pricing tolerance	+- 30%	+- 5%

The Detailed Business Case is going to be used to provide the data that your C-Suite and Board members need to justify and approve this new IT Strategy. It takes a significant amount of effort and time to complete and is very precise with a cost tolerance of only 5%.

Comparing this to our Directional Business Case, which is more high level, it takes a lot less time and resource to create, but costs are just ballpark approximations with a 30% cost tolerance.

The data for each Business Case will come from internal tools, audits, TCO calculators, and Business Case Analysis. But AWS also has some great Services that can help us here, such as the AWS Application Discovery Service or the newly renamed AWS Migration Estimator (formally TSO Logic). We will discuss these tools later in the chapter.

The Business Case should be fair and balanced. It's easy to approach this task with some unconscious bias based on what you think the decision should be. Be aware of this. Sometimes, a move to the cloud isn't the right thing to do at this moment (although it usually is).

Why not? Maybe due to a lack of a Cloud Strategy, no support from stakeholders, no internal Cloud skills, or lack of a relationship with a partner that can help. I've worked with many large Enterprise companies that have halted their cloud projects because they realized that they are just not mature enough to deal with the cultural changes needed to ensure the project is successful.

To make the Business Case valid, you'll need a lot of information from internal sources that may not be readily available. Figure 9-2 provides a simple summary of the costs that should be considered when building your business case.

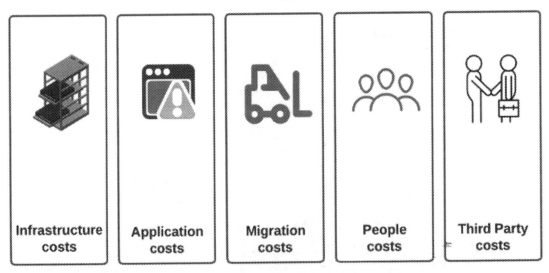

Figure 9-2. *Internal categories to uncover for our Business Case*

Infrastructure costs are fairly easy to calculate. We can find out the cost of the individual physical equipment we have, servers, switches, storage, and so on. Things get a little more complex when we have a mixture of virtual servers in our environment, so we are going to make sure that we add operating system licensing costs to the total – storage costs, including any unused storage, alongside Backup Costs and Media Handling costs too.

Do you own the data center or colocate with a data center provider? Are there per-server management costs or a contracted cost per rack? What are the Power and HVAC costs? Have you got any contractual termination penalties?

As you can see, there is a lot of information to gather, and a lot of it requires some research and investigation. It may surprise you, but often just having a complete list of servers that are currently located inside your data center is near impossible to find. You do not want to get to the end of your Cloud Migration and still find a whole load of equipment that wasn't on the list.

Having a complete, detailed list of your infrastructure is incredibly important when it comes to planning and prioritizing the actual migration but also when we move to the next phase in our Business Case where we uncover costs associated with our applications.

Uncovering your Application Costs relies on the information you've uncovered from the Infrastructure Costs section so that you can start mapping the application you run against the physical servers that run them and uncovering dependencies between applications and other services, whether that's external or internal.

Application Licensing needs to be fully uncovered and understood. Have you purchased the license outright? Is it part of an Enterprise Agreement or SPLA (Services Provider License Agreement)? Do you have the ability to move the license into AWS, and if so, is it tied to vCPU, CPU, Servers, or Sockets?

What SLAs do your applications have and can you provide this with AWS as is? Or do you need to architect a High Availability Multi-AZ approach that will have an impact on costs?

Migration Costs should be covered in our Business Case. Now that we know what workloads/resources we have, and we've taken the time to categorize them, we can now begin to calculate the Migration Costs.

These will typically include the following areas:

- Migration development effort

- Testing effort

- Acceptance into Service

- Deployment

- Tooling costs

- Landing Zone

- Data Migration

Finally, we add into our Business Case the people and third-party costs. People costs should cover both Direct (employees) and Indirect (contractors), and we should dive down into the detail of what covers the tasks that our people complete. You'll find a significant amount of daily work goes into the maintenance/support/operations side of just keeping an IT infrastructure running – patching, releasing code, fixing issues, and so on.

Compare that against what tasks will still be needed when we are running in the cloud. We can automate patching by using AWS Systems Manager or by refreshing our Amazon EC2 infrastructure monthly with fresh AMIs. We can also fully automate code releases using the AWS Code suite of services. If you decide to use Managed Services like Amazon RDS rather than running Amazon EC2 for everything, then that further reduces those housekeeping tasks that take up so much of our time.

Most businesses have been dealing with third-party costs for a long time, whether that's because they've outsourced their IT management or have licensing and support contracts with application providers. All the standard IT management best practices apply here. Understand what you are paying for and understand what is not included and what the cost is for ad hoc requests. We've all heard or experienced horror stories of poor third parties that try to recoup a profit from a Managed Service deal by charging for every small change request.

Are there any contractual lock-ins or early termination penalties? Can we guarantee that the third party will hand over the documented build and operations of the Cloud platform once their contract expires?

AWS Cloud Adoption Readiness Tool (CART)

Is your business ready to move to the cloud? What will the impact be?

AWS has the Cloud Adoption Readiness Tool (CART) available to tell you how prepared your organization is for a move to the cloud. This is a pretty high-level tool to run but can provide you and your teams some insight into which areas you need to focus on to prepare your business for the cloud.

It consists of 16 high-level questions and provides you with a summary report on what your next steps should be. How can it do that with just 16 questions?

The AWS Cloud Adoption Readiness Tool (Figure 9-3) is the customer-facing counterpart of AWS Migration Readiness Assessment which is available to AWS Partners and provides 60 questions that an AWS Partner should ask their potential cloud-ready customer.

The AWS Cloud Adoption Readiness Tool uses a subset of those 60 questions to provide highlights rather than detail into your readiness to run a successful Cloud Adoption program.

The questions asked by the AWS Cloud Adoption Readiness Tool fit into AWS's Cloud Adoption Framework (CAF) perspectives. We discussed CAF in Chapter 8.

I find the reports and visualizations that come out of the AWS Cloud Adoption Readiness Tool to be really effective – the Radar Chart in particular I've used to quickly highlight areas to focus on during a Cloud Adoption project (`https://cloudreadiness.amazonaws.com/#/cart`).

The sole purpose of the AWS CART tool is for organizations to understand their cloud readiness, and my advice for any company here is to either work with an AWS Partner to run through a full Migration Readiness Assessment workshop or conduct their own cloud readiness workshop using the CART tool.

You'll find that different job roles within your organization will answer questions differently and that should lead you to understand a broader perspective of your readiness to cloud adoption.

The Migration Bubble

You'll need to create a process to migrate workloads, and this normally includes a time where you've migrated the individual components that make up your workload and now need to perform some performance and user acceptance testing. If all of these tests are successful, you'll normally take a final cut of the most recently changed data and arrange an out-of-hours cutover to your cloud-based application.

During this time, you are running the workload on-premises as well as in AWS and will be doubling the costs for this workload. There are also other costs the organization must bear, such as bringing in an external consultancy, training, tooling, and so on. This is what defines the Migration Bubble.

It's important to explain this phase to your stakeholders since they'll be looking at costs being reduced when you move to the cloud and may be concerned that costs are initially higher during the migration phase.

The duration of the Migration Bubble (Figure 9-3) makes no significant changes to the cost incurred. For example, if I have a team of five engineers in my Migration Factory, then I could calculate that for X number of applications, the Migration Bubble phase will last 12 months.

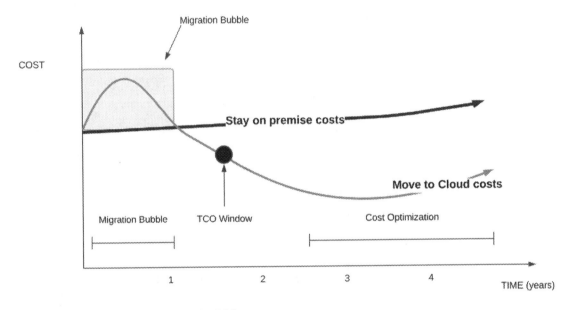

Figure 9-3. *The Migration Bubble*

What if I double the Migration Factory engineers to ten? This could reasonably reduce the Migration Bubble to 6 months, but does this also reduce the costs?

No. The costs are associated with the number of workloads we are moving and not the duration. However, the positive side of reducing the duration of the Migration Bubble is that you get to the payback period a lot faster. This is where you've effectively saved more than enough running in the cloud to pay back the Migration costs. After that will be an ongoing cycle of working at reducing costs, refactoring applications to be more cloud native which also reduces costs, and then exploration of the new AWS services at your disposal and on which you can innovate with.

Cost-Effective Migrations

A Cloud Adoption project can be an expensive business to finance, what with additional skilled headcount, training, and possible help from partners. Bear in mind that one of the biggest drivers to moving to the cloud is the potential cost savings, and you can understand why taking control of Migration costs and having a Migration focused on cost optimization is going to be helpful to the success of the project as a whole.

There are quick wins to be made here such as using consolidated billing to get a holistic view of the spend in your AWS accounts, and we can tie this into the use of tags on every resource you use to enable you to cost and chargeback AWS usage to the other budget-holding parts of your business.

You'll want to ensure that you are sensible around the Services that your users use; is there a need for your developers to have access to the AWS CloudHSM service or perhaps large Amazon EC2 Instance Types? Use services like AWS IAM or AWS Service Catalog to prevent access and protect from accidental usage which would incur high costs.

The biggest change could be in using tagging and automation via AWS Systems Manager to switch off idle resources overnight, ensuring your development, UAT, test, and pre-production environments are only available during times when they'll be in use by your teams.

Tip   If they are not being used, switch off resources.

Moving toward an immutable infrastructure, which we discussed in Chapter 3, will allow your entire infrastructure to be terminated and rebuilt overnight, reducing costs around usage as well as management and patching.

But, by far, the biggest cost reduction will come via the right-sizing of Amazon EC2 Instances compared to what you have been running on-premises.

General industry statistics tell us that on-premises servers have an average usage of 45% (IDC 2017). Obviously, that's an average, and you'll have servers that are more or less utilized than that, but it's a fair starting point. Before we had tools to help us, a lot of companies migrating to AWS chose an Amazon EC2 Instance type that matched the server spec that they were migrating from. Better to overprovision and have spare capacity than underprovision and suffer performance issues.

And overprovisioning was something that we did often when purchasing servers. An extra few gigabytes of RAM, some extra disk space, or a faster processor didn't have a huge impact on a server cost over the lifetime of the server.

But when we are paying per hour for our servers, then choosing the right instance type can add up.

For example, choosing a T3a.XLarge with 4 vCPUs (Virtual CPU) and 16GB RAM rather than an M5a.2XLarge with 8 vCPUs and 32GB RAM will save you in the region of $350 a month. Times that by the number of servers you have, and you can see just how big an impact right-sizing has on your costs.

I feel the reason that companies don't make this a top priority is simply our legacy way of thinking about servers. Previously, we've bought a server with a certain spec and that was that. Unless we really had to, we didn't upgrade it at all, and if we did, that would mean downtime and working in awful data centers overnight. Not recommended.

With AWS, I can change between Amazon EC2 Instance Types with a simple stop and start of the virtual server. The outage is a few minutes compared with a few hours of an on-premises server.

Have I convinced you yet?

Let me show you how easy it all is by using one of AWS's new services, the AWS Migration Evaluator.

AWS Migration Evaluator

In January 2019, AWS announced it had acquired a partner called TSO Logic. I'd been using their services in 2018 as part of a large migration and welcomed the news because the service was really good. On the surface, the TSO Logic software provides Discovery information about a customer's on-premises environment and offers similar functionality to AWS's own Application Discovery Service.

But TSO Logic has a few brilliant tricks up its sleeve, and each of the services offers unique features that the other doesn't. Fast forward to mid-2020 and the service has been rebranded as the AWS Migration Evaluator: *https://aws.amazon.com/migration-evaluator/*.

AWS Migration Evaluator isn't a service you'll find in the AWS Management Console. As a customer or partner, you'll need to engage with the AWS Migration Evaluator team to begin the process of using the tool.

Before we begin, it's worth reiterating the purpose of the tool is to discover what you have running in your data center environment in terms of server details such as server specs, hostnames, what applications are running on the server, and performance data of that server. All of this information is encrypted and sent to the AWS Migration Evaluator service. Your security teams will want to drill further into the details of this process, and in my experience, the AWS Migration Evaluator team is more than happy to answer any questions you or your teams may have.

Once you've engaged with the team, you'll learn that AWS Migration Evaluator has three ways of discovering what you have running on your network. But before you start, you'll need to create a virtual server to act as the Migration Evaluator data collector. Once this server is running, we can choose one of two ways to gather the information – either via a read-only user on your Hyper-V/vmware vCenter hosts or alternatively you can use network discovery via standard TCP/IP management protocols like SNMP or WMI.

However, both methods may require low-impact changes to your infrastructure by either creating read-only access to your VMware hosts or opening network ports to allow SNMP/WMI traffic. This will be early days in your Cloud journey and may make some teams nervous. So AWS Migration Evaluator offers a third choice which is to import your current CMDB database, thus avoiding any internal change requests. However, this will not give you the performance data you require, and although the other methods require some effort, the wealth of data obtained will help you to make more informed decisions further down the line.

Having three methods at your disposal means that you can capture not only the virtual servers in your estate but also the physical servers too.

You'll be working with AWS Project Managers and Solution Architects to make sure you capture all of the data required and at the end of the process are presented with a Business Case Summary (Figure 9-4) that can be used to supplement your own Directional Business Case when evaluating a Cloud Adoption.

Data Insights

Overview of the percentage of time servers were used, environment insights & licensing details.

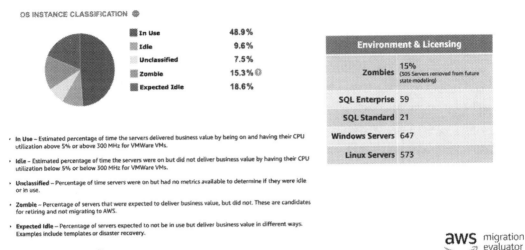

OS INSTANCE CLASSIFICATION	
In Use	48.9%
Idle	9.6%
Unclassified	7.5%
Zombie	15.3%
Expected Idle	18.6%

Environment & Licensing	
Zombies	15% (305 Servers removed from future state modeling)
SQL Enterprise	59
SQL Standard	21
Windows Servers	647
Linux Servers	573

- **In Use** – Estimated percentage of time the servers delivered business value by being on and having their CPU utilization above 5% or above 300 MHz for VMWare VMs.

- **Idle** – Estimated percentage of time the servers were on but did not deliver business value by having their CPU utilization below 5% or below 300 MHz for VMWare VMs.

- **Unclassified** – Percentage of time servers were on but had no metrics available to determine if they were idle or in use.

- **Zombie** – Percentage of servers that were expected to deliver business value, but did not. These are candidates for retiring and not migrating to AWS.

- **Expected Idle** – Percentage of servers expected to not be in use but deliver business value in different ways. Examples include templates or disaster recovery.

aws migration evaluator
Powerly TSO Logic

Figure 9-4. *AWS Migration Evaluator data insights*

Apart from the Discovery information that you'll get from using the service, you'll also receive information related to on-premises server to EC2 instance mapping. This is where your right-sizing information is obtained from, along with the percentage of savings you'll make if you follow the recommendations.

But for me, the area where AWS Migration Evaluator adds a huge amount of value is in its ability to make use of the Microsoft licenses you already own to reduce the costs of your monthly AWS bill (Figure 9-5).

Blended Model – RIs & On-Demand
(SQL Server BYOL)

AWS Modeling Parameters

Location:	US East (N. Virginia)
Instances:	• 3 Year AURI (Prod) • 3 Year AURI – DH (Prod SQL) • On-Demand (Non-Prod)
Modeling:	• TSO Right Sizing
Licensing:	• Windows licenses included • BYOL SQL Server @ $3300/core (Ent) and $1100/core (Std)
Currency:	• USD annually

	On-Prem Estimate	On Demand 8 Hours / Day	3 Year AURI – DH / Shared
Non-Production	$1,073,340	$262,395	
Production	$2,411,763		$436,567
Total	$3,485,103		$698,962
80% Savings			

Figure 9-5. *AWS Migration Evaluator showing license reuse cost savings*

As part of their "white-glove" service, the AWS Migration Evaluator team will work with you to perform an Optimization and Licensing Assessment to fully understand what licenses you own and if they can be reused in AWS. This can significantly increase the cost savings that AWS Migration Evaluator can suggest to you by making right-sizing recommendations that take into account your license obligations as well as introduce Amazon EC2 Dedicated Hosts and Instances to save costs across your AWS bill.

We discussed licensing and the AWS License Manager in Chapter 3.

One final feature of AWS Migration Evaluator is its integration with CloudEndure, an AWS service which provides block-level replication features to support server migrations. After capturing all of the discovery data and making right-sizing recommendations, AWS Migration Evaluator can export all of this data directly into CloudEndure, which gives the service the ability to choose the correct Amazon EC2 Instance type to use when migrating.

AWS Application Discovery Service

Are you getting a sense of déjà vu? AWS also has a different discovery service, and yes, I agree, it does have some overlap with AWS Migration Evaluator when it comes to functionality. However, "everything has a use case" (I'm trademarking that), and AWS Application Discovery Service (ADS) has some nifty features that other services and third-party tools don't.

213

AWS ADS was launched in 2016 alongside its family members, AWS Server Migration Service and AWS Database Migration Service, which all come under the AWS Migration Hub service.

AWS ADS can run as a virtual appliance on both VMware and Hyper-V, similar to AWS Migration Evaluator. However, AWS ADS can also be installed as an agent on each server (Figure 9-6). All the discovery information that it finds is encrypted and sent back to the AWS ADS service in your region.

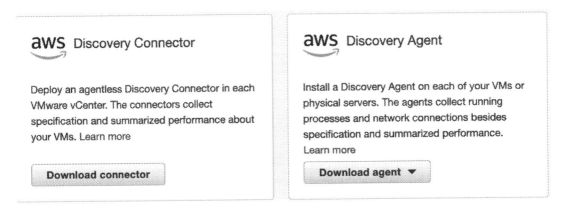

Figure 9-6. *AWS Application Discovery Service*

All very familiar so far, right?

AWS ADS runs in the console, and it's down to you as an AWS user to install it and run it – no "white-glove service" here. If you run AWS ADS as a virtual appliance, then you can gather lots of server details, what applications are running, and so on, the standard stuff you'd expect.

But if you are running AWS ADS via the agent-based approach, then you'll also be able to gather information on network usage and what network connections your server is making. This information can be invaluable to determine whether a workload has some kind of dependency on other workloads, which then will determine how you migrate that workload.

Imagine the scenario where you happily migrate a solitary server that you don't have a lot of information about, only to find out that once a month it transfers data that kick-starts your monthly payroll run. Without an understanding of this transfer, no one will get paid this month. You will not be popular!

Dependency mapping is a very important part of any migration where you don't have full and complete documentation of the workloads you are migrating, which, in reality, is every single migration project that I've ever been a part of.

So, what to use? Keep in mind there are third-party services also, like Deloitte's ATAVision, Flexera, BMC Discovery, and others.

I would certainly recommend AWS Migration Evaluator if I was in the Business Case preparation stage. The data that it will discover and the recommendations it makes will feed directly into your Business Case and will assist in preparing the case for a Cloud Adoption to your stakeholders.

While the decision to move to the cloud is being made, I would look at installing the AWS ADS agents across my estate to capture any network dependencies that I'm not aware of. It could be that you have enough internal knowledge of the workloads not to need it. Personally, I think it's better to be safe than sorry.

I'd then use the output of both services as a base for prioritizing workloads for migration.

Migration Prioritization

I have a confession.

During my first cloud migration project, my CTO asked me what applications we should prioritize first. Our business used approximately 60 applications of all shapes and sizes. We had a lot of small, single server applications used by only a handful of people, and we had a single core application that was used by the entire business and also all of our field agents.

I had zero AWS experience. Before I started the role, I'd never used AWS before, and after 8 years I'm still no nearer to calling myself an expert, and i'm still learning new things every day.

I looked my CTO in the eye and told him the first application we would move is that big, ugly, Microsoft Dynamics CRM core application that everyone uses. My logic was that if we were successful with that, then everything else would be plain sailing.

He looked at me and told me I was an idiot.

He wasn't wrong.

It was a stupid idea but one I'll always remember and a good lesson to learn.

Because when it comes to a Cloud Migration, gaining as much experience and knowledge as quickly as possible is the best way forward. You have to ensure that you understand the nuances of the tools and services you've decided to use, the quirks of internal systems, as well as working with and iterating a migration pipeline process that will allow you to scale the migration when you need to.

You don't do that by spending a month migrating a CRM system; you get that knowledge a lot faster by using that same time period to migrate 30 smaller systems, iterating the process each time and learning more lessons with every application.

You'll need to prioritize which applications to migrate first, and to do that you'll need to map your on-premises application list to a method of migration using the **Seven R's** technique.

The Seven R's is not a proprietary AWS technique; it's been a standard migration approach throughout the IT industry, growing and adapting when new platforms and migration methods arise. Originally coming from Gartner in 2010 and starting with five migration strategies, it has evolved over the last 11 years to move from Rehost, Refactor, Revise, Rebuild, Replace to the current Seven R's as follows:

- Rehost

- Replatform

- Repurchase

- Refactor

- Retire

- Retain

- Relocate

Let's discuss these individually.

Rehost, otherwise called Lift and Shift, is where we take the existing application workload and migrate it to AWS "as is." We don't make any changes to the server workloads; what we have on-premises is what we'll have in AWS.

"What is the benefit of *that*?" I hear you scream?

I understand your concern. On the surface, this may not provide you with the Cloud Nirvana that you've heard about, but it does have its uses. Firstly, this is a very quick way of migrating to AWS. There are no changes, so minimal application testing is required. It worked on-premises; it'll work in AWS. Being a quick method of migration means it's suited for those scenarios where you've got a deadline to close a data center or before a contract expires.

Secondly, Rehosting is usually the start of the journey here. Your migration plan could be to just *get into AWS* as quickly as possible, and once here and saving money, you can then start to transform your workloads.

Finally, you can still add a lot of benefits with a Rehost approach. This could come in the way you can use the services around you. You can use a Rehost approach to right-size your workload based on what performance you actually require rather than what you think you require. There are different forms of storage you can use to give you the performance you require and also save you costs.

Rehosting doesn't mean you can't use Services, so look at what services might work well with the workload and leverage those – whether that's Amazon FSx for shared storage, AWS Systems Manager for managing your workload, or Elastic Load Balancer to distribute traffic. What about augmenting the functionality of the original application by using custom metrics in Amazon CloudWatch or Sidecar architecture patterns?

```
https://aws.amazon.com/blogs/containers/using-sidecar-injection-on-
amazon-eks-with-aws-app-mesh/
```

Rehosting is by far the most popular migration strategy, typically accounting for 40% or more of all migrations.

Don't get all snobby about this. It may not be pretty, but it works very effectively. It's also a migration strategy that is supported by all available tools and lends itself very well to a fully functioning Migration Factory technique that will help you scale your migration across multiple workstreams with a focus on speed.

OK, you want more bang for your buck?

Then can I interest you in a *Replatform*? Otherwise known as Lift, Tinker, and Shift.

With Replatform, we are going to be making changes from the original on-premises server you have running to an AWS-based server that is upgraded in some way. That could be an upgrade to the operating system (OS), service, or application you have running.

If you have out-of-date or out-of-support software running on your on-premises server, then a migration project is the perfect time to slip in some additional changes so that the workload is all shiny and new when it's running on your cloud platform. No one wants to be running out-of-date or unsupported workloads in a brand-new platform. One of your reasons for moving to the cloud might be to reduce the amount of server maintenance you are currently doing, and so migrating workloads that need more maintenance than average doesn't make sense.

Firstly, you'll need a good understanding of the application that you are running. Why does it need to be replatformed? Is the OS out of support? If so, does the application support a newer OS? If it's an application upgrade, then you'll need to work with the application support team to make sure that you can migrate the data and configuration settings you are using.

Secondly, design with the Well-Architected framework in mind (`https://aws.amazon.com/architecture/well-architected/`).

If you are taking the trouble to replatform an application, complete a full design where you also consider reliability, security, cost, operations, and performance. That way, when it's running on AWS, then it'll be running in its best possible form and reducing your housekeeping activities and costs.

Thirdly, test, test, transition, and test. You are making significant changes to a workload. Do not attempt to migrate this to AWS until you are extremely confident that your changes have been successful on-premises. Moving to the cloud when you are not sure will only confuse any investigation should anything hit the fan.

Once you are happy with the Replatformed server, then use standard migration tools to move it into AWS, such as CloudEndure and AWS Server Migration Service.

Unable to upgrade your out-of-support workloads? You'll find information on AWS EMP, the End-of-Support Migration Program, later on in this chapter.

Repurchase is a less common strategy than you may think, just accounting for between 5 and 10% of migrations. Repurchasing covers the replacement of existing applications with brand-new applications – usually, SaaS-type applications that will give you more functionality in a pay-as-you-go manner. A great example of this is the move from on-premises email systems to email services like Gmail or Office 365. Once the migration of existing mailboxes to these services is complete, you can finally switch off all those old Exchange servers that you've had to run 24/7.

Now far be it for me to stop you from using a Service rather than Servers, but you'll need to do your own due diligence here. Will the SaaS service offer the same functionality and configurability that you get currently? It's a common complaint I've heard before from those trying out online SharePoint or Dynamics services where they've been unable to add some of the add-in functionality they use currently. It could be that the benefit of removing ten existing SharePoint servers outweighs the benefit to the business of using a small customization. Only you can decide this.

Refactor is an ambitious migration strategy. It involves redeveloping the existing application, probably to be more cloud native, probably leveraging AWS Services to supplement application functionality such as Amazon SQS or SNS. Maybe the new application will leverage Container services such as Amazon ECS or EKS or go completely cloud native with Serverless AWS Lambda functions.

Whatever your technology choices, one thing is certain; Refactor is not a fast migration method. Instead, it's used for those one or two applications that are out of support or were in need of new functionality anyway.

Typical refactor projects can take upward of a year to complete, which is why it's usual to use a Rehost strategy to first move the workload into AWS and then look at Refactoring applications post migration during a reinvention phase.

There are numerous other ways to refactor an application other than having to redevelop the whole thing – improvements that have little or no impact in terms of functionality but add a huge impact with regard to day-to-day housekeeping, such as using Amazon RDS for the database layer or Amazon SES for email functions. AWS has a lot of ways to help you here.

Retire your application rather than migrate it to AWS. This may be true if you are already running a newer version of the application stack but kept the older version "just to be safe." You may laugh, but I've seen this practice a lot.

According to AWS, this migration strategy covers just 5% of workloads, although in my experience it's a little higher. We can also Retire the application if we've decided to Repurchase a SaaS solution that provides the same or better functionality. Either way, from our perspective, we need to identify these workloads quickly and remove them from our migration planning because they won't be going anywhere.

Retain covers those workloads that won't be moving to AWS for reasons beyond being retired. This could be that a planned refactoring of the workload is underway, and it's this new version that will live in AWS rather than the old legacy version. It could be that the current version is using components that are out of support – hello AWS EMP.

However, the single largest reason is that the workload is running on a hardware platform that is not x86 and therefore not able to run "as is" on AWS. Every Enterprise scale customer I've met has mainframes it uses for critical workloads. So, what do we do with those?

AWS has teams of architects and engineers that can help with these workloads – either using emulation or refactoring to migrate these previously impossible workloads. Ask your AWS Account Manager about this.

Finally, in 2020, AWS added a further R to take us up to the current seven.

Relocate is used for those workloads that reside in specific locations and can be moved rather than migrated. Containers are a great example of Relocate. No changes required, just take the container image and run it on AWS. This can also apply to the VMware Cloud solution that is sold by VMware and fully supported by AWS due to the partnership between the two companies from 2017. VMware's NSX virtual networking technology allows for lightning fast movement between on-premises VMware hosts and AWS.

There's a well-known Customer Case Study of the Massachusetts Institute of Technology (MIT) using VMware Cloud to migrate 3300 virtual machines over the course of 3 months and 550TB of data using the equivalent of one full-time employee (`www.crn. com/slide-shows/virtualization/10-keys-to-successful-vmware-cloud-on-aws-migrations`).

Cloud-to-cloud migrations also fall under this category, and as businesses try out cloud platforms based on how many free credits they receive, then this will be a growing migration strategy.

In this section, we've discussed Migration Business Cases, AWS Cloud Adoption Readiness Tool, AWS Migration Evaluator, Costs, and the Seven R's migration strategies. In the next section, we discuss how we get there using some of the available AWS Services.

Figure 9-7 shows a table of migration complexity. It compares all seven of the migration strategies. It's easy to spot why Rehost and Repurchase are the favored methods of migrations if your workloads are on-premises. They both provide time-efficient ways of moving to the cloud. There are *some* benefits in terms of agility, especially for Replatform where you can use additional services to augment what you already have.

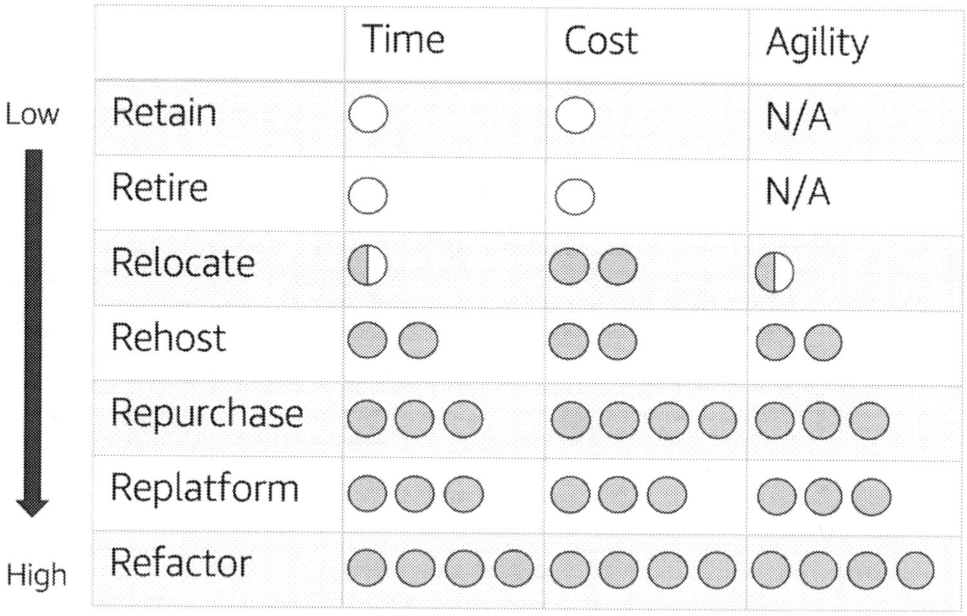

	Time	Cost	Agility
Low ↓			
Retain	◯	◯	N/A
Retire	◯	◯	N/A
Relocate	◑	◯◯	◑
Rehost	◯◯	◯◯	◯◯
Repurchase	◯◯◯	◯◯◯◯	◯◯◯
Replatform	◯◯◯	◯◯◯	◯◯◯
High Refactor	◯◯◯◯	◯◯◯◯	◯◯◯◯

Figure 9-7. *Comparison based on time, cost, and agility*

Obviously, the best in terms of time and cost is Relocate, but this is still a very new approach and focuses on a use case of either using tools like VMware Cloud, containerization, or migration from other cloud platforms. A significant amount of companies are yet to start their first cloud journey, let alone moving between cloud platforms!

Migration Tooling

AWS has a number of Migration Services, and in this section we dive a little deeper into each of them. Firstly, let's begin with a quick overview of AWS Quick Starts.

We discussed AWS Quick Starts during Chapter 4 in relation to quickly creating database solutions, and I also mentioned that there are many more Quick Starts available. One of the most popular Microsoft Quick Starts is SharePoint, and I've used it myself to accelerate a migration. Running the SharePoint Quick Start takes approximately 90 minutes and will save you a good day compared to building a similar solution manually.

Once the Quick Start (Figure 9-8) completes, we can quickly migrate over content and configuration, and we are ready to go. There are Quick Starts covering the majority of Microsoft products as well as a host of other third-party solutions from ISV partners.

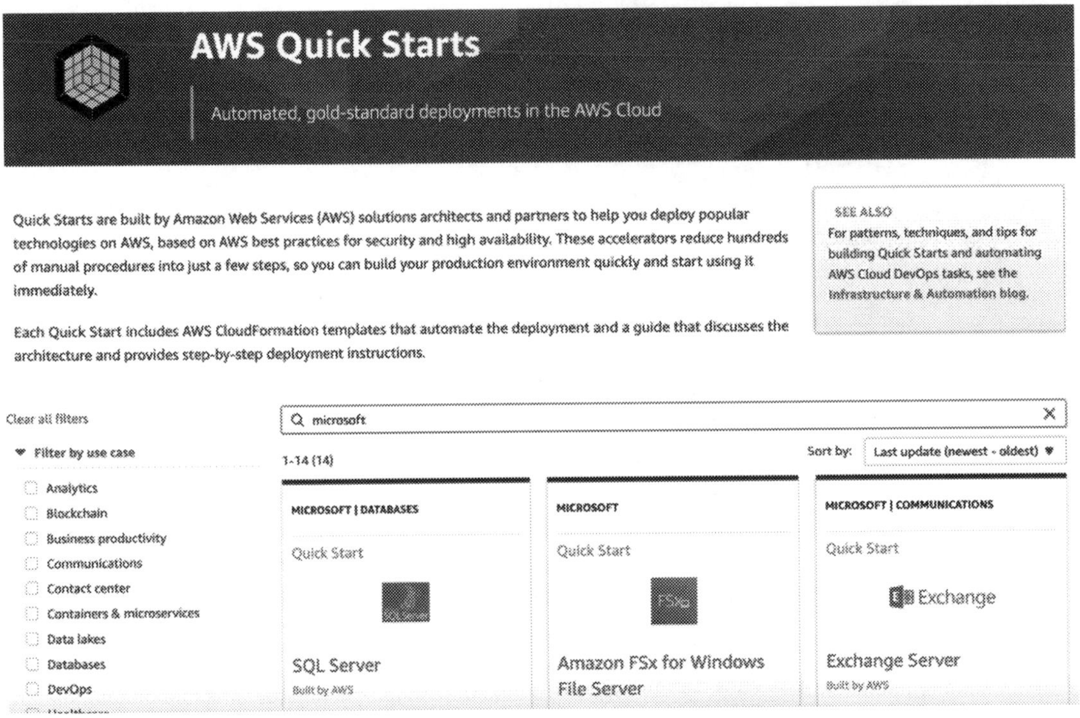
AWS Quick Starts
Automated, gold-standard deployments in the AWS Cloud
Quick Starts are built by Amazon Web Services (AWS) solutions architects and partners to help you deploy popular technologies on AWS, based on AWS best practices for security and high availability. These accelerators reduce hundreds of manual procedures into just a few steps, so you can build your production environment quickly and start using it immediately.
Each Quick Start includes AWS CloudFormation templates that automate the deployment and a guide that discusses the architecture and provides step-by-step deployment instructions.
SEE ALSO
For patterns, techniques, and tips for building Quick Starts and automating AWS Cloud DevOps tasks, see the Infrastructure & Automation blog.
Clear all filters
Filter by use case
Analytics
Blockchain
Business productivity
Communications
Contact center
Containers & microservices
Data lakes
Databases
DevOps
microsoft
1-14 (14)
Sort by:
Last update (newest - oldest)
MICROSOFT | DATABASES
Quick Start
SQL Server
Built by AWS
MICROSOFT
Quick Start
Amazon FSx for Windows File Server
MICROSOFT | COMMUNICATIONS
Quick Start
Exchange
Exchange Server
Built by AWS

Figure 9-8. *AWS Quick Starts*

AWS also has prebuilt solutions in their AWS Marketplace, which provide prebuilt Amazon Machine Images to be used by Amazon EC2. These consist of a base OS along with all of the application components required to run the desired service.

Just choose the solution, create an Amazon EC2 instance using that image, and you'll be ready to go.

There is a huge range of products available to be used, and they are charged using the same pay-as-you-go model as Amazon EC2 where the price includes the normal cost of the type of EC2 Instance you want to run with the cost of the Image bundled on top.

AWS Server Migration Service (AWS SMS)

Before AWS gave us the AWS Server Migration Service, we had the original VM Import/ Export tool which was a command-line tool that converted your VMware (only) VMs to Amazon Machine Images via S3. However, AWS SMS was launched in 2016 and automates a large part of that process for us. It forms part of the AWS Migration Hub service with its focus entirely on migrating virtual machines from the customers' on-premise environments.

It runs as a virtual appliance, called the SMS Connector, which is installed on your existing VMware vCenter, Hyper-V, or Azure environment.

How does it do this? Let's dig a little deeper into the process.

Once the AWS SMS Connector (Figure 9-9) is installed and running, you'll be able to import your virtual machine Server Catalog and then begin the process of either grouping individual servers in Application Groups or selecting individual servers for replication and migration.

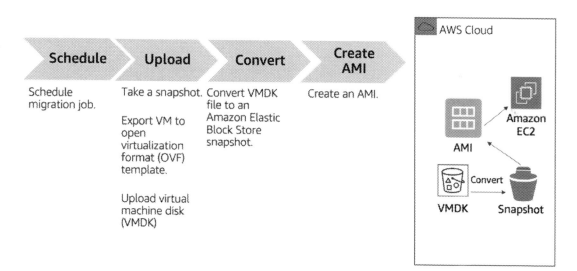

Figure 9-9. *AWS Server Migration Service process*

If you use the Application Groups feature, then AWS SMS replicates the whole application stack and then creates an AWS CloudFormation template to coordinate the launch of the Application Group within AWS. The AWS CloudFormation template launches the Application Group in the following order – database servers, file servers, web servers, and then finally application servers. However, you can obviously edit the template to change the order or add further configuration.

AWS SMS allows you to replicate a virtual machine for up to 90 days. During the replication process, an Amazon S3 bucket is created in your account with an encryption-enabled bucket policy that will delete data after 7 days of use. AWS SMS takes a scheduled snapshot and replicates your on-premises virtual server to this Amazon S3 bucket.

Once you have the snapshot in Amazon S3, AWS SMS creates an Amazon Machine Image (AMI) image from it which then gives you the ability to create an Amazon EC2 Instance from that AMI. Smart.

Although there are some manual steps which can be easily automated, such as creating the Amazon EC2 Instance from the AMI, AWS SMS automates a lot of the process for you.

So why should you get excited by this?

Well, firstly, AWS SMS is wonderfully simple to use, has a solid process that is easy to understand, and has zero cost for running the service – although you will incur Amazon S3 costs for the snapshots and Amazon EC2 costs if you launch instances.

It's also very flexible in allowing you to schedule when and how often replication between your on-premises virtual machine and AWS will occur. So you can kick this off when it's needed, not before.

AWS SMS generates API Events that can be picked up by AWS CloudWatch and CloudTrail, allowing you to automate still further. There's a great example of using an AWS Lambda function to launch an Amazon EC2 Instance when there is a change in the AWS SMS job status: `https://docs.aws.amazon.com/server-migration-service/latest/userguide/cwe-sms.html`. This small piece of automation can be really useful when migrating single servers.

What about migrating from Azure?

It's a very similar process to migrating from on-premises VMware or Hyper-V environments. The first step is to deploy the AWS SMS Connector with onto a virtual machine with at least four VPCs and 8GB RAM in the same Azure region as your Azure virtual machines reside. If you are using multiple Azure Regions, then you'll need to deploy multiple SMS Connectors. You deploy the Connector via a Powershell script that is available via the AWS SMS Service page. Once deployed and configured (which you have to do from a separate VM), you'll then begin to see a valid Azure Connector on the SMS Connectors page, allowing you to import the VMs and scheduling their replication and migration.

AWS SMS is a really useful service, one I've recommended on many a migration project. Other Migration Services may have more features, but I doubt they've migrated as many customer VMs as AWS SMS has.

CloudEndure (An AWS Company)

AWS acquired CloudEndure in January 2019. Where AWS SMS simply creates an AMI from a virtual machine snapshot, CloudEndure replicates the server a disk block at a time via an agent which you have to install. Designing CloudEndure around an agent rather than a virtual appliance gives some immediate benefits.

The obvious first benefit is that you now have the ability to migrate physical servers as well as virtual servers. Other benefits include a more streamlined migration and cutover process and an integration with AWS Migration Evaluator that will bring you huge cost reduction in the form of right-sizing.

The first thing to explain is that CloudEndure is the name of the company, not the service, and they have two distinct services available.

CloudEndure Disaster Recovery is a service that replicates your most critical workloads into AWS with the focus on reducing costs by replicating to a "staging area" and then being able to launch your servers inside AWS, as the name suggests, in the event of an actual disaster. Being able to replicate to a staging area and not a complete like-for-like production environment can save your business significant cost.

What I particularly like about CloudEndure Disaster Recovery is the ability to run a Disaster Recovery Test, something most companies like to do on a quarterly basis, and using this service they'll be able to do that in a very cost-effective and non-impactful way.

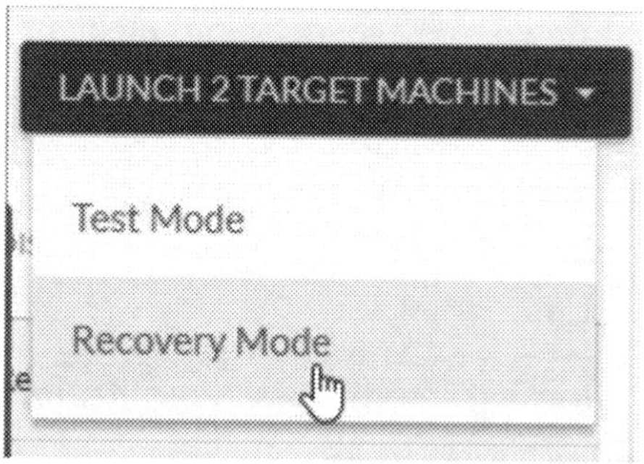

Figure 9-10. *CloudEndure Disaster Recovery test mode*

When the brown stuff hits the fan and you have to launch a recovery for real, CloudEndure Disaster Recovery (Figure 9-10) lets you choose the exact Recovery Point based on the replications that it's been doing in the background – perfect if something has gone wrong and corrupted the current data on the machine.

There is even a *Prepare for Failback* option which is truly amazing. If you've ever been involved in a DR solution, you'll know that the failover is usually the easy part, and the failback is by far the most difficult operation to achieve successfully. This feature makes it easy to recover from a disaster.

AWS Application Migration Service

The other CloudEndure product, and perhaps the most important in the context of this chapter, is CloudEndure Migrations. This has very recently been rebranded as AWS Application Migration Service and integrated into the AWS Management Console. It works in the exact same way as CloudEndure Migrations but now feels a little more integrated and ready for the same treatment that AWS provides to all its services, even the ones it's acquired, which is fast and constant iteration.

AWS Application Migration Service – AWS MGN (AWS AMS had already been taken by the AWS Managed Services team) – is designed for large-scale migrations where you have multiple members in a "Migration Factory." It features rapid cutover between source and target environments. There are a few implementation steps to note before we get there.

Firstly, as mentioned, AWS MGN is agent based, so you'll need to install the lightweight agent onto each of your target machines. Once the agent is installed, it'll start to sync the server to a staging environment in AWS. I've seen a few mistakes in the past where local IT have installed the AWS MGN agent onto every machine overnight. Since you only have 90 days between agent install and cutover before the agent stops working, then installing the agent ahead of time isn't the right strategy to use here.

The agent should be installed a short time before you are actually going to perform a migration of that workload. You'll see in Table 9-2 that it's recommended to install the agent in "Stopped Mode."

Having an agent-based service gives you enormous flexibility in terms of what your source server is. As long as it's x86 based, you'll be fine. That's a huge benefit in comparison to AWS Server Migration Service which only handles virtual servers. Once the agent is installed, then real-time continuous data replication migrates the workloads a block at a time, including the machine state, OS configuration, and applications. This means when we finally cut over, everything will work as expected.

How secure is this? Well, AWS MGN encrypts your data during transit, which can also be via VPN or AWS Direct Connect, and if you are replicating to EBS, then you've got encryption at rest also. Unlike AWS Server Migration Service, the whole process is completely automated, meaning that once you install the AWS MGN agent on your target server, you'll end up with a perfect mirror in AWS once you cut over.

The use of a staging environment allows you to fully test the workload inside AWS before you commence a cutover into production. Any issues and you can stop replication and apply remedial actions before starting replication again.

Table 9-2. *AWS Application Migration Service best practices*

	Action	**Benefit**
Implementation	• Group servers into application groups • Set a cutover date for each application group	This provides a better application user experience
First replication	• Install the agent in stopped mode • Start replication one application group at a time	Avoids overloading our network links
Ongoing replication	Confirm that the replication reaches Continuous Data Protection mode	Target servers can only be launched once replication is complete
Testing	Test application functionality and performance 1–2 weeks before cutover	Ensure you leave enough time to deal with any issues
Cutover	Verify servers are in CDP mode	Shorten cutover window to decrease cutover time

Finally, in this section, Table 9-3 distills all of the information we've learned over this chapter and provides some advice on when to use AWS SMS or AWS MGN.

Table 9-3. *Comparison between AWS SMS and AWS MGN*

	Use Case	Recommendation
Infrastructure Source	Hypervisor based	AWS SMS
	Any source	AWS MGN
Deployment Preference	Agentless	AWS SMS
	Agent-based	AWS MGN
Cutover automation and time	Long cutover	AWS SMS
	Cutover in minutes	AWS MGN

AWS Database Migration Service

The final AWS Migration Service we'll cover is my favorite: AWS Database Migration Service (DMS).

In terms of migrations, moving data is an element that has to be carefully planned. You need to test your migrated workload, and so you'll need a backup of the database in order to test functionality. Database files tend to be big and difficult to transfer. If the only thing between your data center environment and your AWS account is a VPN connection, then you can forget being able to send Multi-TB files over the network and instead need to consider the AWS Snow Family of services – more on those later.

AWS Database Migration Service (Figure 9-11) allows you to migrate databases from a wide variety of sources into a large variety of targets, and along the way, you are able to filter and change data in a whole host of ways.

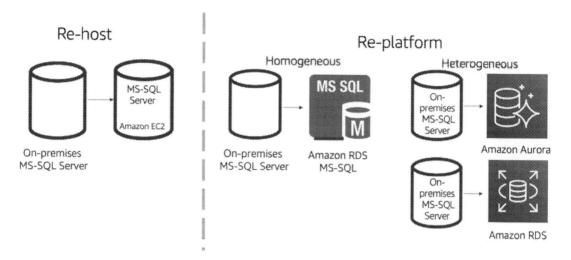

Figure 9-11. *AWS Database Migration Service different migration strategies*

When you use the AWS DMS service for the first time, you'll be asked to create a DMS Replication Instance. The replication instance will live in your AWS Account; you specify which VPC and subnet and the type of instance to use. The Instance type is important; obviously, we need to keep an eye on costs at all times, but if you choose a smaller Instance Type, then the migration will take longer and may cost you more.

You'll also need to choose enough storage for the Replication Instance (Figure 9-12). The default amount is usually sufficient. The storage is used to replicate log files and transactions and not the whole database. It's something to look at if the replication were to fail.

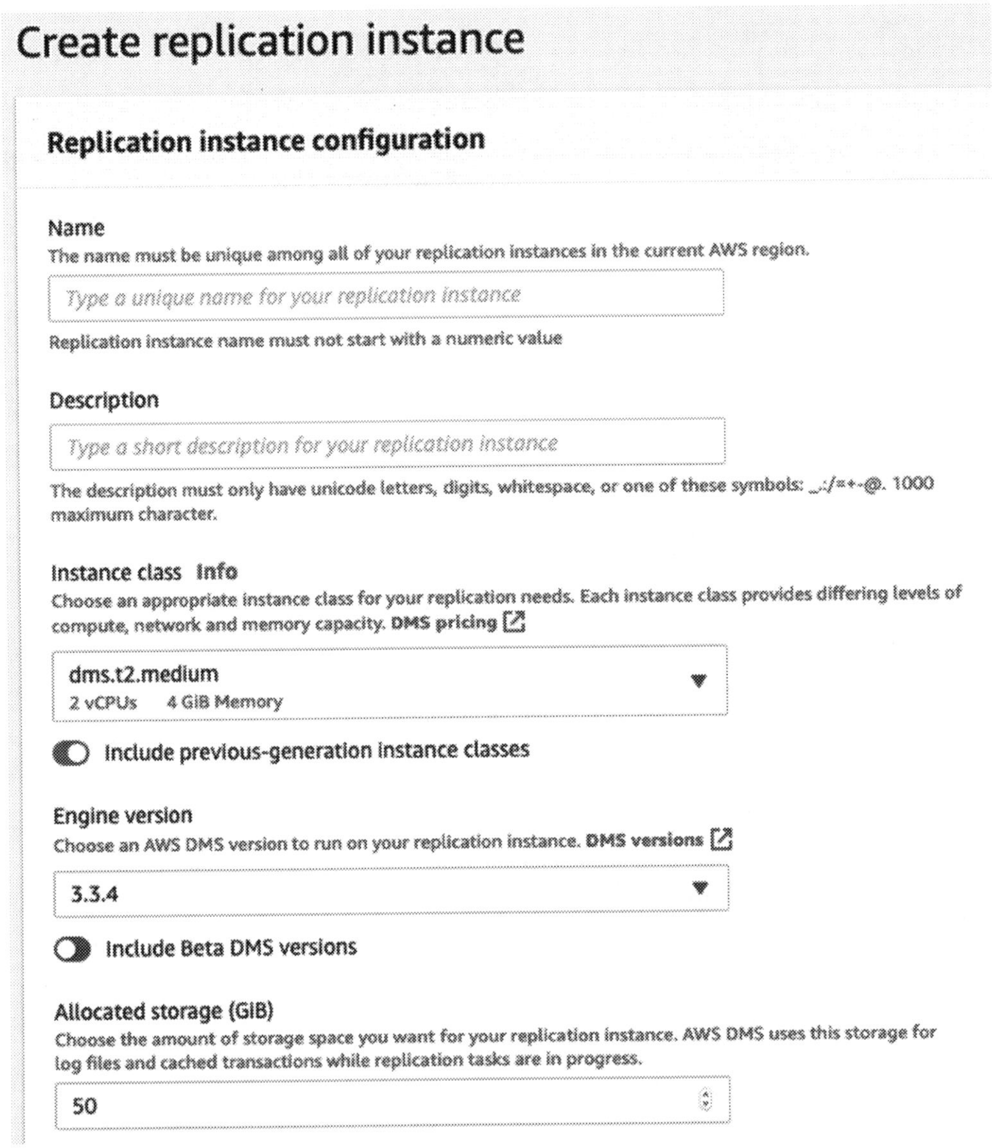

Create replication instance

Replication instance configuration

Name
The name must be unique among all of your replication instances in the current AWS region.

> Type a unique name for your replication instance

Replication instance name must not start with a numeric value

Description

> Type a short description for your replication instance

The description must only have unicode letters, digits, whitespace, or one of these symbols: _.:/=+-@. 1000 maximum character.

Instance class   Info
Choose an appropriate instance class for your replication needs. Each instance class provides differing levels of compute, network and memory capacity. **DMS pricing** ☑

> dms.t2.medium
> 2 vCPUs   4 GiB Memory   ▼

🔘 Include previous-generation instance classes

Engine version
Choose an AWS DMS version to run on your replication instance. **DMS versions** ☑

> 3.3.4   ▼

🔘 Include Beta DMS versions

Allocated storage (GiB)
Choose the amount of storage space you want for your replication instance. AWS DMS uses this storage for log files and cached transactions while replication tasks are in progress.

> 50   ⇕

Figure 9-12. *AWS DMS Replication Instance*

AWS DMS has a range of clever features and a huge amount of flexibility that makes it a favorite. In terms of flexibility, the fact that you can migrate your Microsoft SQL Server from on-premises to Amazon EC2 or Amazon RDS running MS SQL Server is nice enough, but then you also have to factor in that you can use AWS DMS and its companion tool, the Schema Conversion Tool (SCT), to convert Microsoft SQL Server databases to MySQL or Postgres. You can then migrate directly to run via Amazon Aurora and benefit from the performance increases and cost decreases that the service offers.

It's not just Microsoft SQL Server that it works with, there's also a whole host of other database engines like Oracle, DB2, MySQL, Postgres, MariaDB, MongoDB, and SAP.

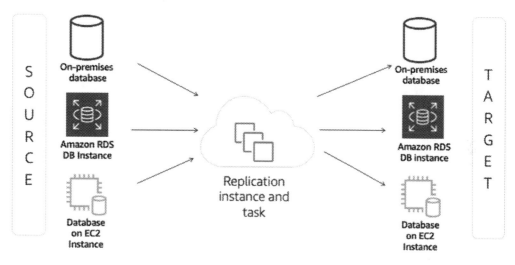

Figure 9-13. *AWS DMS Source and Target options*

And it's not just relational databases, it's interested in either. You can migrate NoSQL, Analytics, and Data Warehouses data using the same service. In terms of the Source and Target, it's fair to say that normally the Source would be an on-premises database, and the Target would be cloud based – not necessarily with AWS DMS. You can actually use the service to migrate from the cloud to on-premises as well as from Amazon RDS to Amazon EC2 and obviously Amazon EC2 to RDS (Figure 9-13). It's simply a matter of configuring your source and targets and clicking Start to replicate!

The AWS DMS Replication Instance runs a thing called a Replication Task. Each task is a migration and requires a Source and Target. Tasks work independently from each other, so with a large enough Replication Instance, you can have multiple tasks running at the same time.

There are a number of options when creating a Replication Task – Source, Target, and so on. There's also a parameter called Replication Type, and it's here that we can provide even more flexibility when it comes to how we migrate our databases.

Migration Type offers three options:

- "Migrate Existing Data" allows you to perform a one-time migration from the Source to the Target.

- "Migrate Existing Data and replicate ongoing changes" performs a one-time migration from the Source to the Target and then continues to replicate data changes until it is stopped.

- "Replicate data changes only" does not perform a one-time migration but instead replicates data from the Source and the Target. This is particularly useful if you've had to copy the initial database load via a different method like AWS Snowball, and then you can use this migration type to replicate the deltas.

AWS DMS Replication Tasks also allow the use of Selection and Transformation rules to select or exclude specific schemas or tables in the source database and to convert character strings on the Target database. Once thing to keep in mind is that AWS DMS uses Change Data Capture which will need to be enabled on the source database and can therefore have an impact on that server. How much of an impact will need to be tested by you.

AWS DMS is one of the most flexible migration tools you'll use, but it becomes even more powerful when it's used in conjunction with its companion tool, the AWS Schema Conversion Tool.

AWS Schema Conversion Tool (SCT)

The AWS Schema Conversion Tool (SCT) is a small downloadable add-in that analyzes your target database and gives you suggestions on what needs to change to move it to a different database engine. See Table 9-4.

Table 9-4. *AWS Schema Conversion Tool*

Source	Target Database
Microsoft SQL Server from version 2008 to current	Amazon Aurora with MySQL
	Amazon Aurora with PostgreSQL
	MariaDB 10.2/10.3
	Microsoft SQL Server
	MySQL
	PostgreSQL
Oracle from version 10.2 to current	Amazon Aurora with MySQL
	Amazon Aurora with PostgreSQL
	MariaDB 10.2/10.3
	Oracle
	MySQL
	PostgreSQL

The AWS Schema Conversion Tool is a standalone Java-based application that facilitates the task of converting a source database schema to a different target schema. AWS SCT also integrates with AWS Database Migration Service by creating Source and Target endpoints to use for the migration.

Once you run AWS SCT, you'll be given a report with guidance on the next steps and any manual actions you'll need to perform. You can see a sample report in Figure 9-14.

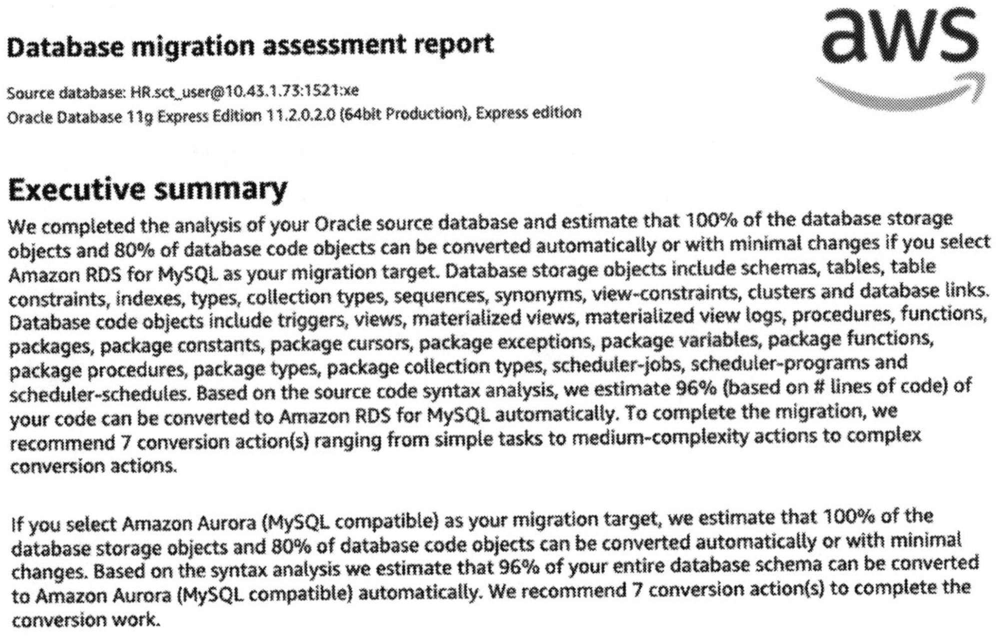

Database migration assessment report

Source database: HR.sct_user@10.43.1.73:1521:xe
Oracle Database 11g Express Edition 11.2.0.2.0 (64bit Production), Express edition

Executive summary

We completed the analysis of your Oracle source database and estimate that 100% of the database storage objects and 80% of database code objects can be converted automatically or with minimal changes if you select Amazon RDS for MySQL as your migration target. Database storage objects include schemas, tables, table constraints, indexes, types, collection types, sequences, synonyms, view-constraints, clusters and database links. Database code objects include triggers, views, materialized views, materialized view logs, procedures, functions, packages, package constants, package cursors, package exceptions, package variables, package functions, package procedures, package types, package collection types, scheduler-jobs, scheduler-programs and scheduler-schedules. Based on the source code syntax analysis, we estimate 96% (based on # lines of code) of your code can be converted to Amazon RDS for MySQL automatically. To complete the migration, we recommend 7 conversion action(s) ranging from simple tasks to medium-complexity actions to complex conversion actions.

If you select Amazon Aurora (MySQL compatible) as your migration target, we estimate that 100% of the database storage objects and 80% of database code objects can be converted automatically or with minimal changes. Based on the syntax analysis we estimate that 96% of your entire database schema can be converted to Amazon Aurora (MySQL compatible) automatically. We recommend 7 conversion action(s) to complete the conversion work.

Figure 9-14.   *AWS SCT summary report*

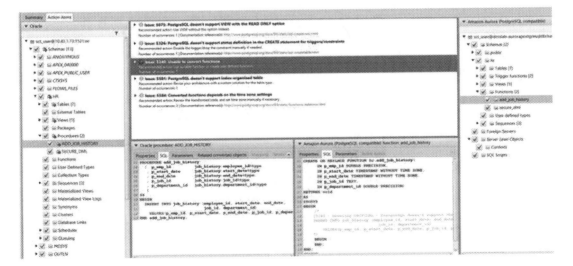

Figure 9-15.   *AWS Schema Conversion Tool in action*

You can see the AWS SCT application in Figure 9-15; you have your Source window on the left and the Target on the right window. The middle windows give you information about what AWS SCT has found.

There is also the AWS SCT Extension pack which provides pre-created AWS Lambda code for any gaps in functionality between your source and target databases.

Not limited to Microsoft SQL Server or Oracle, AWS SCT can also be used for Data Warehouse conversions using the Data Extraction Agents. More details on this can be found here:

https://docs.aws.amazon.com/SchemaConversionTool/latest/userguide/agents.html

Table 9-5. *Phases of a database migration and what tools are required per phase*

Phase of Migration	Phase Description	Tools Needed
1	Remove any unneeded objects from the database	Customer resource
2	Schema conversion assessment	AWS SCT
3	Schema issue remediation	AWS SCT
4	Application conversion/remediation	AWS SCT
5	Data migration	AWS DMS, Snowball, DataSync
6	Data migration validation	AWS DMS
7	Performance tuning	Customer resource
8	Deployment	Customer resource

Moving Large Files

Whether you are migrating databases, applications, or file systems, you will need a mechanism for moving files that are either large in quantity or large in size. AWS have a number of methods for enabling this.

AWS DataSync can be used for your file systems. The AWS DataSync agent runs on a VM in your on-premises environment, connects to Windows SMB or Linux NFS servers, and can transfer files at speeds of 10x faster than traditional open source tools. Files are encrypted during transfer, and the service is integrated with Amazon FSx for Windows File Server.

If you don't have a large enough network connection, then you can opt for moving files to AWS via one of its many Snow devices.

AWS Snowball was launched at re:Invent 2017 and gave us a ruggedized encrypted storage that plugged into a data center switch and presents as an Amazon S3 bucket. You then copy your data into the device and ship it back to AWS where the encrypted data is then copied to an encrypted Amazon S3 bucket in your account.

AWS Snowball has evolved over the years to offer more than just easy storage migration into AWS. There are now two different AWS Snowball options. AWS Snowball Edge Storage Optimized (yes, that really is the full name) provides up to 80TBs of data storage, whereas AWS Snowball Edge Compute Optimized devices provide 52 vCPUs and 42TB of storage. Offering compute devices at the edge offers multiple use cases such as machine learning in disconnected environments.

There are also two other members of the Snow Family, and they couldn't be more different from each other.

AWS Snowmobile is an 18-wheeler truck that can drive right up to your data center and take your data to the cloud. It offers 100PB of storage, GPS tracking to find out where the truck is along with a 24/7 video, and a security escort vehicle.

It's quite a sight and was introduced on stage by AWS CEO Andy Jassy during re:Invent 2017, which can be seen here: https://youtu.be/8vQmTZTq7nw.

On the other end of the spectrum, we have AWS Snowcone which provides the ability to store 8TB of data locally but also includes AWS DataSync agents and edge compute capabilities to allow it to run in remote environments. AWS Snowcone is the only member of the AWS Snow Family that fits into your hand.

Summary

Cloud Migration is a huge topic. It's also a topic that every single business will be wanting to learn more about. Those companies may have possibly had some experience of migrating between data centers or switching from one managed services partner to the next. But moving to the cloud won't be like those other migrations. In this chapter, we've learned about how AWS can help you on this journey. From starting with the creation of a Business Case all the way through to giving you all the services and tools needed to successfully move your business to the AWS Cloud.

We've discussed different types of Business Case and when to use them and how to uncover the costs you'll need to provide a TCO Analysis.

We've talked about tools like AWS's Cloud Adoption Readiness Tool to find out if your business is ready for a cloud adoption, the Seven R's of migration strategy, as well as the Migration Bubble and how to provide a cost-effective migration.

We've covered tools like the awesome AWS Migration Evaluator, Application Discovery Service, Server Migration Service, and the sublime Database Migration Service as well as new additions like AWS Application Migration Service.

We've covered a lot of ground in this chapter. I hope you've found this chapter useful; AWS Migration is a subject close to my heart.

In the next chapter, Active Directory and Identity Management, we discuss one of the fundamental elements of every Microsoft Workload cloud adoption – Microsoft Active Directory.

CHAPTER 10

Identity

I remember having to create a "network user" for myself on every individual server in the office. This was back in the days of using Novell NetWare 3.11 in the early 1990s. Every morning, I'd have to connect and authenticate to several different servers because each one had something different that I needed. One was for printer access, another for my "Home Drive," and the third for office files. In 1993, I asked my boss to allow me a day off to attend a Novell seminar at their UK offices. It was there that I saw NetWare 4.0 for the first time and heard of something called NetWare Directory Services (NDS).

Offering the ability to create a user once only (yes, you heard that correctly) and then provide access and authentication to resources on your network, Novell NDS was light years ahead of what Microsoft was offering at the time. It really wasn't until Windows NT3.5 was released with its PDC/BDC approach that there was even a thing called a Domain.

And if we really are comparing apples to apples, then a comparable Directory to Novell's NDS with its LDAP-style Organizational Unit and Leaf Object structure wasn't available until Microsoft released Windows Server 2000 and a little thing called Active Directory came along.

Microsoft was trying to Active-Everything at the time, but the name stuck as did the product, and today you will find Microsoft Active Directory in 95% of Enterprises and Fortune 1000 companies throughout the world.

Active Directory has been one of Microsoft's most enduring successes. It has had many updates along the way, but the foundations of what was launched in 2000 are largely still relevant and used today.

Active Directory enables access to all of your business resources and files. It allows users to log in to access these resources, and as such it holds the keys to your business.

If it is compromised in some way, then the blast radius would be catastrophic. This is why a conversation with a customer or your business on the placement of Active Directory will be one of the most contentious episodes of your cloud adoption journey.

© Ryan Pothecary 2021
R. Pothecary, *Running Microsoft Workloads on AWS*, https://doi.org/10.1007/978-1-4842-6628-1_10

Active Directory Admins are, quite rightly, very sensitive over their Active Directory Forest, and I've had some memorable meetings with customers discussing which approach to take with implementing Active Directory in the cloud.

Fortunately, for us, AWS offers a whole range of services and solutions that can make even the fiercest AD Admin happy. But before we get to that, let's take a minute to provide a quick overview of AD and some of the common terms we'll be discussing in this chapter.

Active Directory 101

Active Directory is a multimaster database based on the JET engine, used back in the day by Microsoft Access, which can hold approximately two billion objects during its lifetime and allows administrators to create identities which are stored in a centralized system called Active Directory. Active Directory runs on a server called a Domain Controller.

Inside Active Directory, we can have one or more Domains (Figure 10-1) which are logically isolated parts of an Active Directory. Inside Domains, we create User objects and give them permissions to allow those users to access resources in our network. These resources can be files, printers, or access to other computers. To help us administer all of our users, we can create Groups and add our users to those Groups where they have a common requirement, such as needing access to the Sales files.

We can further control what our users can do by creating and applying policies to manage their environment. This could be something simple like displaying a Legal Access message when a user tries to log on to a machine, warning them that they should only log on if they are authorized to do so.

We can place our User and Resource objects into Organizational Units (OUs), and we can apply different policies to different Organizational Units.

For example, you may need to enforce Hard Drive encryption on the Sales OU since the Sales team travels to customers' sites often. You may not need such a policy for the Marketing department who are normally office workers.

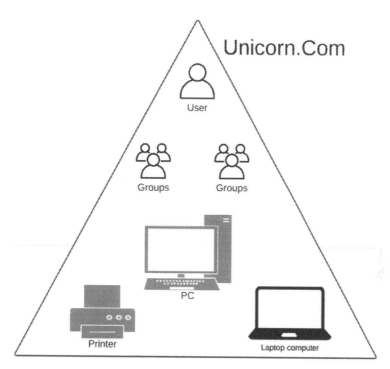

Figure 10-1. *Single Active Directory Domain*

When a user tries to log in to a system with a username and password, a lookup is made to the nearest Domain Controller (DC) to see if the username and password are valid. If so, the User is authenticated to the Domain. Once a User is authenticated, the Local Security Authority (LSA) creates an Access Token.

The Access Token contains a Security Identifier (SID) for the user, the Security Identifier for all of the Active Directory Groups that the User belongs to, and also the User Privileges. All wrapped up in one token.

When a User tries to access a resource, the operating system hosting that resource checks the permissions assigned to that resource against the Access Token provided by the User and queries whether the user is able to perform that action. If they are, then the operating system grants access to the resource.

With Active Directory providing such an important and integral role for our end users, we need to protect our Active Directory from failure. We also need to place our Domain Controllers close to the resources to avoid any delays due to network latency. Together this means that we require more than one Domain Controller.

Having more than one Domain Controller means we need a way to replicate the Active Directory database across all of our Domain Controllers so that they have the very latest version of the database. This replication happens automatically across the Active Directory Forest.

When you create your first domain, you'll need to give it a Domain Name such as Unicorn.com. If you then need to create subdomains such as Rental.Unicorn.com, you'll be creating a Domain Tree (Figure 10-2).

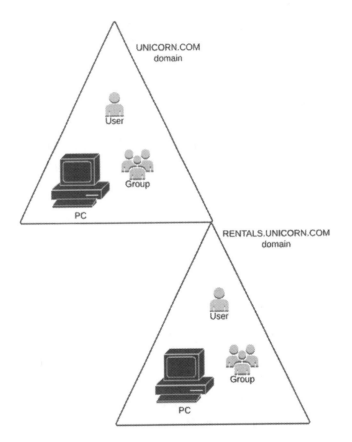

Figure 10-2. *An Active Directory Domain Tree*

An Active Directory Forest is made up of one or more Active Directory Domain Trees. Each Forest has a unified database; it represents a complete Active Directory. The Domains inside that Forest share a common structure and have a single Schema.

A Schema defines the types of objects and attributes that the Active Directory can use. It allows an out-of-the-box Active Directory implementation to grow and expand as you add more elements to it. For example, if you were to install Microsoft Exchange in your environment, it adds a whole host of mailbox objects into your Active Directory. Having this "extensibility" was high on Active Directory's list of benefits, but in reality few applications really used it.

One final thing to note here. As new versions of Windows Server are released, they typically contain updates to Active Directory. The changes are fully backward compatible with previous versions, and we call these the Domain or Forest Functional Level.

I can add a new Windows Server 2019 instance to a Domain whose Forest Level is Windows Server 2008. But this doesn't mean that the Domain can use any of the new AD features the Windows Server 2019 has. To upgrade your Functional Level, you will need to upgrade all of the Domain Controllers to this version first.

Since Domains are logically separate from each other, how do we get access to resources from one domain to another?

Easy. We create a Trust Relationship between the domains. Trusts are very powerful but very often misunderstood; there are several different types of Trusts, but the most important thing to understand right now is the direction of the arrows in Figure 10-3.

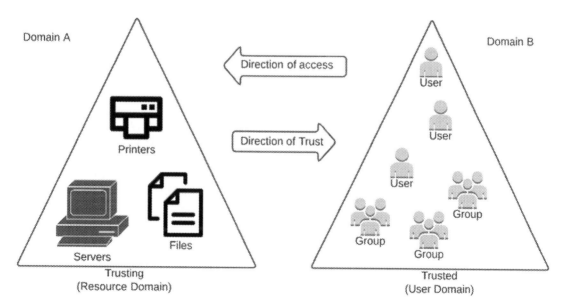

Figure 10-3. *Standard one-way Domain Trust*

In Figure 10-3, you can see two domains (A and B). Domain A has some resources like printers and files that Domain B's users want to access. We create a single one-way Domain Trust from Domain A to Domain B so that Domain A is **Trusting** Domain B to access its resources.

As you can see, the direction of the Trust is from Domain A to Domain B, allowing access from Domain B to Domain A.

Domain A is **Trusting**; Domain B is **Trusted**.

Looking at this example, we can see that in no way does Domain B trust Domain A, meaning that if there were users in Domain A, they wouldn't have access to anything in Domain B.

Make sure you are clear on this before we proceed as we will be using Trusts later on in this chapter.

Before we do that, let's take a moment to discuss a few elements of Active Directory security.

Having centralized access management using Active Directory is great, but we no longer live and work in a centralized way. We have branch offices and manufacturing plants spread over the globe, and so we place Domain Controllers in these environments as well. Having multiple Domain Controllers isn't a bad idea if they are properly configured in their respective sites, but security starts being a concern if we no longer have physical security of our Domain Controllers. In September 2020, it was announced that hackers could use the Zerologon exploit to compromise Domain Controllers if they are on the same Local Area Network segment.

Remember, due to replication of your Active Directory database, if you can compromise one Domain Controller, you compromise them all. This means somebody then has access to all of your IT resources. The idea of limiting the impact of such a breach resulted in the creation of Read-Only Domain Controllers (RODC) with Windows Server 2008. An RODC contains a cached copy of the AD Database, and users locally to the RODC can access this to help them authenticate and log in to services. You can further limit RODC access to only cache accounts and passwords for staff at this branch office.

Managed Service Accounts allow you to create an account in AD that is linked to a specific computer. These have been replaced in Windows Server 2016 by **group Managed Service Accounts (gMSA)** that provide the same functionality, but this time over multiple computers. The benefit of gMSA is that it allows for increased security by limiting the permissions required for that service account to run automated tasks, scripts, services, and applications. The password for the account, which is randomly generated and rotated, is completely handled by Windows Server.

It's best practice that you do not allow Internet access or Remote Desktop access to your Domain Controllers. There really is no need to allow these things, and it'll prevent a large risk to your most important servers. Microsoft has created the Security Compliance Toolkit that you can download and run in conjunction with the Security Configuration Wizard to produce configuration baselines for Domain Controllers.

This configuration can be enforced by Group Policy Objects via the Domain Controller Organizational Unit inside your Active Directory Domain.

Active Directory in AWS

One of the many benefits of using AWS is the flexibility it offers when it comes to creating solutions. How you use Active Directory in AWS is a prime example of this. You not only have the choice of using Amazon EC2 to run your own Active Directory services, but AWS provides you with a number of fully managed services that can also do the task.

But before we look at the options we have, let's discuss the question of whether we should be using Active Directory in AWS. You'll be surprised by how many times this question comes up.

Since my prior advice to you when it comes to moving to the cloud has been to challenge everything, then it's a fair question. I can understand why people ask it. There's a general perception from new users that the cloud is not as secure as your own data center. Added to that is the fact that the AWS Cloud is not under their direct control, which results in putting trust into the hands of a company you don't really know. It's perfectly natural to feel that way; the only way past it is to earn your businesses trust over time.

Now, add your company's Active Directory to this nervousness, and you'll see why people ask the question. The truth of the matter is that your Active Directory as well as your applications and data are at least, if not more, secure running in AWS.

I normally tackle this issue by introducing architecture patterns that make use of AWS's own Directory Service and one-way Trust relationships that add a further layer of security to your existing Active Directory strategy.

If you decide not to use Active Directory in AWS, there will be a number of things your decision will impact.

Firstly, access control methods for both Windows and Linux servers. You might get around this by using a Privileged Access Control service like Centrify or Okta. But, these cost money to purchase, whereas Active Directory is built into the Server operating system. You'll also be unable to use AWS Services like Amazon RDS for SQL Server which relies on AWS Directory Service as does Amazon FSx for Windows Server, Amazon WorkSpaces, Amazon Connect, Amazon QuickSight, and Amazon Chime, among others.

Active Directory on Amazon EC2

What if introducing the fully managed AWS Active Directory service is a step too far at this stage? Or perhaps the AWS Directory Service has a constraint that you can't live without? As a customer, you can create an Amazon EC2 Instance and use Microsoft's own instructions[1] to install the Active Directory Domain Service (ADDS) onto it. This section details how you go about that.

If you've chosen to install ADDS on Amazon EC2, then you'll be aware of your responsibility when it comes to ensuring security and best practice are followed. You are the administrator of the Amazon EC2 instance. You'll need to install and configure ADDS in line with your current design, and most importantly, you'll be responsible for its ongoing operational and security tasks.

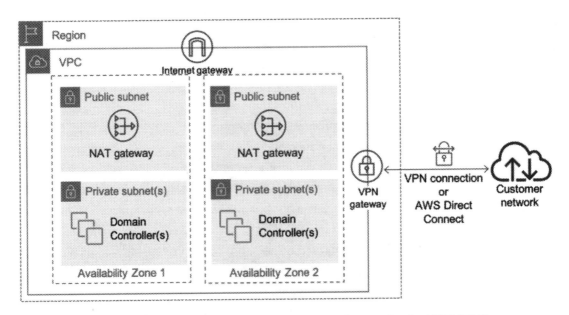

Figure 10-4. *Active Directory on Amazon EC2 within a single AWS VPC*

In Figure 10-4, you'll see Amazon EC2 running Microsoft ADDS on Domain Controllers in private subnets in separate AWS Availability Zones within a single VPC within a single AWS Region.

---

[1] https://docs.microsoft.com/en-us/windows-server/identity/ad-ds/deploy/
install-active-directory-domain-services--level-100-

It's always been best practice to create two Domain Controllers so that if one should fail, you can recover easily. That's not the case if you've just got one Domain Controller, and you have to restore from backup.

You are not limited to two; have as many as you need. You'll also notice that the Domain Controllers are in private subnets. Implementing Domain Controllers in a public subnet, where potentially they can be compromised, will mean you'll never get a good night's sleep again.

One final piece of best practice advice is to ensure that you put all of the Domain Controllers that are within a single AWS Region in a single Active Directory Site. Active Directory uses Sites to understand the network layout of your environment and will ensure that you contact the nearest Domain Controller to you rather than a Domain Controller on the other side of an expensive network circuit.

But what if you are using multiple AWS Regions, what do you have to do to ensure things still work?

Well, firstly, the AWS global infrastructure is amazing and will easily cope with multi-regional replication traffic, plus you can use AWS VPC Peering or AWS Transit Gateway (Figure 10-5) to ensure private communication for your Domain Controllers. Similar to the preceding advice, make sure that each of your Domain Controllers in each Region is spread across multiple Availability Zones and belongs to an Active Directory Site. You'll need an Active Directory Site per Region.

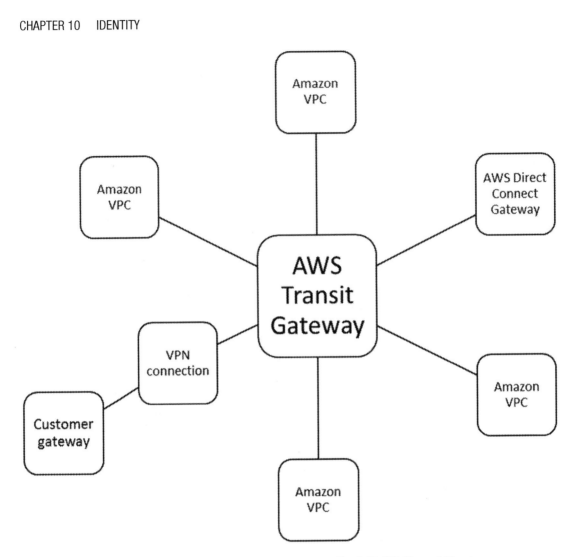

Figure 10-5. *AWS Transit Gateway to connect all AWS VPC and Regions together*

Your Amazon EC2 Domain Controllers will have to have a Security Group attached to them, and this is going to be something you'll need to manage carefully because it requires a lot of network ports to be open.

A full list of required network ports for Active Directory can be found here:

`https://docs.microsoft.com/en-us/previous-versions/windows/it-pro/`
`windows-server-2008-r2-and-2008/dd772723(v=ws.10)`

You'll also want ICMP enabled from your clients to your Domain Controllers to ease troubleshooting. Yes, that's a lot of network ports. Since every network engineer will want to restrict any open ports to the least amount possible, they get very nervous when it comes to Active Directory. Microsoft's advice is not to restrict open ports on internal subnets or use VPN if you have to.

As you can see, there's no nice answer here.

An example of Active Directory Security Groups can be found in Table 10-1.

Table 10-1. *AWS Security Group details from the ADDS Quick Start Template*

Security Group	Associated with	Source	Ports
DomainController SG	Domain controllers	VPC CIDR	TCP5985, TCP53, UDP53, TCP80, TCP3389
		DomainControllerSG	IpProtocol-1, FromPort01, ToPort-1
		Domain MemberSG	UDP123, TCP135, UDP138, UDP137, TCP139, TCP445, UDP445, TCP464, UDP464, TCP49152-65535, UDP49152-65535, TCP389, UDP389, TCP636, TCP3268, TCP3269, UDP88, TCP88, UDP67, UDP2535, TCP9389, TCP5722, UDP5355, ICMP
DomainMember SG	Remote Desktop Gateways	ADServer1_EIN, ADServer2_EIN	UDP88, TCP88, TCP445, UDP445, TCP49152-65535, UDP49152-65535, TCP389, UDP389, TCP636
RDGWSecurity Group	Remote Desktop Gateways	RemoteDesktopGatewayCIDR	TCP3389

Manually building your Active Directory environment is time consuming. Fortunately, AWS has a Quick Start template[2] that is ready to run and provides you a best practice implementation of two Domain Controllers in different Availability Zones within a single AWS Region.

This Quick Start provides three different scenarios for creating an Active Directory infrastructure in AWS.

The first scenario, option 1 (Figure 10-6), implements an Active Directory Domain Service on Amazon EC2 ready for you to manage yourself. It creates a brand-new Active Directory domain that is entirely self-contained. It'll save you time by creating the networking layer and EC2 servers.

---

[2]https://aws.amazon.com/quickstart/architecture/active-directory-ds/

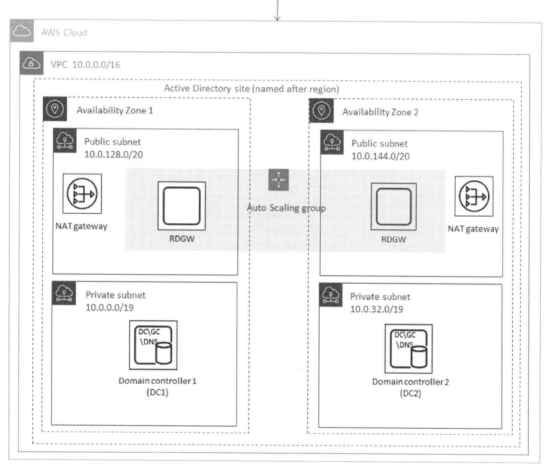

Figure 10-6. *AWS Quick Start to create Active Directory on Amazon EC2 - option 1*

The second scenario (Figure 10-7) allows you to extend your current Active Directory into AWS using Amazon EC2 which you'll then be responsible for managing. This is similar to our option 1 but forms an extension of the organization's existing Active Directory Domain into the Amazon EC2 Domain Controllers.

It uses the AWS Systems Manager Automation capability to install the Active Directory roles onto EC2 and then uses AWS Secrets Manager to securely manage and rotate passwords.

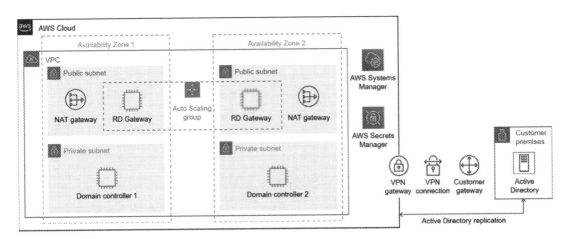

Figure 10-7. *AWS Quick Start to extend your current AD Domain into AWS - option 2*

Finally, the third scenario automatically sets up your Active Directory environment, using the AWS Directory Services service (Figure 10-8).

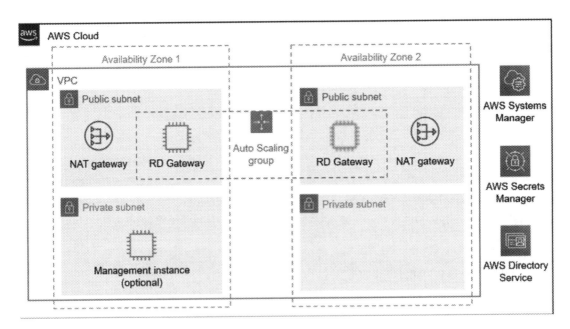

Figure 10-8. *AWS Quick Start using AWS Directory Services - option 3*

Managing DNS When Using AD on Amazon EC2

When you install Active Directory Domain Services on your Amazon EC2 instance for the first time, it also requires DNS to be installed. It's entirely feasible for you to use an independent DNS Server like BIND. However, the best practice and general ease of use mean that for the vast majority of use cases, you'll be installing Microsoft DNS Server at the same time. But before you start introducing a full-blown DNS Server in the middle of your VPC, you'll need to understand the impact of such a move and how DNS resolution will work in conjunction with the built-in AWS DNS Service that is part of every VPC.

We will look at how DNS works at the VPC level before we introduce ADDS. First, a quick overview of VPC Networking – each AWS VPC that you create is based on a CIDR range that you specify, such as 192.168.0.0/16 or any such RFC1918 address range. Within that CIDR block of address, you'll create subnets such as 192.168.1.0/24 which gives you 254 possible IP addresses to use; however, a small number of addresses are reserved.

- .0 is the network address and not usable.

- .1 is the AWS router address.

- .2 is reserved by AWS for its DNS service.

- .3 is reserved for future use.

- .255 is the network broadcast address. AWS does not support broadcasts but reserves this address.

You can see in Figure 10-9 a standard AWS VPC with two Availability Zones (AZ) with an Amazon EC2 instance in each AZ. You can see that when the EC2 instance sends a DNS request for a domain name lookup, the default solution is to use the VPC's .2 address.

When you try to resolve a DNS name on an Amazon EC2 instance within a subnet, it will send the query to the subnet's .2 address. This forwards the query to the Amazon Route 53 DNS Service which acts as a resolver.

The .2 address lives on the Amazon EC2 Host as part of the Hypervisor and forwards DNS traffic to the Amazon Route 53 Resolver service. The Resolver service then has a choice of three different destinations, depending on the query.

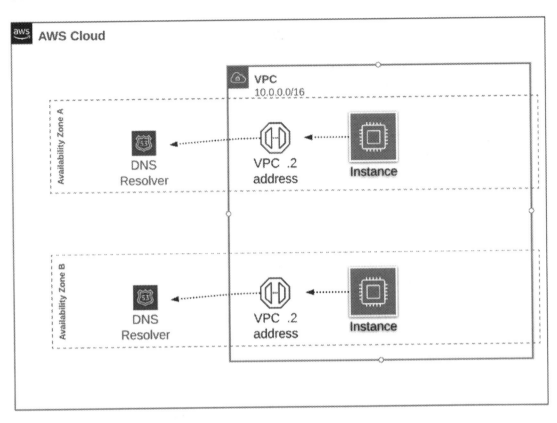

Figure 10-9. *DNS resolution using .2 address*

Amazon Route 53 in this context is classifying queries (Figure 10-10). It's looking at the query name and which VPC the query came from. It checks whether a Route 53 Private DNS Zone has been created; if so, it'll send the query there. The Amazon VPC DNS handles hostnames of Amazon EC2 instances. If neither of those is a match, then it'll forward the query to the Public DNS.

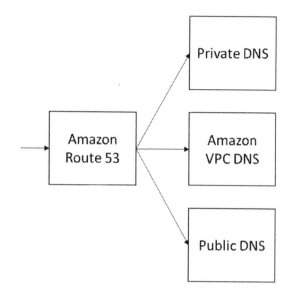

Figure 10-10. *Route 53 resolution destinations*

So how do we add a Microsoft DNS Server in the middle of all this without breaking it all?

Amazon EC2 Instances receive their network configuration via AWS's own DHCP Servers. The network configuration includes a private IP address and the address details of what DNS Servers to use.

If you are running Active Directory Domain Services on Amazon EC2, then the recommendation was to update the DHCP configuration to include the DNS Servers' IP address of two Domain Controllers. You can update the DHCP configuration by creating the DHCP Option Set and then associating it with a VPC. Please see Figure 10-11 for details.

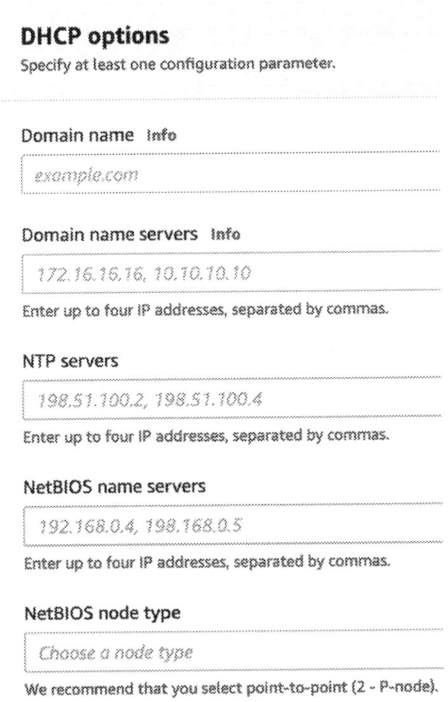

DHCP options

Specify at least one configuration parameter.

Domain name   Info

example.com

Domain name servers   Info

172.16.16.16, 10.10.10.10

Enter up to four IP addresses, separated by commas.

NTP servers

198.51.100.2, 198.51.100.4

Enter up to four IP addresses, separated by commas.

NetBIOS name servers

192.168.0.4, 198.168.0.5

Enter up to four IP addresses, separated by commas.

NetBIOS node type

Choose a node type

We recommend that you select point-to-point (2 - P-node).

Figure 10-11. DHCP Option Set

The configuration in the DHCP Option Set is delivered to each and every Amazon EC2 Instance that is created inside the VPC in which the DHCP Option Set is assigned.

This is applicable to Linux instances as well as Windows Instances.

So, effectively, your Active Directory domain becomes the single source method to resolve internal and external DNS addresses.

To allow resolution of non-AD Domain names, we have to set up a Conditional Forwarder on the Microsoft DNS Server that is part of the Domain Controller (Figure 10-12). This Conditional Forwarder must redirect all non-AD Domain resolution to the AWS DNS Resolver service inside your VPC, which is found on the .2 address.

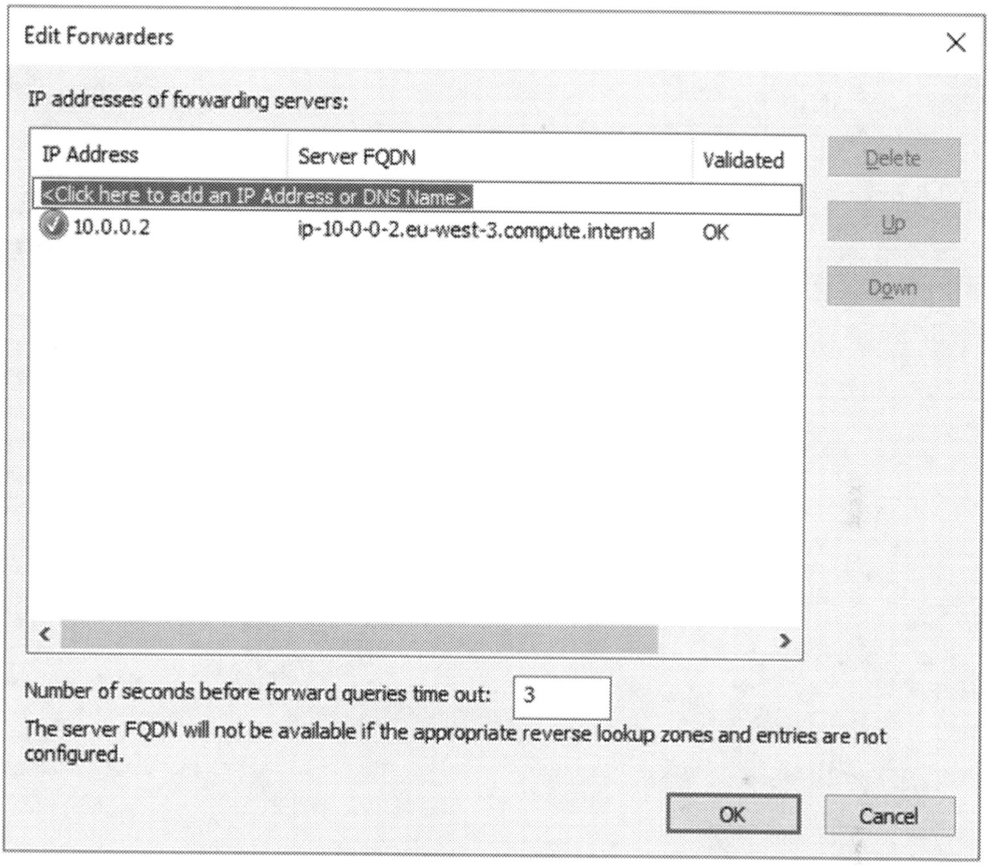

Figure 10-12. *Conditional Forwarder from the AWS ADDS Quick Start*

Figure 10-13 provides a high-level overview of the DNS resolution process using Domain Controllers on Amazon EC2 configured with DNS Conditional Forwarders to resolve via the VPC .2 address which then uses Amazon Route 53 to resolve the query.

There are downsides to this design. In practice, Windows as well as Linux servers tend to favor the first Nameserver on the list, which means that although we have two DNS Servers, one of them will be significantly more utilized than the other.

This causes an issue since there is a hard limit of 1024 packets per second on the VPC .2 Resolver. It places strain on the Amazon EC2 Domain Controllers and also adds a further step to resolving DNS names. It works, but is not ideal.

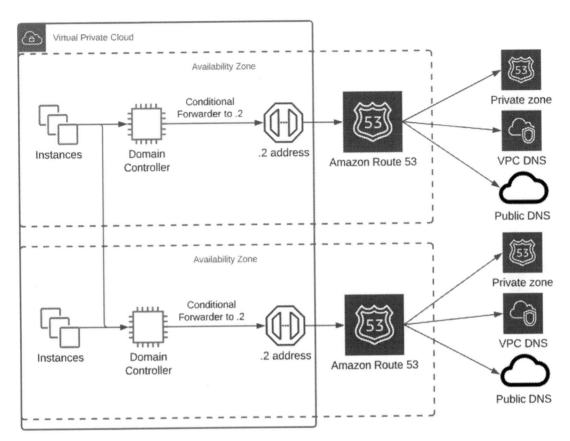

Figure 10-13. *Amazon EC2 Domain Controllers and Conditional Forwarders*

How can we solve the issues with this design? Enter the Amazon Route 53 Resolver.

Launched prior to AWS re:Invent 2018, the Amazon Route 53 Resolver allows the creation of outbound and inbound DNS endpoints that make name resolution within your VPC a lot better, especially when using Active Directory.

Before you create an Outbound Resolver, gather some information:

- The IP addresses of your Amazon EC2 Domain Controllers/DNS Servers

- The name of the Active Directory Domain

- VPC ID

- Subnet IDs

- Security Group ID that covers your Domain Controllers

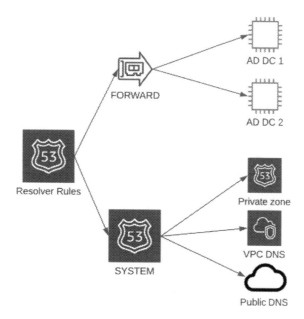

Figure 10-14. *Route 53 Resolver Rules*

AWS's previous best practice for Amazon EC2–hosted Active Directory was to update the VPC's DHCP Option Set. But since the launch of Amazon Route 53 Resolver, this now provides you with a much better solution for AD DNS.

During the creation of an Amazon Route 53 Resolver, you'll also create whatever Resolver Rules you require. Figure 10-14 shows where Resolver Rules fit in with VPC DNS resolution. There are two rules that you can use, FORWARD and SYSTEM. FORWARD rules match to a domain name you enter and then forward all requests for that domain name to a specific IP address. SYSTEM rules override any broad FORWARD rules for specific domains.

Using the Amazon Route 53 Resolver with Outbound rules provides us with what you see in Figure 10-15.

Figure 10-15 looks like a complex design, but using Amazon Route 53 Resolvers actually reduces complexity as well as provides a much more performant solution.

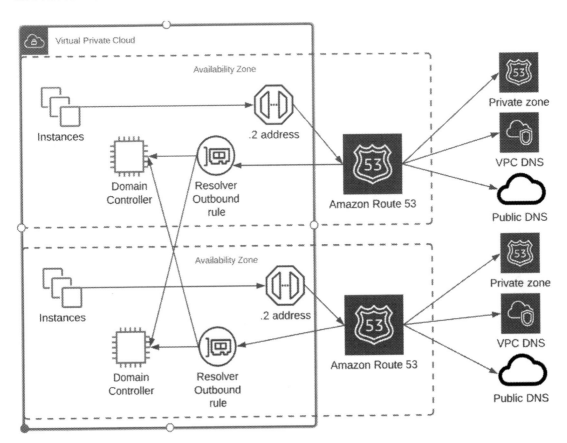

Figure 10-15. *DNS resolution using Amazon Route 53 Resolvers for Active Directory on Amazon EC2*

AWS AD Connector

Using Amazon EC2 to run your Active Directory infrastructure is a common use case. It's something that everyone can relate to since we've been running Active Directory on virtual and physical servers since the technology was released all those years ago. The common design for running Active Directory on Amazon EC2 is when the customer has a current Active Directory Domain in place on-premises and wants to connect both the cloud and on-premises together in a single Domain.

The immediate issue that springs to mind is one of network connectivity.

Active Directory uses a *lot* of network ports over the protocols TCP, UDP, and ICMP. If you choose to go down this route, then you are faced with opening up subnet NACLS and Security Groups to all of these ports and managing them in life. Not nice.

This is why AWS created the AWS AD Connector. This allows you to create a Kerberos proxy between your AWS VPC and your on-premises AD Domain over three network ports. The AWS AD Connector is a fully managed service. There is nothing to manage in life, no patching or backups to worry about, and if it fails, it gets replaced automatically. You can create an AWS AD Connector via the Directory Services console.

Here, the first question you'll be asked is what size of AD Connector you'll need. See Figure 10-16.

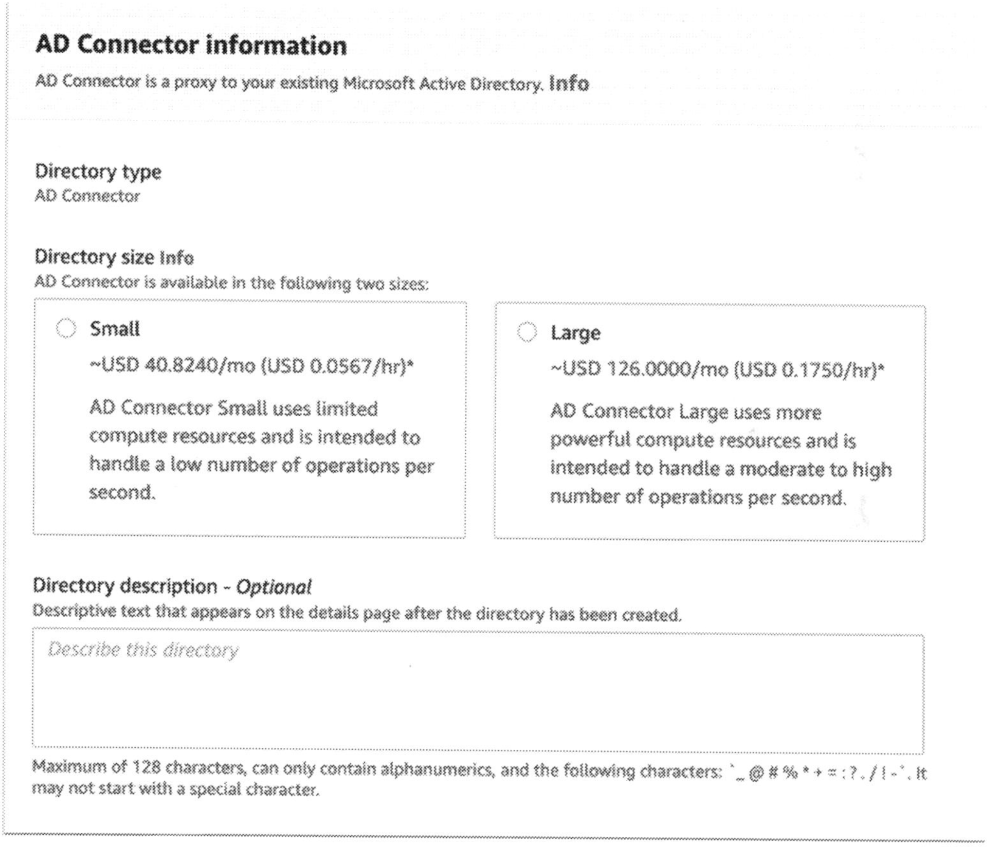

AD Connector information

AD Connector is a proxy to your existing Microsoft Active Directory. **Info**

Directory type
AD Connector

Directory size **Info**
AD Connector is available in the following two sizes:

○ **Small**

~USD 40.8240/mo (USD 0.0567/hr)*

AD Connector Small uses limited compute resources and is intended to handle a low number of operations per second.

○ **Large**

~USD 126.0000/mo (USD 0.1750/hr)*

AD Connector Large uses more powerful compute resources and is intended to handle a moderate to high number of operations per second.

Directory description - *Optional*
Descriptive text that appears on the details page after the directory has been created.

Describe this directory

Maximum of 128 characters, can only contain alphanumerics, and the following characters: `_ @ # % * + = : ? . / ! - `. It may not start with a special character.

Figure 10-16. *AWS AD Connector*

Effectively, what you are choosing here is the size of the Amazon EC2 Instance that will run the proxy software used by the connector. It is important to note that AD Connector sizing is approximate and is a function of transaction type and TPS (transaction processing system). The limits mentioned are more of a guideline that shows reasonable performance at that scale. If there is no expectation that the performance during high login periods will outstrip the AD Connector, you can scale to much larger numbers.

Since the AWS AD Connector is a fully managed service with built-in High Availability, you'll need two subnets in separate AZs, as a prerequisite. Similar to AWS's full-blown AD service, Directory Services, the AWS AD Connector does not place Amazon EC2 Instances inside your VPC. Instead, it hosts these in an internal management network outside of your VPC, and all you get to see are two AWS Elastic Network Interfaces (ENIs) which are connected to the service.

Next, you'll need an Active Directory Domain Controller to connect to.

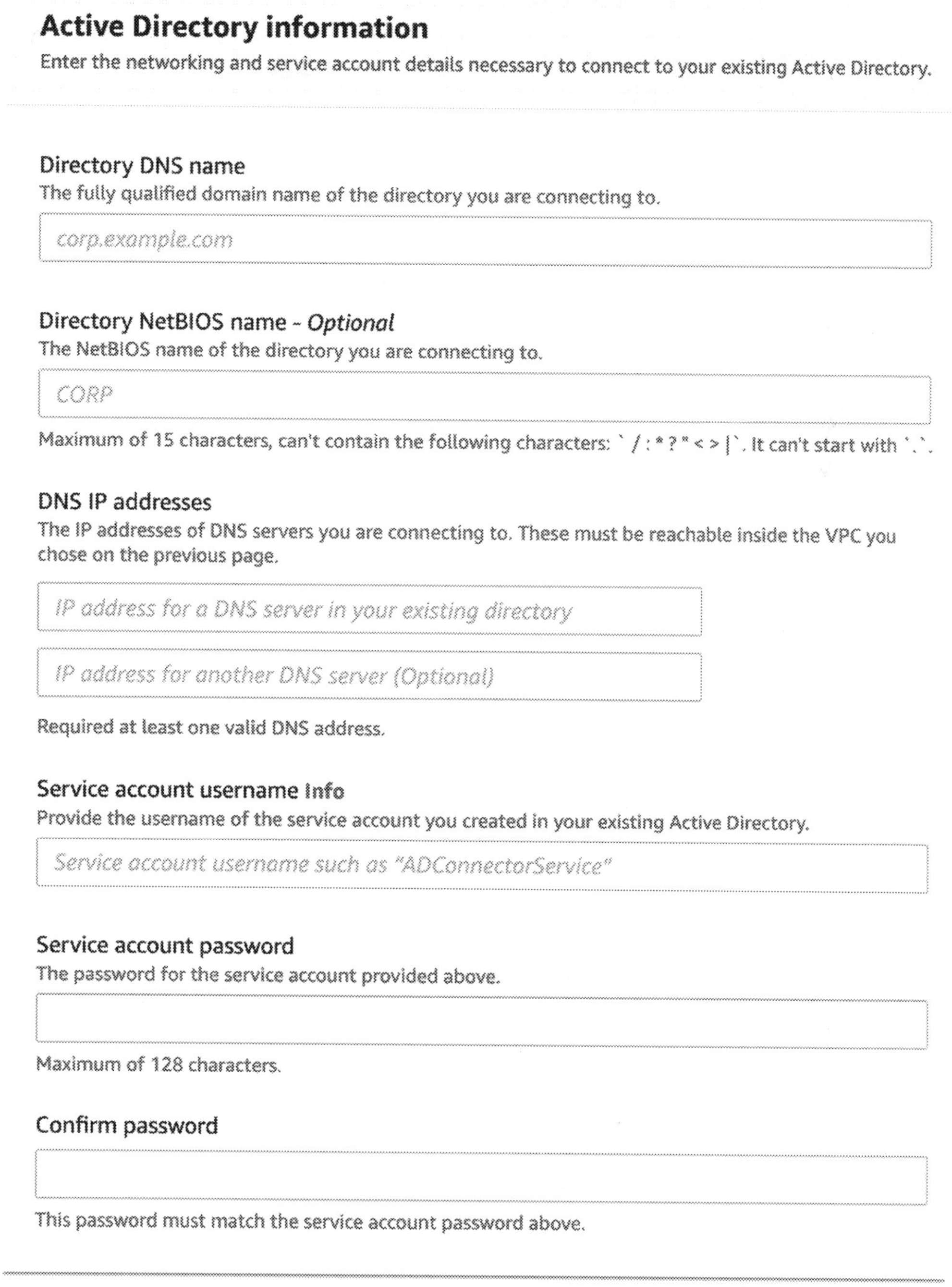

Active Directory information

Enter the networking and service account details necessary to connect to your existing Active Directory.

Directory DNS name

The fully qualified domain name of the directory you are connecting to.

> corp.example.com

Directory NetBIOS name - *Optional*

The NetBIOS name of the directory you are connecting to.

> CORP

Maximum of 15 characters, can't contain the following characters: ` / : * ? " < > | `. It can't start with `.`.

DNS IP addresses

The IP addresses of DNS servers you are connecting to. These must be reachable inside the VPC you chose on the previous page.

> IP address for a DNS server in your existing directory

> IP address for another DNS server (Optional)

Required at least one valid DNS address.

Service account username Info

Provide the username of the service account you created in your existing Active Directory.

> Service account username such as "ADConnectorService"

Service account password

The password for the service account provided above.

Maximum of 128 characters.

Confirm password

This password must match the service account password above.

***Figure 10-17.** AWS AD Connector configuration details*

On this screen (Figure 10-17), you'll provide your AD Domain name, IP addresses of internally reachable Domain Controllers/DNS Servers, and a Service Account username. The Service Account must have the following privileges in your Active Directory Domain:

1. Read Users and Groups

2. Join computers to the Domain

3. Create computer objects

I know you may be tempted to just add the Service Account to the Domain Admins group; please avoid this temptation. You know that it's not best practice and goes against our "Least Privilege" way of working.

Finally, the firewall on your own network must have the following ports enabled to the AWS-based IP address of the Elastic Network Interface presented by the AWS AD Connector service:

- TCP/UDP 53 – DNS

- TCP/UDP 88 – Kerberos

- TCP/UDP 389 – LDAP

Once everything is configured, you can test out that you have network connectivity by running the DirectoryServicePortTest application (Figure 10-18):

https://docs.aws.amazon.com/directoryservice/latest/admin-guide/samples/ DirectoryServicePortTest.zip

```
DirectoryServicePortTest.exe -d <domain_name> -ip <server_IP_address> -tcp
"53,88,389" -udp "53,88,389"
```

```
Testing TCP ports to 10.00.8.205:
Checking TCP port 53: PASSED
Checking TCP port 88: PASSED
Checking TCP port 389: PASSED

Testing UDP ports to 10.0.8.205:
Checking UDP port 53: PASSED
Checking UDP port 88: PASSED
Checking UDP port 389: PASSED
```

Figure 10-18. *DirectoryServicePortTest*

AWS AD Connector works very well, and it's certainly preferable to use this service than to have to manage all those open network ports if you are going to run your Active Directory on Amazon EC2.

Running Active Directory on Amazon EC2 is a common solution. There are no significant changes required to your existing Active Directory Domain, and particularly if you use the AWS AD Connector, then there are fewer network ports required for its use. However, it still leaves you with some issues that you have to reconcile.

You'll have some more Amazon EC2 instances to manage, patch, and maintain. You'll also have these instances running 24/7 (we *do not* switch off Domain Controllers), and so you'll need to be sensible about what Instance Type to use. Currently, a pair of T3.Large Instances is going to set you back about $2200 a year if using on-demand pricing.

The other concern is one of security.

Putting your Active Directory Domain Controllers in AWS is perfectly safe, certainly as secure as they are in your current data center. But if for whatever reason they are compromised, then, as mentioned at the start of this chapter, the blast radius is huge. We can agree that this is a situation we face no matter where our Domain is, correct? But what if I can show you a service that adds an extra layer of security to your existing Domain, and you don't have to manage anything?

Interested?

AWS Directory Services for Microsoft Active Directory

I really wasn't a huge fan of the AWS Directory Services for Microsoft Active Directory service when it launched in October 2014. I come from an Active Directory administrator background, and I got used to how things worked and the fact that I had all the permissions I needed, which was always without fail, Domain Administrator or Enterprise Administrator.

Does this mean that Active Directory Administrators are lazy, just giving out God-like access to everyone who asked for it? Well, no. Active Directory has never lent itself to provide granular access in the same way that AWS IAM does today. And so, AD Users tended to be in either the Domain Users or Domain Admins groups.

As a Domain Admin, you had complete control over the entire Active Directory Domain and all subsequent Organizational Units (OUs) below the root of the Domain.

This changes when using AWS Directory Services for Microsoft Active Directory.

AWS Directory Service is a fully managed Active Directory. It is also a service used by numerous other AWS services such as Amazon RDS, AWS WorkSpaces, and so on.

Those services put objects into the same AWS Directory Service Domain, and being able to modify or delete those objects will make those services fail.

To mitigate against this issue, an Organizational Unit is created on the root of the domain using the NetBIOS name of the Domain. For example, if the domain you create is Example.com, then you'll find you've got an OU called Example in the root of your newly created Domain. You have full Administrator-level permissions to everything below the OU, but no permissions to the root of the Domain.

I'll let you breathe that in for a moment.

This is the part where some AD Admins stop and decide that using Amazon EC2 rather than AWS Directory Services is the way forward.

It was certainly my own experience when confronting the service for the first time. But in reality, we all have a responsibility when it comes to security, AD Admins especially, and working in a Least Privilege manner gives you a better night's sleep.

The other impact AWS Directory Services has is the fact that you must create a brand-new AD Domain when using it. It cannot be a subdomain of an existing AD Forest. The implication is that there must be an AD Trust between your on-premises Domain and the new AWS Domain.

This used to be a problem.

When launched, AWS Directory Services were limited to a specific Virtual Private Cloud (VPC). If you had more than one VPC (which you almost certainly would have), then it would require a new AWS Directory Service Domain.

The alternative was to configure AWS to use a "Shared Services" VPC design where you have a single VPC which hosts AWS Directory Services and any other management tools you have. This is then peered with your other VPCs and can be seen in Figure 10-19.

Typical multi-account designs use the service AWS Organizations to provide some structure and ease of use in creating and applying security.

AWS created guidance on designing for a multi-account strategy, which can be found here: https://aws.amazon.com/organizations/getting-started/best-practices/.

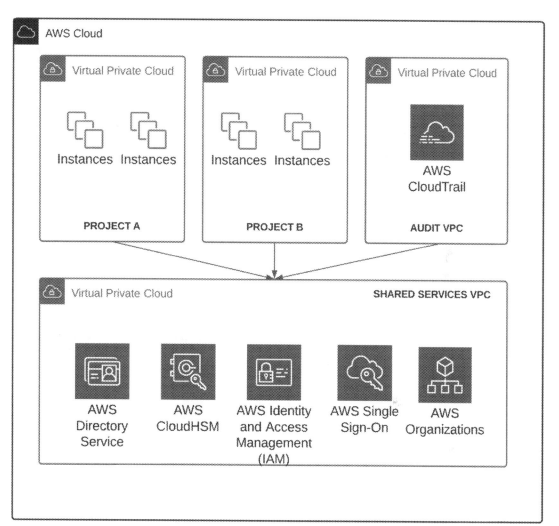

Figure 10-19. *Shared Services VPC*

A Shared Services VPC was a good solution which reduced the number of AWS Directory Services needed, therefore reducing cost and the number of AD Trusts you'll need. However, there's a massive increase in the amount of VPC Peering connections required to maintain, and pretty soon it could all get out of hand.

AWS Transit Gateway[3] is a great service that addresses this issue, allowing you to manage all these inter-VPC connections as well as external connections.

---

[3]https://aws.amazon.com/transit-gateway/

However, if you work in a multi-account or multi-regional manner, then you would still have to create multiple AWS Directory Services.

AWS Directory Services added the ability to share a directory with other AWS Accounts and VPCs way back in 2018, and finally as part of pre:Invent 2020 (the features and services released before AWS re:Invent) came the ability to share a single directory across multiple regions.

Let's go back to the beginning and run through creating an AWS Directory Service.

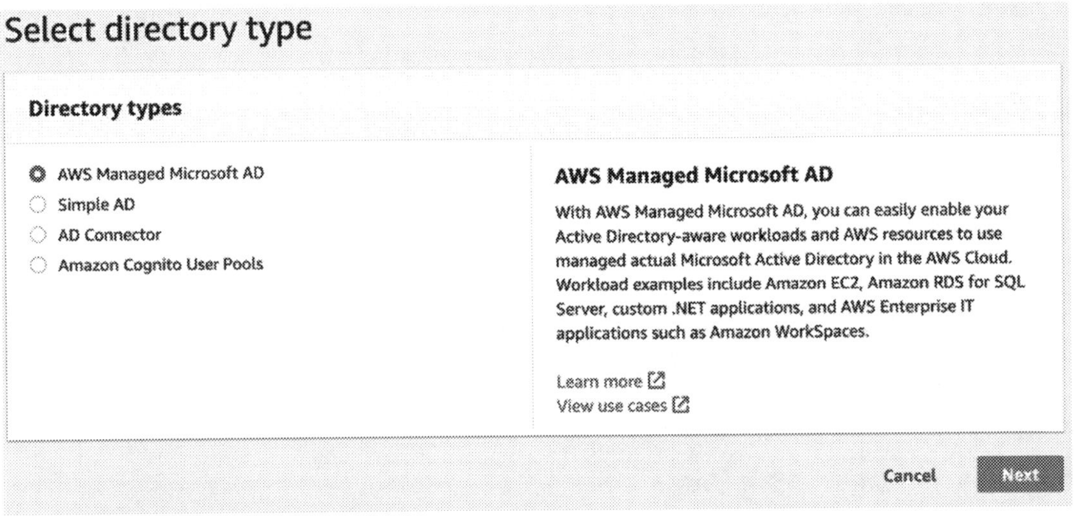

Figure 10-20. *AWS Directory Service options*

The first question you'll be presented with when you choose to "Set up Directory" is what type of directory you wish to use. There are several to choose from.

We've already covered AWS AD Connector, and this section covers AWS Managed Microsoft AD (or AWS Directory Services). We've also got Amazon Cognito and AWS Simple AD.

I'll very briefly cover the use cases of both of those later on in the chapter, but we will continue to focus on AWS Directory Services for Microsoft Active Directory.

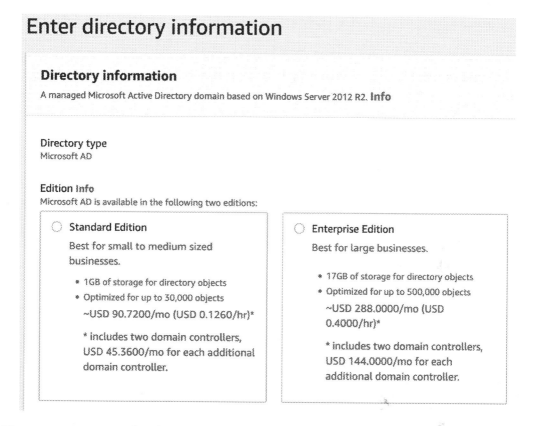

Figure 10-21. *Standard and Enterprise Editions*

Once you've chosen AWS Managed Microsoft AD, the next screen will ask a further question about the size of Active Directory Domain you wish to use. See Figure 10-21. My advice here is not to get too hung up on this. Firstly, the figures used in the examples are an approximation. If you happen to use a Standard Edition and have 30,001 objects in your Domain, then the Domain Controllers will not explode.

Also, it's a little known fact, and AWS don't advertise it widely, but you do have the ability to move from a Standard Edition to an Enterprise Edition. It'll require you to create a Support Ticket to AWS Tech Support which you can do from the AWS Management Console. This change only works for Standard to Enterprise editions, not from Enterprise to Standard.

You'll see there is a significant price difference between the options, so ensure that you take this into consideration.

Once you are happy with your choice, the same screen asks for your configuration information. This is very important. Any mistakes here and you'll typically end up deleting and re-creating the Directory afresh which takes about 30 minutes to achieve.

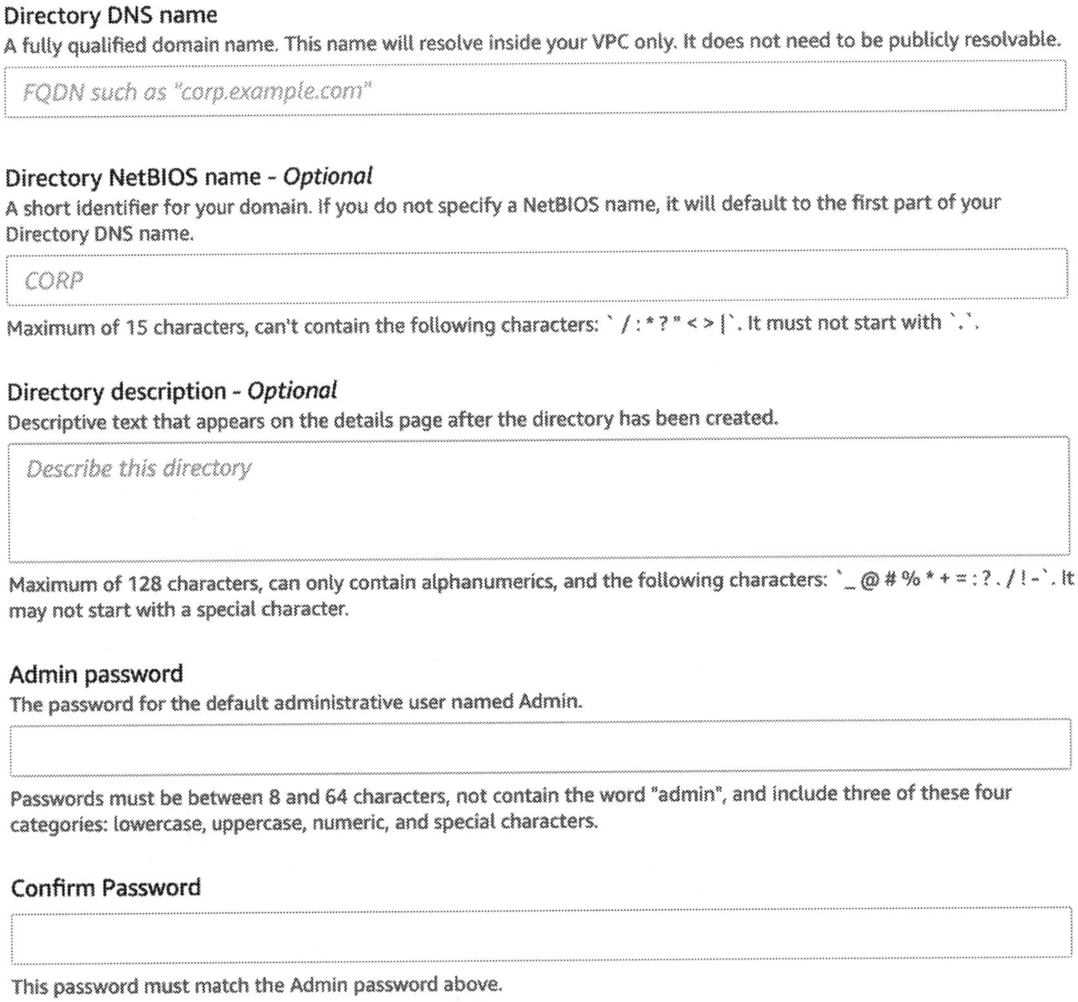

Directory DNS name

A fully qualified domain name. This name will resolve inside your VPC only. It does not need to be publicly resolvable.

> *FQDN such as "corp.example.com"*

Directory NetBIOS name - *Optional*

A short identifier for your domain. If you do not specify a NetBIOS name, it will default to the first part of your Directory DNS name.

> *CORP*

Maximum of 15 characters, can't contain the following characters: ` ` / : * ? " < > | ` `. It must not start with ` `.` `.

Directory description - *Optional*

Descriptive text that appears on the details page after the directory has been created.

> *Describe this directory*

Maximum of 128 characters, can only contain alphanumerics, and the following characters: ` `_ @ # % * + = : ? ./ ! - ` `. It may not start with a special character.

Admin password

The password for the default administrative user named Admin.

>

Passwords must be between 8 and 64 characters, not contain the word "admin", and include three of these four categories: lowercase, uppercase, numeric, and special characters.

Confirm Password

>

This password must match the Admin password above.

Figure 10-22. *AWS Directory Services configuration*

Remember that you are creating a *brand-new domain* in a new Active Directory Forest. This domain will not be part of your existing on-premises AD infrastructure except via AD Trust relationships.

The password that you enter (twice) is going to be the Admin user that you'll use to initially administer the Domain. The configuration screen (Figure 10-22) asks you which VPC and subnets to place the Elastic Network Interfaces (ENI) in for the two Domain Controller instances that live in the AWS Management network (and out of your reach). One final confirmation screen and you are done. Go grab a coffee; the service will take about 20 minutes to create.

There are a few more steps to complete in order to get everything working seamlessly. You now have a fully managed Active Directory service running inside your VPC which you will administer by means of running the Microsoft AD tools on a separate Instance. You will not have access to the Domain Controllers running AWS Directory Service nor should you ever need to. Everything you need to log in to a Domain Controller can be done via the standard management tools or the AWS Management Console – including full authoritative restores.

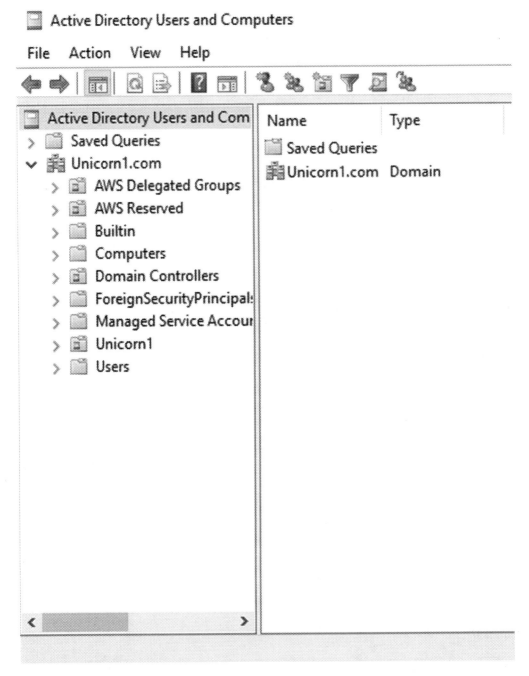

Figure 10-23. *AWS Directory Service Domain*

You'll see from Figure 10-23 that the Active Directory Domain running on AWS Directory Services looks very familiar.

There are three Organizational Units that are created that won't be in a standard AD Domain:

- AWS Delegated Groups – Used to store all of the domain Groups that you can use to delegate AWS-specific permissions to your users.

- AWS Reserved – This OU stores AWS-specific accounts used for management.

- <Domain>/<yourdomain> – This is the OU that is created when you enter the Domain Name in the creation process. You have full control of every object under this OU.

There is a large amount of functionality for your new directory provided via the AWS Management Console.

- Creating a Trust Relationship to your existing AD infrastructure

- IP Routing allowing routing to public IP addresses

- Client-side LDAPS for application-level encryption to your directory

- CA Certificates allowing you to register your own certificates

- Log Forwarding to Amazon CloudWatch Logs

- MFA for an existing RADIUS server

- Notifications using Amazon SNS

- Snapshots which allow you to create extra snapshots or restore existing ones

- Schema Extensions if you have a valid LDIF file

- Application access to allow AWS Services to use your Directory

Further information on all of these can be found in the excellent AWS documentation:

```
https://docs.aws.amazon.com/directoryservice/latest/admin-guide/
directory_microsoft_ad.html
```

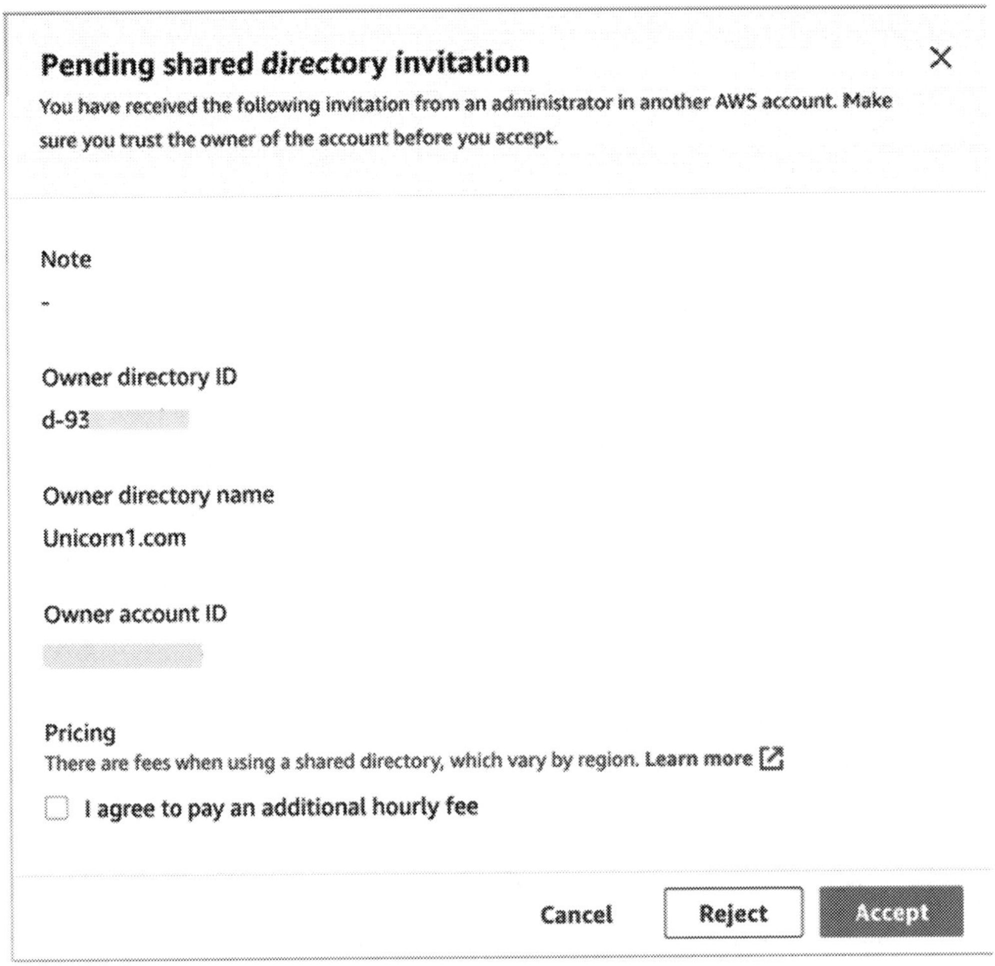

Pending shared *directory* invitation   ✕

You have received the following invitation from an administrator in another AWS account. Make
sure you trust the owner of the account before you accept.

Note

-

Owner directory ID

d-93

Owner directory name

Unicorn1.com

Owner account ID

Pricing
There are fees when using a shared directory, which vary by region. **Learn more** ☐

☐   I agree to pay an additional hourly fee

Cancel   Reject   Accept

Figure 10-24.   *Sharing directories*

As I mentioned, you can also share this directory with other AWS Accounts and
VPCs (see Figure 10-24). Selecting the option under the Scale & Share tab in the AWS
Management Console, you can create a new shared directory and enter the AWS Account
Number you wish to share with.

This process provides access to a Directory shared from your Directory Provider (the
account which shared the directory) to a Directory Consumer (the account you share the
directory with).

You must then accept the sharing invite in the same AWS Region in the account you
shared with, unless your accounts are part of an AWS Organization hierarchy, in which
case the invite is automatically accepted.

Although you'll be able to see the Shared Directory, you won't be able to use it until you create a VPC Peering request between the Directory Provider VPC (the VPC where you created the Directory) and the Directory Consumer VPC (where you want to share with).

The VPC Peering process is very straightforward and is covered here: `https://docs.aws.amazon.com/directoryservice/latest/admin-guide/step1_setup_networking.html`.

You'll end up with a confirmation screen as seen in Figure 10-25.

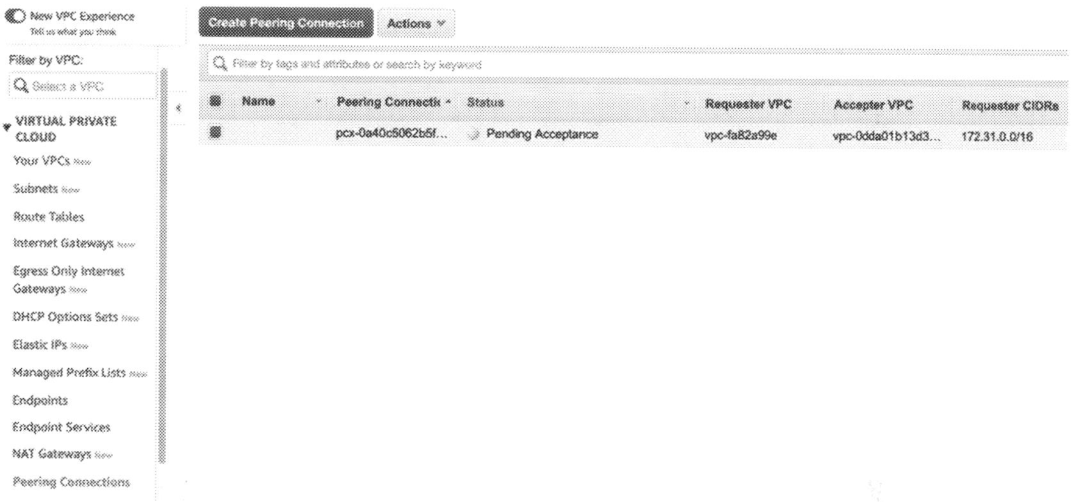

Figure 10-25. *VPC Peering confirmation*

One final aspect we will cover with AWS Directory Services is the ability to provide seamless AD Domain joining of your Amazon EC2 instances.

There are two main actions to complete this. The first involves changing how your VPC handles DNS requests. The second is to provide an AWS IAM role to give your Amazon EC2 Instance permissions to add it to the Domain.

Let's cover DNS first. You know that our Active Directory Domain Controllers also act as DNS servers; they do this whether you are running AWS Directory Services or Microsoft ADDS on Amazon EC2 Instances. Now since each AWS VPC has a direct DNS Resolver via the .2 IP address (see earlier in the chapter), we need to change this to point to our Domain Controller/DNS Servers. The simple reason is that Amazon Route 53 will not handle dynamic DNS entries in the same way as Microsoft DNS Server does.

Making this change is straightforward.

Before we make the change, you'll need two items of information – the ID of your VPC and the IP addresses of both of your AWS Directory Services servers. You'll find both in the AWS Directory Services console (Figure 10-26).

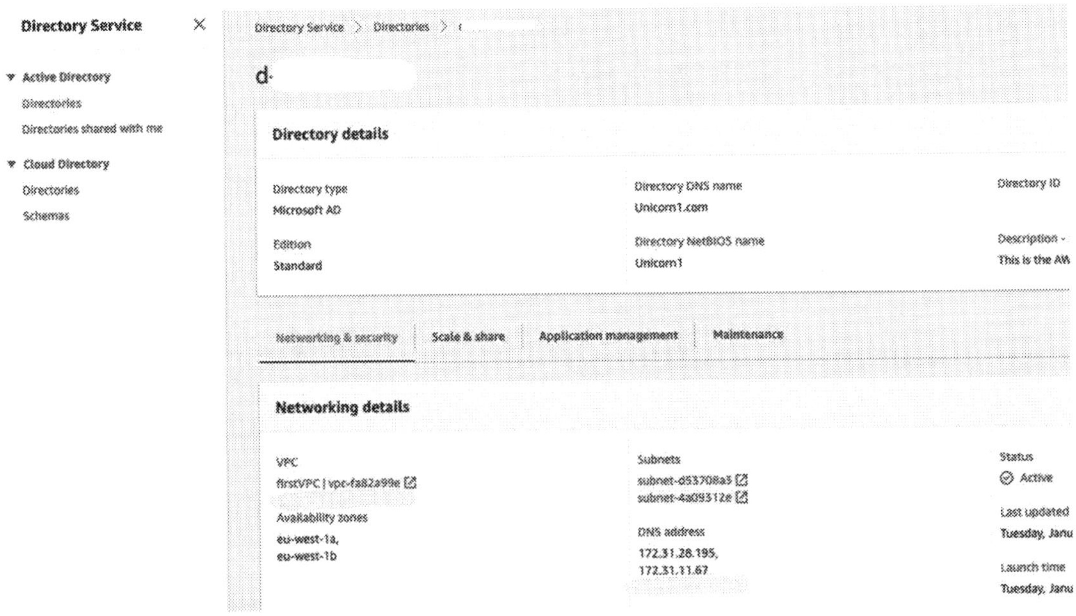

Figure 10-26. *AWS Directory Services details*

Armed with this information, go to VPC in the AWS Management Console, and on the left-hand side menu, you'll find DHCP Option Sets.

Once this is created, you'll need to assign it to the VPC containing your AWS Directory Service Domain.

The next step is to create an IAM role to allow seamless Domain join. This role will allow the Amazon EC2 service to elevate its permissions temporarily to perform an action using the AWS Systems Manager service.

The full process is described here: `https://docs.aws.amazon.com/directoryservice/latest/admin-guide/launching_instance.html`.

The AWS IAM role uses two managed policies called `AmazonSSMDirectoryServiceAccess` and `AmazonSSMManagedInstanceCore` in order to invoke the AWS Systems Manager Run Command which performs the Domain join action during the Amazon EC2 first-run startup process.

With everything in place, you'll be able to launch an Amazon EC2 Instance, select an AD Domain and IAM role, and automatically join your AD Domain when it launches.

Other Directories

Earlier on in this section, we also mentioned two other services which come under the AWS Directory Services banner: Amazon Simple AD and Amazon Cognito.

Amazon Simple AD was the precursor to the current AWS Microsoft Managed AD service. It was also a fully managed service, but rather than running Microsoft Active Directory, it used the open source Samba tool instead. This allowed for the creation of users and groups in an AD-like environment using the standard Microsoft AD tools. All very familiar so far? Unfortunately, Samba isn't a pure Microsoft Active Directory, and there are compatibility problems with some applications, also AWS Simple AD doesn't support AD Trusts which made its use case very cloud-centric.

But everything has a use case, right?

If you need a quick, cost-effective, and easy directory for some testing or development, then AWS Simple AD could be the right choice for you. Although it's no longer being actively enhanced with more features, it will still be available in the console or via API, the same as every AWS Service.

Amazon Cognito provides authentication and authorization and uses management services for your mobile and web applications.

It's a fully managed service that provides authentication to Identity Providers like Amazon, Facebook, or Google as well as federation back to your own Active Directory. As a fully managed service, it can scale to hundreds of millions of users (should your mobile app really take off!).

Amazon Cognito is split into two areas. These are Amazon Cognito User Pools which are Directories that provide authentication, sign-in or sign-up functionality, for your app users. There's also Amazon Cognito Identity Pools which provide authorization services to allow your users to access AWS Services.

If you want to find out more about Amazon Cognito, then head over to `https://docs.aws.amazon.com/cognito/index.html`.

AWS Single Sign-On

The final service we will discuss in this chapter is the newest, and that's AWS Single Sign-On (AWS SSO). At the start of this chapter, I described the pain of having to log in to every individual server in the office at the start of the morning. Thinking back now, at most, that was maybe five to six servers. Just take a moment to think about the number of services we use these days!

A 2019 report by the *Wall Street Journal* details that small companies have around 73 internal applications, whereas large companies have over 200.[4]

But that's not all.

We have web services, social media, shopping, and so on, all of them requiring us to log in at some point.

Single Sign-On has been around for some time and is now a mature technology thanks to authentication protocols and frameworks such as SAML, SCIM, OAuth2, and OIDC. It's a technology you doubtless already use, but if this is a new area for you, then the AWS SSO Service is very easy to set up and manage.

AWS SSO was launched during AWS re:Invent 2017. It allows you to log in to a web portal, and from there you can access all of your AWS Accounts as well as a host of third-party services such as Microsoft Office 365, Jira, Confluence, Salesforce, and so on. It also allows you to create your own SAML-based integrations, so you can configure the service to SSO to your own internal applications.

AWS SSO is tightly integrated with AWS Organizations (`https://aws.amazon.com/organizations/`).

There are two options when configuring AWS Organizations. This is detailed in Figure 10-27. You can create an Organization that creates a single payer account and handles centralized costs, provides you the ability to create new accounts or invite existing accounts into this Organization, and also gives you the ability to create policies that are applied throughout the AWS Accounts that are part of your Organization.

This is the most common option. However, there is another option which is to create an Organization to handle consolidated billing features. This provides the financial features but without the ability to apply policies throughout the Organization.

The benefit of consolidated billing is that you'll receive a single AWS bill every month for all the usage in all your accounts. It will also detail per-account spend, so that you can charge back to projects or groups within your business.

---

[4]`www.wsj.com/articles/employees-are-accessing-more-and-more-business-apps-study-finds-11549580017`

Create organization

This creates an organization that:

- ⊘ Provides single payer and centralized cost tracking

- ⊘ Lets you create and invite accounts

- ⊘ Allows you to apply policy-based controls

- ⊘ Helps you simplify organization-wide management of AWS services

| Create organization | Learn more |

Or you can create an organization with only consolidated billing features.

After you create an organization, you cannot join this account to another organization until you delete its current organization.

Figure 10-27. *AWS Organizations options*

Once you have created your AWS Organizations, you can invite any additional AWS accounts to be a part of that Organization. AWS Organizations is a great service that allows you to set up and provision a multi-AWS account strategy, providing governance and shared services to any accounts associated with it.

For more information on AWS Organizations, please see `https://aws.amazon.com/organizations/getting-started/`.

All it takes is a click of the Enable AWS SSO button to begin the configuration process for the AWS Single Sign-On service.

Welcome to AWS Single Sign-On

AWS Single Sign-On (SSO) enables you to manage SSO access to your AWS accounts, resources, and cloud applications centrally, for users from your preferred identity source. Learn more

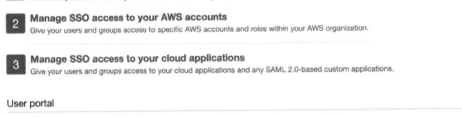

You successfully enabled AWS SSO

To get started, go to the Users page and add your users, or use the Settings page to choose a different identity source. After setting up your identity source, you can manage permissions to your AWS accounts, roles, and cloud applications.

Recommended setup steps

1 Choose your identity source
The identity source is where you administer users and groups, and is the service that authenticates your users.

2 Manage SSO access to your AWS accounts
Give your users and groups access to specific AWS accounts and roles within your AWS organization.

3 Manage SSO access to your cloud applications
Give your users and groups access to your cloud applications and any SAML 2.0-based custom applications.

User portal

The user portal offers a single place to access all their assigned AWS accounts, roles, and applications.

User portal URL:

Figure 10-28. *AWS SSO configuration screen*

We can see in Figure 10-28 there are three elements that can be configured.

First, we have to choose whether to create individual users or select an existing Identity Provider to use.

When AWS SSO is created, it comes with a default directory. This default directory is actually an AWS managed service and lives outside of your account in the AWS Management area. The only interaction you have with the default directory is to add Users and Groups via the AWS SSO Console.

This is why one of the first configuration steps is usually to add your own Active Directory Domain or External Identity Provider.

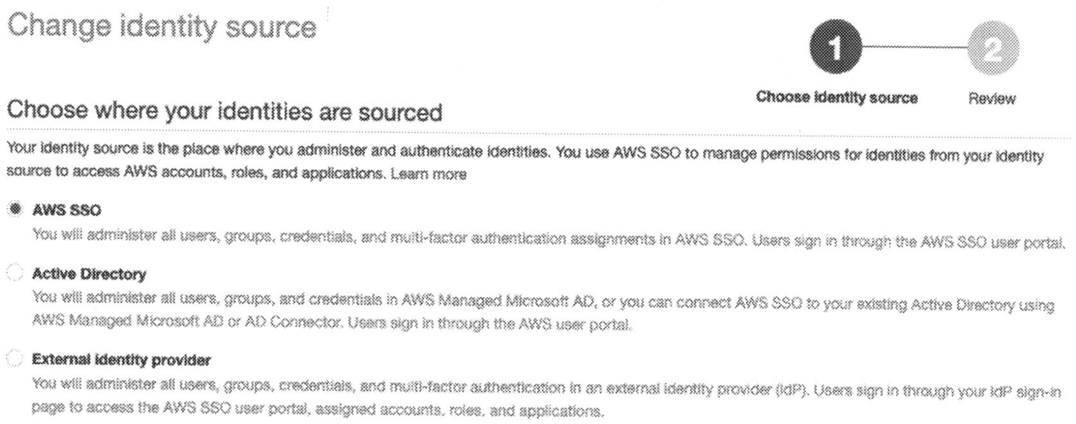

Change identity source

Choose where your identities are sourced

Your identity source is the place where you administer and authenticate identities. You use AWS SSO to manage permissions for identities from your identity source to access AWS accounts, roles, and applications. Learn more

● **AWS SSO**
   You will administer all users, groups, credentials, and multi-factor authentication assignments in AWS SSO. Users sign in through the AWS SSO user portal.

○ **Active Directory**
   You will administer all users, groups, and credentials in AWS Managed Microsoft AD, or you can connect AWS SSO to your existing Active Directory using AWS Managed Microsoft AD or AD Connector. Users sign in through the AWS user portal.

○ **External identity provider**
   You will administer all users, groups, credentials, and multi-factor authentication in an external identity provider (IdP). Users sign in through your IdP sign-in page to access the AWS SSO user portal, assigned accounts, roles, and applications.

Figure 10-29. *AWS SSO Identity Source*

There are three options here (Figure 10-29).

Firstly, we can continue to use the default directory that AWS SSO provides.

Secondly, we can choose to target an Active Directory domain. Here, you'll see any AWS Directory Services managed AD Domains you have running. You can also use AWS AD Connector to target an Active Directory running either on-premises or on an Amazon EC2 instance within AWS. Either way, it'll get picked up by AWS SSO.

Thirdly, we can integrate with a SAML 2.0 Identity Provider such as Microsoft Azure AD.

This is shown in Figure 10-30 and discussed later on in this section.

If you move away from the default AWS SSO Directory, a number of things change. Most importantly, if you've added any Users and Groups to the default directory, they will be removed. There will also be a change to the access URL, although customizing that URL would lower the impact.

The URL currently has a suffix of .awsapps.com/start but is in the process of migrating to .signin.aws. If you provide filtering for the URLs your users can access, please include both URLs as this will save you a headache later on.

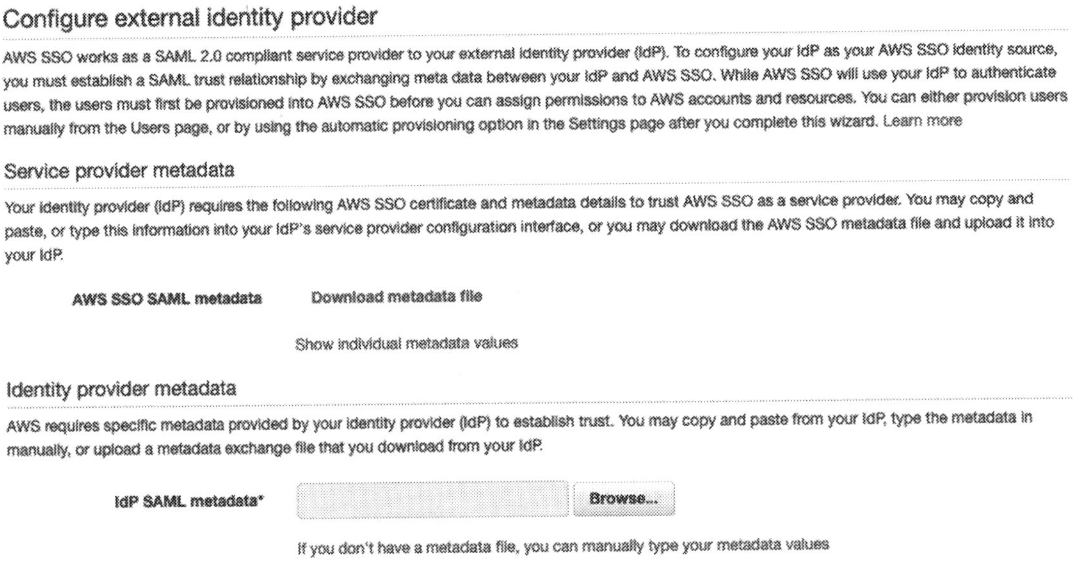

Configure external identity provider

AWS SSO works as a SAML 2.0 compliant service provider to your external identity provider (IdP). To configure your IdP as your AWS SSO identity source, you must establish a SAML trust relationship by exchanging meta data between your IdP and AWS SSO. While AWS SSO will use your IdP to authenticate users, the users must first be provisioned into AWS SSO before you can assign permissions to AWS accounts and resources. You can either provision users manually from the Users page, or by using the automatic provisioning option in the Settings page after you complete this wizard. Learn more

Service provider metadata

Your identity provider (IdP) requires the following AWS SSO certificate and metadata details to trust AWS SSO as a service provider. You may copy and paste, or type this information into your IdP's service provider configuration interface, or you may download the AWS SSO metadata file and upload it into your IdP.

AWS SSO SAML metadata   Download metadata file

Show individual metadata values

Identity provider metadata

AWS requires specific metadata provided by your identity provider (IdP) to establish trust. You may copy and paste from your IdP, type the metadata in manually, or upload a metadata exchange file that you download from your IdP.

IdP SAML metadata* [   ] Browse...

If you don't have a metadata file, you can manually type your metadata values

Figure 10-30. *AWS SSO – configure external Identity Provider*

Once you've chosen your Identity Source, you can then move on to the next step in the configuration which is to "Managed SSO Access to your Accounts."

This will provide full single sign-on access to your AWS accounts via either the AWS Management Console or the CLI (command-line interface). Here, we can assign Users to allow for SSO access.

We also have the concept of Permission Sets during this step.

Permission Sets define the level of access that users have to a specific AWS Account. Permission Sets are cumulative, so a user can have more than one, which allows the user to select a given Permission Set and level of access when they sign in.

This is a great feature. Rather than a user having a single set of permissions every time they sign in to the console (which would almost certainly have more permissions than actually needed), the user selects a level of access that fits the task they wish to accomplish.

There are two options when you create Permission Sets (see Figure 10-31).

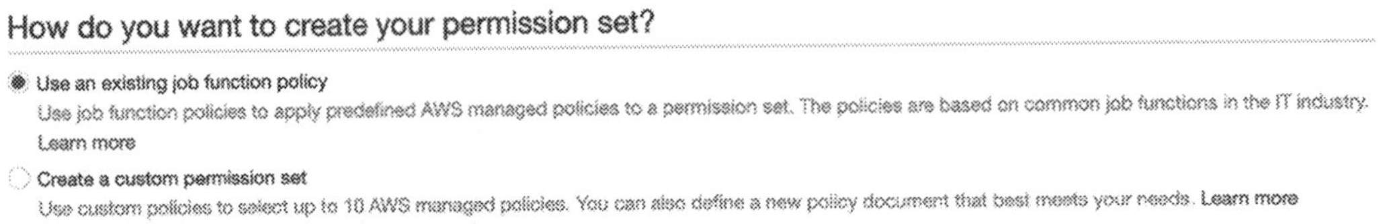

How do you want to create your permission set?

⦿ Use an existing job function policy
  Use job function policies to apply predefined AWS managed policies to a permission set. The policies are based on common job functions in the IT industry. Learn more

○ Create a custom permission set
  Use custom policies to select up to 10 AWS managed policies. You can also define a new policy document that best meets your needs. Learn more

Figure 10-31. *Permission Set options*

Using an existing job function policy gives you access to already created AWS managed policies that fit around common job roles (Administrator, Database Admin, Network Admin, View-Only access, etc.). By selecting these job function policies, you are just saving some time from having to create the policy from scratch yourself.

You always have the ability to edit the policy and add/remove access to a very granular level using AWS IAM.

The other option is to create a custom Permission Set. Once again, you'll use AWS IAM to create the policy, but here you have the ability to change the session duration, which is the time the user has in the account before being automatically signed out.

If the thought of creating your own policy gives you the chills, don't worry; there are lots of AWS managed policies already built, and you can duplicate and update these to accommodate your specific requirements.

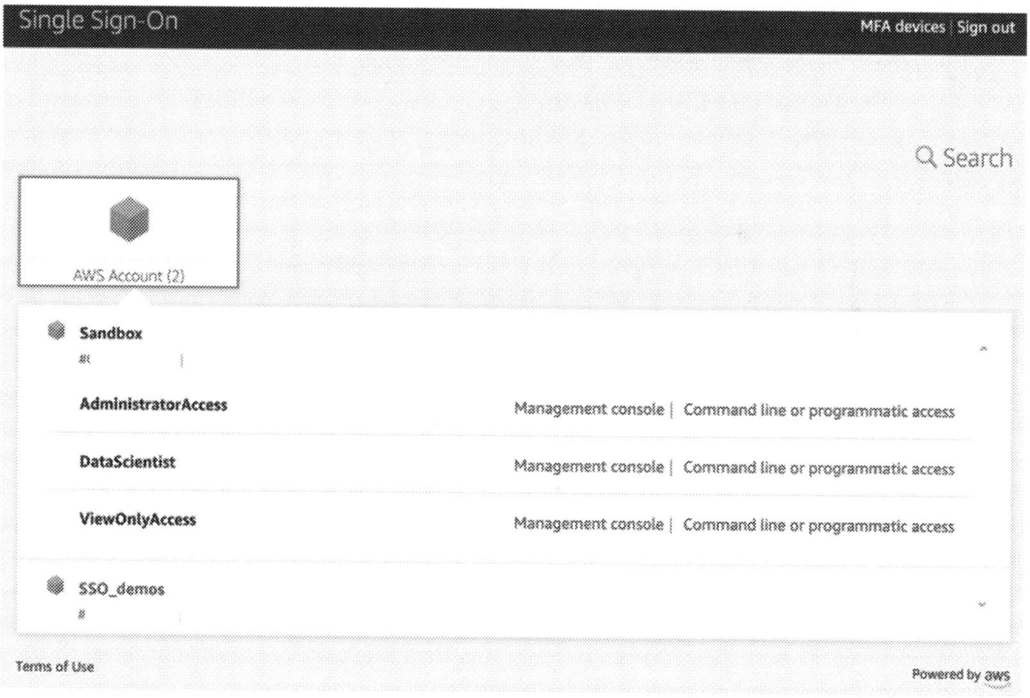

Figure 10-32. Single sign-on access to AWS Accounts

The last step in this process is to select the Users or Groups from your connected Active Directory and assign them to one or more Permission Sets (Figure 10-32).

The final part of the AWS SSO setup is to provide single sign-on access to your other cloud-based applications.

There are now a significant number of third-party services that are ready to be configured, including Microsoft's Office 365.

AWS SSO will give you all the SAML URL and metadata needed to create the SSO link to your application. Each Cloud application has a different method of configuring single sign-on, and I would always consult the services' own support center on how to configure SSO. However, AWS SSO also includes instructions for each Cloud service on how to configure their application for single sign-on.

Summary

In this chapter, we have covered the broad topic of Identity and how it relates to creating and running Microsoft-specific solutions on AWS. We started with a brief overview of Microsoft Active Directory and then discussed one of the most common scenarios we see in AWS, running Active Directory on Amazon EC2.

We explored how to provide DNS resolution using the DHCP Option Sets and also Amazon Route 53 Resolvers. We looked at how AWS AD Connector complements this solution and can help streamline access to Active Directory on-premises or even running on Amazon EC2.

Then we explored AWS's own fully managed Active Directory service called AWS Directory Services for Microsoft Active Directory which I refer to as AWS Directory Services although that's an umbrella that covers the fully managed Active Directory service as well as AWS Simple AD and Amazon Cognito.

Finally, in this chapter, we run through an AWS Single Sign-On installation providing single sign-on to other AWS accounts and a host of external SaaS applications.

Identity is going to be incredibly important to your AWS and Cloud adoption journey. It's one of the core elements you'll need to talk through, agree upon, and implement securely before you even think about migration or running application services for real.

Index

A, B

R. Pothecary, *Running Microsoft Workloads on AWS*, https://doi.org/10.1007/978-1-4842-6628-1

Printed in the United States
by Baker & Taylor Publisher Services